MW00788336

LGBTI Rights in Turkey

The LGBTI community in Turkey face real dangers. In 2015, the Turkish police interrupted the LGBTI pride march in Istanbul, using tear gas and rubber bullets against the marchers. This marked the first attempt by the authorities to stop the parade by force, and similar actions occurred the following year. Here, Fait Muedini examines these levels of discrimination in Turkey, as well as explores how activists are working to improve human rights for LGBTI individuals living in this hostile environment. Muedini bases his analysis on interviews taken with a number of NGO leaders and activists of leading LGBTI organisations in the region, including Lambda Istanbul, Kaos GL, Pembe Hayat, Social Policies, Gender Identity and Sexual Orientation Studies Association (SPoD), and Families of LGBTs in Istanbul (LİSTAG). The original information provided by these interviews illuminates the challenges facing the LGBTI community and the brave actions taken by activists in their attempts to challenge the state and secure sexual equality.

FAIT MUEDINI is the Frances Shera Fessler Professor of International Studies at Butler University. He is the author of *Sponsoring Sufism: How Governments Promote "Mystical Islam" in their Domestic and Foreign Policies* (2015) and *Human Rights and Universal Child Primary Education* (2015).

LGBTI Rights in Turkey

Sexuality and the State in the Middle East

FAIT MUEDINI
Butler University

CAMBRIDGE
UNIVERSITY PRESS

CAMBRIDGE
UNIVERSITY PRESS

University Printing House, Cambridge CB2 8BS, United Kingdom

One Liberty Plaza, 20th Floor, New York, NY 10006, USA

477 Williamstown Road, Port Melbourne, VIC 3207, Australia

314–321, 3rd Floor, Plot 3, Splendor Forum, Jasola District Centre, New Delhi – 110025, India

79 Anson Road, #06–04/06, Singapore 079906

Cambridge University Press is part of the University of Cambridge.

It furthers the University's mission by disseminating knowledge in the pursuit of education, learning, and research at the highest international levels of excellence.

www.cambridge.org
Information on this title: www.cambridge.org/9781108417242
DOI: 10.1017/9781108265133

© Fait Muedini 2018

This publication is in copyright. Subject to statutory exception and to the provisions of relevant collective licensing agreements, no reproduction of any part may take place without the written permission of Cambridge University Press.

First published 2018

Printed and bound in Great Britain by Clays Ltd, Elcograf S.p.A.

A catalogue record for this publication is available from the British Library.

Library of Congress Cataloging-in-Publication Data
Names: Muedini, Fait, author.
Title: LGBTI rights in Turkey / Fait Muedini.
Description: New York : Cambridge University Press, 2018- I Includes bibliographical references and index. Contents: Part 1. Sexuality and the state in the Middle East
Identifiers: LCCN 2018021305I ISBN 9781108417242 (hardback) I ISBN 9781108404730 (paperback)
Subjects: LCSH: Sexual minorities–Civil rights–Turkey. I Sexual minorities–Legal status, laws, etc.–Turkey. I Gays–Legal status, laws, etc.–Turkey. I Lesbians–Legal status, laws, etc.–Turkey. I Transgender people–Legal status, laws, etc.–Turkey. I Human rights–Turkey. I Civil rights–Turkey.
Classification: LCC KKX2467.G38 M84 2018 I DDC 342.56108/7–dc23
LC record available at https://lccn.loc.gov/2018021305

ISBN 978-1-108-41724-2 Hardback
ISBN 978-1-108-40473-0 Paperback

Cambridge University Press has no responsibility for the persistence or accuracy of URLs for external or third-party internet websites referred to in this publication and does not guarantee that any content on such websites is, or will remain, accurate or appropriate.

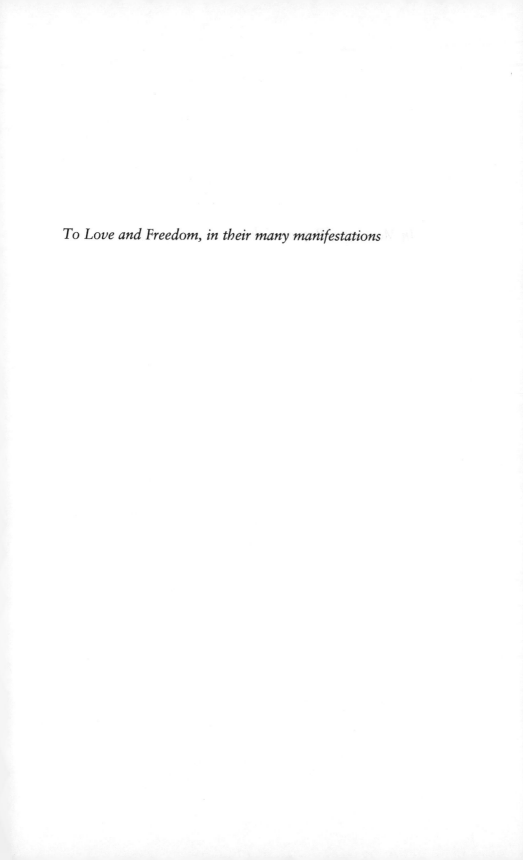

To Love and Freedom, in their many manifestations

In Memory of Boysan Yakar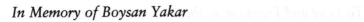

Contents

Acknowledgments

There are so many people that I indebted to, without whose help this book would never have been possible. I want to begin by thanking all of the activists in Turkey who allowed me to interview them. I want to thank Sedef Çakmak, Cihan Hüroğlu (SPoD), Murat Köylü (Kaos GL), Janset Kalan (Pembe Hayat), and Murat Renay for their time and willingness to allow me to interview them about their work. I will also always remember the kindness of the late Boysan Yakar in taking the time to speak with me about his activism and the LGBTI rights movement. I am grateful for having met him and for learning about, and from, his life.

I want to thank Megan Day, Katie Morford, and Autumn Tyler for their role as research assistants. They not only helped in collecting published stories on LGBTI rights in Turkey, but they also worked tirelessly in transcribing the interviews. I also want to thank Butler University for its support through the BAC Grant and the Desmond Tutu Center in Indianapolis, Indiana, for providing a research fellowship for me to carry out this work.

I also want to thank William Felice for his comments about the manuscript and all reviewers for their detailed suggestions for improving the manuscript. In addition, I want to thank my students and colleagues with whom I have had conversations regarding LGBTI rights in Turkey and the Middle East.

I also want to thank my editor at Cambridge University Press, Maria Marsh, for understanding the importance of such a project and for her excitement regarding the manuscript. I am very fortunate to have an editor who is so passionate about publishing such research on the Middle East, on Turkey, and on LGBTI rights. This book could never have been published in such a timely manner had it not been for Maria's strong belief in the work. In addition, I want to thank Abigail Walkington, Shaheer Husanne, and Thomas Haynes for their help with the production of the final manuscript. I also want to thank Joe Fitzgibbon for all of his work in copyediting the book.

Of course, none of this could have been possible without my family. I want to thank my wife, Kaltrina Muedini, for her continued support and encouragement during the fieldwork in Turkey and throughout the entire writing process. I also want to thank my children, Edon and Dua Muedini, and my parents, Atli and Mudzefer Muedini.

Introduction

Joining [the] Gezi resistance, being the very first in the very first stage with some important groups, we took our pride back from society. It was important. It was ... stolen from us ... with their homophobic words and discrimination. But ... we took it back.

Boysan Yakar

On Sunday, June 28, 2015, police interrupted the Lesbian, Gay, Bisexual, Transgender, and Intersex (LGBTI)[1] Pride March in Taksim Square – and on Istiklal Street – in Istanbul, Turkey. Officers used tear gas, as well as rubber bullets, against those walking in the march, forcing the protesters to move out of these areas (*Public Opinion*, 2015). Some people were actually able to capture video on cell phones, which showed police also using a water cannon against the marchers (Heavy.com, 2015). This sort of direct violent behavior was new for Turkish police; the 2015 Pride March was the first time that authorities attempted to stop the parade with force. As to why the police attempted to halt the Pride March during that particular year, authorities argued that they decided to interrupt the march because the event took place during the Islamic month of Ramadan (*Public Opinion*, 2015). This is a holy month in the faith, when Muslims believe the Prophet Muhammad first received divine messages from God.

What transpired in 2015 was not the only instance of Turkish police breaking up LGBTI Pride Marches; similar actions occurred the following year. For example, in 2016, a Pride parade in Izmir was cancelled because of what authorities said was "intelligence that there will be terror propaganda" (Uras, 2016). Then, on June 19, 2016, according to reports,

Taksim was put under police blockade prior to another Pride March, the 7th Trans Pride March (organized by Istanbul LGBTI Solidarity Association), which was scheduled to start at 17:00 ... Cumhuriyet Monument at Taksim

1

Square was surrounded by barriers; water cannons and police vehicles were positioned on Taksim Square, Istiklal Avenue, Cumhuriyet Avenue, Tarlabaşı Boulevard and various streets that lead to Taksim where a high number of riot police were assigned to. After 15:00, transphobic groups started gathering along Istiklal Avenue. A group that got off Taksim metro station chanted "Ya illah bismillah Allahuakbar" and "Faggots don't be surprised, don't test our patience." At 16:00, metro services were cancelled. A poster that reads, "Dear Passengers, our vehicles will not be stopping at Taksim station for a temporary duration" was hung on the metro. (Tar, 2016)

The police prohibited this Trans Pride March from taking place (although some activists still went to the location of the Pride March). Then, when individuals – including the organization committee – wanted to make a statement to the press about what transpired (Tar, 2016), over 300 police (NBC, 2016) used tear gas, as well as rubber bullets, to break up the crowd of dozens of protesters (BBC, 2016b). Similar to the arguments made in 2015, authorities said they stopped the parade because it took place during Ramadan, and because of "security concerns" (Sezer, 2016), specifically arguing that they acted this way in order to "safeguard security and public order," (Sezer, 2016), even though the Islamists and ultranationalists – despite threats – never showed up (NBC, 2016). Again, human rights activists were quick to challenge the police decision. For example, Ebru Kiranci, the spokesperson for the LGBTI Solidarity Association said, "(The) holy month of Ramadan is an excuse. If you are going to respect Ramadan, respect us too. The heterosexuals think it's too much for us, only 2 hours in 365 days" (Sezer, 2016).

Officials in Istanbul issued similar orders for the larger LGBTI Pride March that was to take place on June 26, 2016, saying that they would not allow it to occur based on similar "security concerns," and that those who tried to take part in the march could see a police intervention (Williams, 2016). While activists used social media to stress the importance of participating in the Pride March, the police still urged people to not attend the event. Despite claims by the LGBTI Pride March organizers that they applied for permission to hold the event, the authorities denied this, saying (over a week before the event) that "[a]n application is required to conduct a procession, parade or race in Istanbul and the governor's office must be informed. As of today, no such request has been received by the governor's office" (Uras, 2016). The claim that they did not receive a request for permission contradicts a statement by the LGBTI rights organization Kaos GL (2016b), which said on their website that an application was "not approved." Then, when some activists still decided to still carry out the Pride March, the police disrupted the march for the second year in a row. Similar to their actions during the previous marches, plainclothes police officers used tear gas (*Los Angeles Times*, 2016) and rubber bullets to break up the crowds, and then also arrested a total of twenty-nine activists. One individual that was detained was Volker Beck, a member of the German Green Party (*Los Angeles Times*, 2016). Beck stated, "They [the police] ripped my passport away from me and pushed me around. It was a massive and arbitrary police attack that we saw" (Paton, 2016). This crackdown began after "[d]ozens of activists assembled on Istanbul's main pedestrian street to publicly read a statement marking the end of the gay, lesbian and transgender pride week and to denounce the ban. Several of them were detained, however, before they could speak" (*Los Angeles Times*, 2016). LGBTI rights activists were very upset at what they saw as yet another attempt by the government to restrict the rights of the LGBTI community in Turkey. They continued their demonstrations elsewhere, but were quite critical of the state position, stating on social media that the government's decision was a "flagrant violation of the constitution and the law" (Williams, 2016). Kaos GL (2016b), an LGBTI rights organization in Turkey, posted on their website the following message:

Our popular Pride Marches, held for 12 years with great joy, are a space where we celebrate our existence, our persistence to live a proud life, and our exponentially growing organized movement. They influence not only LGBTI+ individuals' lives but everyone. Pride March allows humanity to dream: If this world were different, what kind of people would we be? What would we wear, desire, do, say? What would the streets of this city look like? If we organized with love, what could tear us apart from each other? If we held our bodies, work, and future in our own hands, what would happen? The ban on Pride March is an effort not only to stop us from leading dignified lives but also to stop us from dreaming of this world.

As alluded to earlier, the government's unwillingness to allow the 2016 Pride March also came after threats by conservative Muslim groups in Turkey against the LGBTI community. On June 13, 2016, an organization named the Anatolia Muslim Youth Association (MAG) said that they would carry out an "intervention" against what they called an "immoral" Pride March (Korkmaz, 2016). Then, one day later, another youth conservative group by the name of Alperen Hearths – which is linked to the nationalist Great Union Party (BBP) in Turkey – said that they would do what they could to make sure that the 2016 Pride March would not take place. The president of the organization, Kürşat Mican also said, "They can do whatever they want by gathering somewhere, but we definitely don't want them to walk naked on the sacred soil of our country in the blessed month of Ramadan" (Korkmaz, 2016). Other statements included: "Dear state officials, who close your eyes and ears to this immorality and allow this, we are calling on you to perform your duties to stop this immorality. Otherwise the Alperen Hearths, who are the representatives of the people, will perform their duties on this soil, which was passed to us from our ancestors" (Korkmaz, 2016).

Like the year before, authorities took a similar approach to the 2017 Pride March. The Istanbul government disallowed a Pride March protest to take place, issuing a statement saying, "The march will not be allowed after considering the security of citizens, especially the participants themselves, and tourists who will be in the area" (Uras, 2017). However, despite this ban, some activists assembled anyways, as they viewed this ban as unjust. Police in Istanbul responded by breaking up the Pride March in Istanbul, shooting rubber bullets, as well as tear gas towards the demonstrators. While the government used the "Ramadan" argument for why the protests were shut down, the 2017 protests did not occur during the month. This led Lara Guney Ozlen, an LGBTI activist and spokesperson for the Pride Week to say that "[f]or the last two years, the march overlapped with Ramadan. This year it does not. So, that is not an excuse [to prevent it] either. I believe the ban is about not accepting our sexual orientation and it is a reaction to the movement getting stronger" (Al Jazeera, 2017). As evidenced by their recent decisions, the government has shown little sign of a willingness to allow LGBTI individuals to gather and march in pride parades.

The situation facing the LGBTI community in Turkey today is a very dangerous one: there exists a real threat to those who are LGBTI in Turkey by those who wish to repress their human rights. The LGBTI community continues to be discriminated against in a country that claims to be an open society for those living within its borders. Again, this topic of LGBTI rights abuses is not limited to violations in Turkey.

The issue of LGBTI rights as a whole is an issue that has been receiving a great deal of attention in domestic and international media. LGBTI individuals in many parts of the world continue to face discrimination, from public statements by political leaders condemning homosexuality (this has been observed in many places across the globe) to murder. LGBTI individuals are often viewed as targets by governments and homophobic members of civil society.

Again, unfortunately, such tensions between LGBTI activists and government leaders (often conservative parties and groups) are quite common not only in Turkey but elsewhere. Yet, what makes Turkey an interesting case for analysis is that leaders of the state have attempted to argue that the country – through its constitution and national law – offers a series of human rights protections to those living within the country. Political elites in the government have tried to sell Turkey as a progressive state that is not only in line with international human rights law norms, but they have also tried to convince the world that Turkey provides full rights to all members of its society. This, coupled with a strong economy, they argue, shows why Turkey would also be an excellent partner and state for economic and political international organizations such as the European Union. However, as I shall argue throughout this book, this perception of Turkey is merely an illusion, one becoming clearer as the days and months pass. As Amnesty International researcher Andrew Gardner explains, "[Turkey] is a tolerant society but also a country badly served by its government and its media in terms of the negative stereotypes about gay people. There has been a long history of negative statements by public officials and the government is incredibly reluctant to recognize that people have rights or any protection in law" (Jamieson and Akyavas, 2015). Gardner also goes on to say that while LGBT celebrities are often more accepted in Turkey, they are but the few, as those who are not nationally or internationally known, or those who are not perceived to be part of the higher socioeconomic levels or statuses in Turkish society, are not viewed positively, nor are they accepted (Jamieson and Akyavas, 2015). However, it must be noted that even the celebrities and well-known LGBTI figures are rarely seen as equal to those not of the LGBTI community in Turkey.

Given the hostile conditions facing the LGBTI members in Turkey, my reasons for writing this book are to examine the history and levels of sexual orientation discrimination in Turkey, to understand the role

of religion as it is used in the context of LGBTI rights, and to explore
how activists are working within this space to improve human rights
for LGBTI individuals. While there is a larger body of literature
looking at same-sex rights movements in the West, there are far fewer
studies that examine this issue outside of the region (Engin, 2015) and
fewer still situated in the Middle East itself.[2] The primary goal of this
book is to explore the various facets of LGBTI rights in Turkey,
shedding light not only on rights abuses but also on how individuals
and NGOs are – in very difficult climates – working to improve
conditions for sexual minorities. The central themes of this book center
on the examination of the legal, political, economic, social, and cultural conditions facing members of the LGBTI community in Turkey,
and also the activism strategies by LGBTI activists in Turkey. But along
with the attention to LGBTI rights-based activists, I am also interested
in exploring the relationship between the use of religion and such
human rights. I examine how groups attempt to use religion to justify
their positions against homosexuality, as well as whether activists
approach LGBTI rights from the lens of Islam itself. Thus, this book
aims to analyze the issue of sexual orientation rights from a series of
perspectives, each one ultimately intersecting with the others.

In the work, I begin with a discussion about public opinion of
homosexuality in the "Muslim World" and Turkey, showing the high
level of anti-LGBTI sentiment that exists and also how people use
Islam and religion to "justify" their anti-LGBTI positions and behavior. I then look at whether activists use religion to advocate for LGBTI
rights. In the next chapter, I examine the history of same-sex rights in
Turkey, which will center on the various conditions facing the LGBTI
community. As I show, the Turkish government has been using
ambiguous state laws to discriminate against lesbian, gay, bisexual,
transgender, and intersex individuals. While Turkey technically does
not ban homosexuality, I will discuss how the interpretations of the
law make it quite easy for the state to ignore equal protections for the
LGBTI. But human rights violations towards the LGBTI are not in any
way confined to the actions of the government. In fact, many members
of society within Turkey have also committed crimes against LGBTI
individuals.

Then, I discuss the history of the LGBTI movement (and subsequent
government responses to the rights movement), interpretations of
domestic law as they relate to LGBTI rights, and statements by public

figures regarding homosexuality, Next is a chapter on how the government, and other state institutions such as the police, have carried out human rights violations towards LGBTI, be those violations are related to politics, economics, or many other aspects of life. However, despite the challenges that the LGBTI face, I then shift the focus to how LGBTI activists are working to improve human rights conditions in Turkey. Before examining their specific tactics in Turkey, I review the academic and policy literature on LGBTI rights activism over the past decades. I look at what strategies LGBTI activists have taken in the Middle East and elsewhere, and within this lens, show what has been more successful as it relates to advancing LGBTI rights. Then, I present my findings with regards to how activists are working to improve LGBTI rights in Turkey. I devote additional attention to specifically examining the question of same-sex marriage in Turkey. I then discuss challenges LGBTI activists face, and what they see as the course of action to take.

In this book, not only do I examine state law and reports of rights abuses but I also interview a number of NGO leaders and political human rights activists who have been fighting for LGBTI rights in some shape or form for years. During my time in Turkey (the in-person interviews took place during the summer of 2015, with follow-up (and additional) interviews in the Spring of 2016), I spoke with activists of leading LGBTI organizations, which include Lambda Istanbul,[3] Kaos GL, Pembe Hayat, Social Policies, Gender Identity and Sexual Orientation Studies Association (SPoD), and Families of LGBT's in Istanbul (LİSTAG). I also interviewed the founder of a well-known LGBTI digital magazine, *GZone Magazine*, as well as municipality workers Sedef Çakmak and the late Boysan Yakar. Through these various interviews, I was able to gain insight into the histories of these organizations and the strategies employed by LGBTI activists in their pursuit of domestic and international justice. The timing of the interviews began less than two weeks following the police breaking up the 2015 Pride March and went through the new onset of the civil war in southeastern Turkey, the state's continued fight against ISIS, a series of terror attacks in Turkey, and the cancellation of the 2016 Pride March. Because the interviews occurred during this period, this allows for detailed documentation and analysis of how these different domestic and international events have affected the progression (or regression) of LGBTI rights. I received consent for all interviews. I had copies of consent forms in Turkish as well as English, but all interviews were conducted in English. I used a convenience sampling method, reaching out to various activists and organization leaders, wanting to interview anyone who would grant this request.

It is my belief that this work will be useful not only in documenting LGBTI rights abuses in Turkey but also in showing just how LGBTI rights-based activists in Turkey are willing to risk their lives in challenging authorities on matters of ensuring full rights for the LGBTI (and all individuals) in Turkey. The hope is that others in the international community will recognize the work done in Turkey. This is not only important for the sake of learning about what is transpiring in Turkey but it is also with the goal that others can be inspired by the work these activists are doing in the country, and in turn they themselves can possibly provide any additional needed support through a rights advocacy network with local activists. Moreover, it is also a hope that the same LGBTI rights-based activists elsewhere can also apply some of the strategies and tactics to their own work wherever else they may be working on these human rights issues.

Unfortunately, LGBTI community members face what seems to be perpetual discrimination in various parts of the Middle East, Africa, Asia, Europe, and elsewhere. Yet, regardless of the challenges and outright discrimination, people are continuing to fight for change. It is within this vein that I hope to detail the level of commitment, the various strategies, and the successful results of LGBTI rights activism, and also any challenges that continue to exist. Every person in the world should live freely, without any form of discrimination whatsoever. There should be no judging of people, and there must also be direct and continued condemnation of any forms of discrimination, whether this discrimination is based on race, ethnicity, economics, gender, religion, or one's sexual orientation.

1 | Islam, Public Opinion, and Homosexuality in Turkey and the "Muslim World"

You can try ... and ... bring in a very interesting voice of a Muslim person who is respected, and speaks out in a good way about homosexuality, and you have the right media to support that idea and present that in a good way ... [Y]ou can have that, but it's not easy right now. [It's] very risky. If you don't do it in a good way, it backfires.

Cihan Hüroğlu

The LGBTI community experiences horrible conditions throughout much of the world. Sadly, it is all too common to see news of LGBTI individuals who are attacked and killed or targeted because of their sexual orientation. In many instances, their very own governments are either responsible for some of the crimes, complicit in not holding perpetrators accountable, or are also themselves behind treating the LGBTI community as inferior to heterosexual members of society. Whether it is murder or other forms of physical violence; a lack of equal access to housing and/or employment; the denial of a fair judicial system; not possessing the right to marry who they wish or use a bathroom based on the gender with which they identify; LGBTI individuals face dire situations in their everyday lives. As I shall discuss later, homosexuality is against the law in a number of countries in the world, and is punishable by jail time, not to mention the "unofficial" punishments imposed by radicals who detest LGBTI people. While such disturbing conditions exist throughout the world – and are perpetuated by out by perpetrators of different religions – an unfortunate reality is that a number of such rights abuses take place within Muslim-majority societies, under governments who go out of their way to ensure that LGBTI rights are not guaranteed.

As we shall see throughout this book, one of the reasons those who disprove of granting equal rights based on sexual orientation commonly cite against LGBTI rights in Turkey by comes from what these individuals perceive homosexuality to be in regard to their Islamic faith. For such people, they view the LGBTI community as "sinful." To these individuals, Islam prohibits homosexuality, and because of this, they do not believe in equal rights for those who are LGBTI, since this is "what their religion says." In fact, there are many instances where Muslim religious leaders have spoken out against homosexuality (Yip, 2008).

Discussion of Islam and homosexuality was brought to the forefront of international affairs following the mass shooting at an LGBT nightclub in Orlando, Florida, on June 12, 2016. Given that the shooter, who killed forty-nine people, was a Muslim, questions about the compatibility of "Islam and homosexuality," as well as the attitudes of Muslims on the issue of LGBTI community and same-sex rights, were raised.

While many within the Muslim community came out to condemn the murders – and continue to do so throughout their respective communities and networks – it would be incorrect to say that there is even a majority within Muslim communities who are openly supportive of LGBTI rights. In fact, as we shall see, based on public opinion surveys, Muslims who view homosexuality positively are statistically in the minority. What makes matters even worse is that leaders of respective states, police, and other holders of power often have similar homophobic attitudes. Indeed, we have witnessed numerous homophobic comments by leaders in the Muslim world. For example, in 2017, when asked about whether there were homosexuals in Chechyna, Ramzan Kadyrov, the leader of the Chechen region in Russia, was quoted as saying, "We don't have such people here. We don't have any gays. If there are any, take them to Canada. Praise be to God. Take them far away from us. To purify our blood, if there are any here, take them" (Sterling, 2017). While one might counter this by suggesting that such leaders posess negative attitudes about homosexuals and just happen to be Muslim, their comments are often defended based on what they deem to be "Islamic values" and that they are merely speaking about the "problem" of homosexuality from the perspective of Islam. For political leaders of Muslim-majority countries, these sorts of viewpoints have in turn influenced domestic and foreign policies. For example, in May 2016, LGBTI human rights organizations were not allowed to attend a United Nations conference organized on the theme of the AIDS virus. Fifty-one Muslim states, led by Egypt, opposed these lesbian, gay, bisexual, and transgender organizations participating in the AIDS conference. The Egyptian leadership, who was "representing the Organization for Islamic Co-operation, wrote to the General Assembly president to object to the participation of 11 groups" (BBC, 2016a). While Egypt did not give a reason for their letter (BBC, 2016a), Muslim-majority state representatives have brought up what they view as an "incompatibility" between homosexuality and the Islamic faith. This led to some officials condemning the move by these Muslim-majority states. For example, US Ambassador to the United Nations Samantha Power wrote: "Given that transgender people are 49 times more likely to be living with HIV than the general population, their exclusion from the high-level meeting will only impede global progress in combating the HIV/Aids pandemic" (BBC, 2016a). Yet, despite the importance of including LGBTI voices in this conversation and work, these Muslim state leaders continue to exclude LGBTI rights groups from important international initiatives, and many of them also strongly resist allowing these organizations to have an open platform in their respective states. As Mutua (2011) has noted, "homophobia has long been a hallmark of the two Abrahamic faiths [Islam and Christianity]" (452). This homophobia has been historically advanced by groups of these religions since the era of colonialism (Mutua, 2011). Yet we continue to still see homophobia in more-recent iterations by some religious groups, such as the Christian Right in the United States (Felice, 2016). When speaking about Islam and homosexuality, it is tough to know exactly how interpretations of Islam affect all individual attitudes and potential change in positions with regard to the issue of gender. Nevertheless, "it is a safe bet that Islam will continue to be critical for the configuration of sexuality in the Middle East. Islam is the most powerful cultural vehicle in the region, and whoever can get his or her message carried by Islam will stand to achieve a measure of social and cultural ascendency" (Uhlmann, 2005: 10).

Despite the fact that Muslim government leaders are so easily willing to discriminate against citizens who are LGBTI (Mutua, 2011), a similar sentiment exists among much of the population in most Muslim-majority states. Public opinion in most Muslim-majority countries continues to be quite strongly against the LGBTI community. There have been a series of studies conducted with regard to Muslim attitudes related to homosexuality. Here, I summarize just some of the more recent studies and their findings on this issue. For example, in 2013,

the Pew Research Center conducted a survey on Muslim-majority countries. Within the survey, they asked a series of questions related to social
life and issues of morality. One of the questions asked was what
individuals thought about homosexuality. In the thirty-six Muslim
countries featured in the study, the vast majority of respondents viewed
homosexuality negatively. This number was over 75 percent of the
entire population interviewed in thirty-six of the countries surveyed. In
fact, "[o]nly in three countries do as many as one-in-ten Muslims say
that homosexuality is morally acceptable: Uganda (12%), Mozambique
(11%) and Bangladesh (10%)" (Pew Research Center, 2013).

Along with this cross-sectional study, additional country-specific
public opinion polls show similar results. In an earlier 2009 study –
entitled the "Gallup Coexist Index of Muslims and non-Muslims in
Britain, France, and Germany" – "[n]one of the 500 British Muslims
interviewed believed that homosexual acts were morally acceptable ...
By comparison, 35% of French Muslims found homosexual acts to be
acceptable" (Butt, 2009). Then, in a controversial 2016 survey of
British Muslims, 52 percent of those surveyed believed that homosexuality should be illegal (Hume and Greene, 2016).[1] There have also been
a few other public opinion surveys measuring Muslim (and other religious groups') attitudes towards homosexuality (Markoe, 2016). For
example, "[a]s of 2011, U.S. Muslims were somewhat split between
those who said homosexuality should be accepted by society (39%) and
those who said it should be discouraged (45%), although the overall
Muslim population had grown considerably more accepting of homosexuality since a similar survey was conducted in 2007" (Lipka, 2015).[2]

Public Opinion about the LGBTI Community in Turkey

While studies measuring attitudes towards homosexuality have been
conducted across several Muslim countries, specifically gauging public
opinion with regard to support for same-sex rights in Turkey alone has
been somewhat more difficult. There are different reasons for this. For
example, as late as 2010, there existed no study directly tailored
towards public opinion of LGBTI individuals in Turkey. The most
recent public opinion poll on the issue at that time was a 2009 World
Values Survey entitled "Radicalism and Extremism" (Esmer, 2009),
in which the surveyors asked whether they would like to have a

homosexual living near them as neighbors; 87 percent of Turkish respondents said that no, they would not want LGBT individuals as their neighbors (Esmer, 2009, in COWI, 2010).[3]

In 2013, the Pew Research Center's thirty-nine-country poll of individuals and their thoughts on homosexuals included Turkey.[4] In their question on whether society should accept homosexuality, 78 percent of the Turkish respondents said "no," whereas 9 percent of those polled said "yes" (Pew Research Center, 2013a). This figure actually declined from a 2007 poll in which 14 percent of Turkish respondents answered "yes" to the same question. Other than France (83 percent "yes" in 2007 to 77 percent "yes" in 2013), this was the largest drop (−5) of any country that had the poll conducted in both years (Pew Research Center, 2013a). It is also interesting to note that the question has been previously posed to the Turkish public (through Pew public opinion surveys) in 2002, 2007, and 2011, and that the percentage of those who believed that society should accept homosexuality actually declined from 2002 onwards. In 2002, 22 percent of those surveyed felt that society should accept homosexuality. This figure dropped to 14 percent in 2007, 11 percent in 2011, and then 9 percent in 2013 (Pew Research Center, 2013b).

In the more recent 2013 survey, scholars also looked at whether there were any disparities in the responses to the question based on demographic categories, such as age differences. It is worth pointing out that while they found that there existed an age gap in a number of countries (with younger individuals tending to be more accepting of homosexuality), this was not really the case with Turkey. In Turkey, 9 percent of those age 18–29 said that homosexuality should be accepted, as did 7 percent of those age 30–49 and 10 percent of those age 50+ (Pew Research Center, 2013a). Again, these low acceptance numbers are not merely isolated to Turkey; they seem to be a rather consistent trend among many Muslim and sub-Saharan African states (Pew Research Center, 2013).[5,6]

Islam and Homosexuality

Given the high numbers of Muslims (in Turkey and elsewhere) with an unfavorable view of homosexuality, this leads one to wonder why they might feel this way, and if their interpretations of Islam could have anything to do with such sentiments. There is a long history of conversations about homosexuality within Islam and Islamic jurisprudence, where Islamic scholars have examined the issue of homosexuality within the faith for centuries. From the legality of sexual acts to debates over punishments for homosexuality, jurists in various Islamic schools of study have offered their opinions and rulings on these matters. While the discussions have been highly complex, and looked at from many different positions, it continues to hold that for most *imams* and Muslim populations, homosexuality is interpreted as being *haram*, or a prohibited act that goes against God and the faith. Those who hold such positions within Islam have tried to cite the Quran (Islam's holy religious text) in attempts to justify their position. For example, one of the most referenced verses with regard to Islam's position on homosexuality is Surah 7:81–82, which states: "And We sent Lot who said to his people: "Do you commit lewdness such as no people in creation (ever) committed before you? For you practice your lusts on men in preference to women; you are indeed a people transgressing beyond bounds." According to their interpretation of the story of Lot, the reason that God punished Sodom and Gomorrah was because of homosexual behavior committed by inhabitants of those cities.

Similar to Quranic references of the story of Lot, others also point to *Hadiths* (sayings of Muhammad) as further evidence of a disapproval of homosexuality (despite the fact that "the hadiths were written down almost two centuries after the prophet lived, and their authenticity has been repeatedly questioned – as early as the ninth century by the scholar Imam Nesai – and they can be questioned anew today" (Akyol, 2015)). Nonetheless, many Muslims interpret the Lot story only in this way, and take the Hadiths as truth, without understanding multiple interpretations of the story of Lot, as well as questions on the validity of hadiths.

Another reason why some have viewed homosexuality as a sin in Islam has to do with interpretations about sexual relations as pertaining to marriage. As Kutty (2014) explains, "The prohibition is derived from the normative Islamic position that the institution of the family (preservation of which is one of the *maqasid al Shari'ah*, higher objectives of the Sharī'ah) created through marriage is the only sanctioned avenue for sex. This policy objective is reinforced through comprehensive regulations found in classical fiqh, which is the human articulation of God's will as expressed in the *Sharī'ah.*" So, for these individuals, because they view marriage as that between a man and a woman, homosexuality, falling outside of the scope of what they define as a permissible marital relationship, has led to the opinion that homosexuality and homosexual relationships are against the Islamic faith. Others have even tried to say that homosexuality is a choice; some Islamic scholars have also attempted to "use science" to advocate their positions that homosexuality is either "unnatural" or a choice by an individual. There have even been some who – when looking at the studies about the naturalness of homosexuality in humans – argue that there is no clear evidence that homosexuality is viewed as "natural."

But while these individuals want to make the argument that Islam is "clear" on the issue of homosexuality, there actually is no consensus position agreed upon by jurist and non-scholar Muslims. For example, there exists a camp of scholars and others within Islam who have argued that while – in their minds – homosexuality continues to be a sin in Islam, LGBTI individuals should not be punished. In fact,

[a] growing number of contemporary traditionalist Sunni and Shia scholars including Shaikh Mohamed El-Mochtar El-Shinqiti and Zaytuna College's Shaikh Abdullah Bin Hamid Ali – while affirming the immorality of the act – assert that there is no temporal punishment stated in the two primary sources of Islamic law, the *Quran* and the *Sunna* (teachings and sayings of the Prophet), for merely being homosexual. Prominent Iranian scholar Abdolkarim Soroush argues that any persecution or discrimination on the basis of sexual orientation would be wrong. (Kutty, 2014)

Historically, there have been additional scholars making similar statements, For example, in arguing against punishment of LGBTI individuals, Hamid Ali

quotes Shaikh Yahya b. Sharaf al-Nawawi (1277 CE) as writing that "there is no blame, censure, sin, or punishment on this type [one acting out of natural inclination] because he is excused by virtue of having no hand in that condition." Shaikh Ali also refers to classical jurist, Hafiz Ibn Hajar al-Asqalaini (1448 CE) who cited Imam Ibn Jariri al-Tabari (922 CE) to conclude, that when men exhibited feminine characteristics due to their innate nature then rather than being condemned they should be taught to gradually unlearn this, because they may have been created this way. (Kutty, 2014)

More recently, on May 3, 2016, it was reported that a well-known Saudi Arabian scholar by the name of Dr. Salman al-Ouda also spoke out against the punishment of homosexuals. Now, al-Ouda was not saying that homosexuality is acceptable; he still viewed it to be a "sin" against Islam. What al-Ouda was saying was that people should not punish these individuals. According to al-Ouda, "Even though homosexuality is considered a sin in all the Semitic holy books, it does not require any punishment in this world. It is a sin that will accompany its committee in the life after death." He also said, "Homosexuals are not deviating from Islam. Homosexuality is a grave sin, but those who say that homosexuals deviate from Islam are the real deviators. By condemning homosexuals to death they are committing a graver sin than homosexuality itself" (Duffy, 2016). It is important to note that al-Ouda continues to view homosexuality as a problem; his position is not one of full acceptance. Rather, for him, he seems to take issue when individuals want "to show their feelings in public."

Again, this is in no way justifying the idea that homosexuality is a sin – since to do so opens up the allowance of discrimination – but in the case of these scholars, it has been argued that there is at least some movement away from the position that because of homosexuality, an LGBTI person can be punished. These imams who have at the very least said that the LGBTI community should not be punished have often done so by often citing earlier Muslim scholars who worked on the same question. Others still have looked to the Prophet Muhammad and the early Muslim community as to how he, and they, dealt with LGBTI issues. As I shall discuss in the next section, there is another group of scholars looking to reinterpret these stories and hadiths, and when doing so, are finding that Islam is not homophobic, but rather, supports different sexual identities.

Reinterpretations of Islam and Homosexuality

As I mentioned, while many Muslim imams and scholars say that homosexuality is not compatible with Islam, there have also been countercurrents of scholars, writers, and activists working within the Islamic tradition to argue that Islam itself does not ban homosexuality activity, nor does it punish homosexuals or those who are transgender. There are also scholars who say that there has been recognition within the Islamic tradition of people who may have nonheterosexual feelings (Kutty, 2014). Thus, upon closer examination of Islam as it relates to the topic of homosexuality, it becomes rather evident that interpretations are much more complicated than a simple position of homosexuality being "forbidden" within the Islamic faith.

For example, take the issue of sex between a man and a woman outside of the institution of marriage. While many "traditionalists" argue that the Quran's references of a man and a women when addressing the topic clearly indicates Islam's position on the matter, Scott Siraj al-Haqq Kugle has argued that such interpretations need to be reexamined, and that, through this reinterpretation of the Quran and other early Islamic sources, he finds that there are many reasons to believe that Islam is not opposed to the idea of homosexuality. There is a great amount of evidence to support this position. For instance, despite claims to the contrary, the Prophet Muhammad himself never condemned homosexuality nor punished anyone because they were homosexual. In fact, one could argue that the Quran actually understands that some people are not heterosexuals, and says nothing about punishing them, or about this being a "sin." For example, there is a specific verse in the Quran which speaks about "men who are not in need of women," which has been interpreted as recognition that there are some males who are not sexually attracted to females. The Surah 24:31 of the Quran reads as follows:

"Let them [Muslim women] not display their beauties except to their husbands, or their fathers, or the fathers of their husbands, or their sons, or the sons of their husbands, or their brothers, or the sons of their brothers, or the sons of their sisters, or their womenfolk, their slaves, or their followers among the men who have no wiles with women or children who do not recognize the sexual nakedness of women."[7]

This verse alone is significant evidence that even in the early foundations of Islam, from the most important of sources, homosexuality was something that was understood and accepted. In addition to the Quranic verse on the matter, Muhammad himself showed great acceptance of members of the LGBTI community. For example, Muhammad's wife Umm Salama had a friend by the name of Hit who was *mukhanath* (what today would be referred to as transgendered). According to reports, not only did Muhammad not condemn Hit to some sort of punishment, Muhammad also never criticized or condemned Hit's sexual orientation. In fact, "[u]nlike other men, Hit was allowed to enter both men's space and women's space – Muhammad even trusted the mukhanath enough to let . . .[Hit] enter the private women's space of the Prophet's household" (Kugle, 2010b). And while critics of homosexuality have pointed out that Muhammad at one point did prohibit Hit from being in the areas where other women were staying, scholars explain that

[i]n the case of Hit, Umm Salama's mukhanath friend, Muhammad did "punish" Hit in a way, but not for his sexuality. Muhammad found out that Hit described a woman's body to a man – which he could do because Hit was able to enter both women's and men's spaces. At that point, Muhammad told his wife not to allow Hit into the women's quarters anymore. However, Muhammad did not criticize Hit for his sexuality or for "acting like women" – he only criticized Hit for not respecting the privacy of women." (Kugle, 2010b)

One could also look at additional Quranic verses to suggest that God's message (according to Muslim belief) does not discriminate against LGBTI individuals. For example, in Surah 42:49–50 of the Quran, it states, "To God belongs dominion of the heavens and earth. God creates whatever God wills and gives to whomever God wills females and gives to whomever God wills the males, or pairs them as male and female. And God makes whomever God wills not reproducing, for God is One who knows all, One capable of all things." As Kugle (2010a) argues, this reference seems to include individuals who are heterosexual, homosexual, and those who may be either transgender or are "gender-ambiguous" (66). The Quran seems to not only directly mention individuals who are not sexually attracted to a sex other than their own, but the holy text also makes no mention of punishing someone who is LGBTI (contrary to arguments anti-LGBTI individuals attempt to provide).

Another Quranic reference discussing protocol for women and men when a man is entering a private room in which a female may possibly be naked sheds further light on the support for nonheterosexual individuals. The verse reads:

Yet if your children have reached sexual maturity, then require them to ask permission before entering, like those mentioned before, for in this way God clarifies for you God's signs, and God is a knowing One, One most wise. Of the women, those not reproducing who do not wish for intercourse, it is no harm for them to lay aside their clothing as long as they do not overtly display their beauty (in the company of men). (Q.24:60)

As Kugle (2010a) notes, the specific part of the verse that is applicable here is "those not reproducing who do not wish for intercourse." He argues that "[t]his description could apply to lesbian women" (67–68). Kugle (2010a) also says that this verse could also be open to persons without a sexual drive (or asexual individuals) (68).

Along with more direct references to the Quran, some have also cited historical examples from Turkey's literary and poetic past to make the argument for love and acceptance. For example, Diva (2015) cites Jalaladin Rumi, Turkey's most noted Sufi poet. Rumi's verses were filled with references to Divine Love, and his legacy extends to include respect and acceptance for a variety of religious faiths. The same can be said for the other Sufi references in the article, such as Yunus Emre, who also wrote extensively on themes of love and respect. Diva uses Sufi arguments of love with the Divine, and Divine Love itself, to connect to any form of love, citing Rumi's love for Shams as an example of Divine Love. It is within this Sufi tradition that one escapes notions of gender or sex, elevating their understanding of love to one outside notions of social constructions and of even time itself.

As Kugle (2010a) notes, Sufi tradition stresses the importance of the soul outside of any material conditions or labels, which include notions of body. He says that "[i]t is the goal of Sufis to highlight this vast difference between body and spirit and to encourage the Muslim believer to explore the spirit, to desist from identifying solely with the body, to leave behind the limitations of its appetites, drives, and obsessions" (237). For the Sufi, attention is primarily on the heart and, of course, the soul. While individuals may want to – in their definition of "I" –include gender as a part of one's overall identity, the Sufi tradition points out that while we are centered on ideas of gender duality, God is behind such identities and is genderless (Kugle, 2010a: 237).

The last argument for the position of Islam not being against homosexuality has to do with the story of Lot. As mentioned, those looking to say that Islam hates homosexuality often reference this verse as "proof" that God is so upset with homosexuality that God punished those in Sodom and Gomorrah for engaging in homosexual acts with travellers in these cities. However, other interpretations argue that the real sin was not homosexuality but rather that those in these towns used rape as a weapon against visitors. So, the most heinous crime was sexually violating those who should have been given hospitality. Their crime: "Do you commit an obscenity not perpetrated before you by anyone in all the worlds?" (Quran, 7–80:81). Homosexuality was known during (and before) Islam. So it would be difficult to argue that what was being talked about was homosexuality itself. However, what may have never been done before is a group committing such acts of rape and violence on those visiting Lot (Kugle, 2010a). Punishment was not given because of homosexual behavior but because of the various crimes that were committed by those who intended to turn away from Lot's prophethood (Kugle, 2010a). Again this interpretation is very different than the one often stated by those looking to condemn homosexuality.

So, not only are there Quranic references that are interpreted as understanding various sexual identities, evidence exists that Muhammad himself knew and accepted at least one person who was *mukhanath*, there is a different argument for the events that took place to in Sodom and Gomorrah. It seems that there is ample support for LGBTI rights within the early Islamic tradition (Kutty, 2014). At the same time, we must also understand that Muslim opinions on sexual minority rights were, at times, also influenced by colonialist positions. It is thus important to understand that, while religious arguments in the name of Islam are used, history also suggests non-Islamic sources for the opposition to sexual minorities. Yet, even with this, many within Muslim communities today continue to believe that homosexuality is the crime committed against Islamic law, which has led to more hatred against the LGBTI community. Turkey has not been immune from this sort of attitude toward and response to sexual minorities.

Looking at the issue of same-sex rights in the history of Turkey, homosexuality has not been officially criminalized in Turkey for over a century and a half, when the Ottoman Empire adopted the Napoleonic Code in 1853 (Cole, 2015), which led to the decriminalization of homosexuality in 1858 (Tokyay, 2015)[8] and then in 1923 under the new secular regime of Mustapha Kemal Ataturk (after establishing the modern-day state of Turkey). Despite historical legal protections, this is not to say that Turkish law does not violate the human rights of LGBTI individuals, since there exist a number of laws that, while not directly discriminating against the LGBTI community, are written (and often interpreted) in a way that directs bias towards the group. In the next chapter, I shall show just how these laws are interpreted in ways that make life for sexual minorities in Turkey extremely difficult.

LGBTI Rights Advocacy through the Use of Religion

As discussed in the introduction, one of the most consistent arguments that many within the Muslim world who are anti-LGBTI rights attempt to make is where they suggest Islam prohibits homosexuality, and more directly, that such acts and relationships are "sinful" within the religion. Again, their criticisms seem to revolve around the idea that the faith prohibits homosexuality, and thus, for many, this is the end of the discussion about the issue. However, an underlying question related to this is: What would their opinions be if they were introduced to ideas suggesting that Islam does not prohibit homosexuality, that same-sex relationships are not "sinful?"

One of the best ways to change the minds of those who are religious is to present information from within the same religious framework. As Harrison and Michelson (2015) note, people are much more likely to be supportive of LGBTI rights if the pro-same-sex message comes from a religious cleric than if it comes from a secular voice. Thus, this can be a highly effective strategy: advocate for same-sex rights through the same religious discourse. If people can see that there are individuals within the Islamic faith that advocate for these positions, then they might be more likely to accept the LGBTI community.

This was an important question that drove much of my research. As well as documenting overall advocacy approaches, I was also curious to see whether LGBTI organizations were using similar religious-based strategies in their fight for equality. Knowing that many within Turkey might identify themselves with Islam, and that those people may also view themselves as more religious, the concern is that they would say that they would not accept or support LGBTI rights because of their faith. But if these nongovernmental organizations were able to use Islam and work with Islamic leaders who also support LGBTI rights, then this might have much more sway for those hearing the message. Eliminating the so-called contradiction between Islam and homosexuality, to their minds, could lead to much greater acceptance of these rights. Therefore, a question posed to the human rights advocates was whether they used Islam, or strategies related to Islam, in their LGBTI rights work. More specifically, did they try to find ways to reference the faith when speaking about LGBTI rights? What I found was that, for many of the organizations, even if they were quite secular in their personal makeup, or this was the official position of the group, they were still quite open to using religion as a strategy to help increase awareness and acceptance about LGBTI rights despite this tactic not being central to their approaches

This idea of using Islam, or religious arguments generally, to change opinions on LGBTI rights is not new. In fact, if one takes a look at many same-sex rights movements, it becomes evident that the clergy or religious leaders have played a critical part in ensuring that they presented an alternate position on LGBTI rights, one that was not restrictive but preached a message of love and inclusivity. While it is outside the scope of this book to look at this question in full detail, the topic of religious movements related to LGBTI rights is surely another research strand worth examining. I do, however, want to briefly mention a couple of cases where activists have used religion or religious messages (from religious leaders or through new presentations of holy texts) for the advancement of LGBTI rights.

One noted case where this has been quite successful is with Christian clergy in South Africa. Archbishop Desmond Tutu, for example, has made some of the most powerful statements about his understanding of God as it relates to same-sex rights. Tutu has been quoted as saying that he "would not worship a homophobic God" (BBC, 2013) and that he "would refuse to go to a homophobic heaven. No, I would say sorry, I mean I would much rather go to the other place," and that for him, this issue of same-sex rights is at the same level of concern as was his work against apartheid (BBC, 2013). He even called this struggle "the new apartheid" (Curry, 2014).

Along with Tutu, one of the other leading South African clergy on the issue of LGBTI rights has been Dr. Reverend Allan Boesak. He was a founder of the Uniting Reformed Church. In 2011, Boesak also served as "chair of a synodical committee" within the church. It was at this time that Dr. Boesak presented his synod committee with a detailed paper summarizing his position on same-sex rights issues. "The report, which included a lengthy exegesis of the implications of the Belhar Commission for the topic, recommended full acceptance of homosexuals in loving and faithful relationships to the ministry of the

Church" (Banner, 2011). He spoke about the importance of the Belhar Commission as a human rights text not just for guaranteeing racial equality but equality for all within South Africa. However, this was not well received by the delegates. Many were upset, and they did not accept his demands. Because of this, Boesak resigned from his position (Banner, 2011).

The work of Tutu and Boesak are illustrations of how religious leaders can advocate for same-sex rights through a religious-based message. They are not the only ones doing so. For example, "[t]he current head of the Anglican Church in Southern Africa, Njongonkulu Ndungane, has been an outspoken supporter of including homosexuals in the Church community, putting himself in a strong-worded conflict with other African Church leaders" (Afrol News, 2010). These sorts of actions by religious leaders send a powerful message to individuals. People within (and outside) the church pay attention when a reverend or archbishop offers their voice for the rights of the oppressed. Therefore, this can help increase acceptance for same-sex individuals within religious communities. Again, having an "insider" advocating the message will likely lead to much better results with regard to changing opinions on LGBTI rights.

I also wanted to examine whether NGOs and human rights advocates thought that using Islam as a way to call for LGBTI rights was an effective strategy, and why or why not. In addition, for those that felt it was a useful approach, I was curious to see if they were actively using this approach. Now, it might be expected that if a group feels that the strategy is a good one, they would be likely to employ it. While this was the case in many instances, it was not always so. Again, while most of the human rights organizations were not opposed to the idea of using Islam as an argument point for LGBTI advocacy, the organizations did not have this strategy as a central component within their overall work. The reason is that most activists are simply not well versed on the matters of Islam as it pertains to homosexuality and LGBTI rights; this is not their area of expertise. These activists have worked on LGBTI rights for over a decade (and more) but have done so through the advocacy of rights through the secular, constitutional law. It seems that they are more comfortable working to change conditions through secular arguments.

Sedef Çakmak, a member of the *Cumhuriyet Halk Partisi* (Republican People's Party, CHP) is a city council member and civil servant in

the Department of Social Equality in the Beşiktaş municipality of
Istanbul (Research Turkey, 2015). She is also one of the leading LGBTI
activists in Turkey. Çakmak spoke about some of the challenges with
approaching advocacy from a position of religious issues, saying that
while they have done some work related to this approach, it was not
the primary strategy for Lambda Istanbul, which, founded in 1993, is
one of the largest LGBTI human rights-based organizations in Turkey.
Çakmak explained that Muslim scholars such as Muhsin Hendricks
have been invited to speak about the different ways to interpret Islam
with regard to homosexuality, especially regarding the story of Lot and
how it relates to punishment for rape and not homosexuality. Çakmak
notes that "[t]he first time I heard this theory was from Muhsin
Hendrix. We, in 2006, we invited him to a conference in here ... and
there were lots of people from religious groups that attended it because
they really wanted to learn more about it." Even so, Çakmak goes on
to say that "we never use religious discourse" in their approach to
LGBTI rights.

Elsewhere, Çakmak explains that part of this has to do with the fact
that they are not as knowledgeable about these Islamic interpretations,
saying that "a few years ago when we want to talk about conservati-
vism or we want to talk about religion and the LGBT issues, we
couldn't reach out to anyone knowledgeable about this issue. We had
several conservative intellectuals and we would be asking them whether
they would like to come to our conference and they would be saying to
us 'Are you trying to get me killed? I cannot say this out in public.'"
Çakmak argues that things have changed a bit recently, where "in the
last two years we're seeing more things written on this issue, we're
seeing more people stating that they're conservative and they're gay
even though they, for example, hide their faces but they'll still be giving
some interviews, and these are beginning. So I think this will be better.
But it is ... hard because ... you have to face your family ... [P]eople
are killed by their families in this country because they are gay or
transgender, so this is ... one of the real threats in Turkey." There is
an overall fear that coming out will lead a person to be ostracized from
their communities. Çakmak admitted that she doesn't speak on issues
of religion because that is not what she is versed in, but she does cite
other Muslim intellectuals to people who want to make the argument
that homosexuality is a "sin" in Islam. Çakmak did mention there is
some contact with Muslim organizations, particularly those that were

active in the Gezi Park protests. So while this approach is not a cornerstone of the LGBTI rights strategies, Gezi Park was at least able to bring different groups together based on common causes and objectives – ideas of freedom, justice, and human rights.

I also conducted two interviews with Janset Kalan. Kalan is the international affairs coordinator at Pembe Hayat. Pembe Hayat is an organization based out of Ankara that is concentrated on the rights of the transgender community in Turkey. It was the first organization in Turkey created to focus on transgender rights. In my second interview I asked Kalan about whether the organization was working through discussions of Islam as an advocacy approach with regard to how conservatives view the LGBTI community and LGBTI rights. I was curious to see if using an Islamic-based framework to speak with those who argue that "homosexuality is a sin" in Islam might be more likely to change their position if they are presented with an argument based within their faith-based system. Kalan mentioned that Pembe Hayat does not use this approach as a strategy for their LGBTI rights advocacy. Kalan also said

It usually comes with the hate speech argument. So if it is about hate speech, usually what we do is go to the court, bring the case to the court, and actually evaluate [the situation to see] if [it is] better [that] the court or better [that] the judge will decide in our favor or in their favor. But on the other hand, if there is only a religious sect and they are talking there[,] like spreading their anti-LGBTI discourse in their own group, there is nothing we can do actually, because it is their belief and what we can do is come up with our own discourses. But, we do not use religious argument[s] from within their perspectives.

Regarding why this is the case, Kalan mentioned that there are some partnerships with religious groups, but there are many more groups and sects that exist. Kalan explained that they also don't work with conservative religious groups "[b]ecause it also puts us, and also the larger LGBTI community, into a sort of a risk situation. Because ... if you try to challenge them, and they are so determined about their own ideas and what their own discourse is ... it becomes sort of a clash. We do not want to have these kinds of clashes, actually." They face a threat of physical violence from these groups.

However, one interesting article posted on the Pembe Hayat (Pink Life) website was called *"Din ve Eşcinsellik"* (*"Religion and*

Homosexuality"), by Madi Diva (2015). The article poses a series of commonly asked questions with regard to Islam and homosexuality, and Diva responds to them, specifically discussing people's views of interpretations of Islam as related to the issue of homosexuality. One of the questions asks whether Islam views homosexuality as a sin. Diva responds by saying "What Islam?" This implies that they are various interpretations of the faith, with some within conservative patriarchal societies offering one view, and others having other opinions on the question (Diva, 2015). This is important to say because it allows people to get out of their comfort zone that there is only one Islam, and that "Islam says" this or that, and that the position is then final. This is far from the case. The NGO, by posting this article, is challenging the idea that there is only one way to interpret Islam. By doing this, hopefully readers can call into question what they believe merely because some religious leader said that this is how the faith should be interpreted with regard to the issue of homosexuality, or any other topic for that matter.

I also spoke about this issue with Murat Köylü, who works as the External Affairs Coordinator for Kaos GL Association of Turkey, which is based out of the capital, Ankara. Köylü said that the organization should be taking this approach, but that they were not "very talented or we are very skilled in this. Personally, I am not very skilled." He also said that

we don't have any [such] strategy because to have a strategy you should feel very powerful in that direction, right? So we don't see ourselves very powerful at that moment because religion itself is a very controversial issue in Turkey at this moment, at these times. LGBTI organizations or [the] LGBTI movement, even the other movements are kind of hesitant to ... [approach] some issues and because we are not that powerful ... But we never, never close our doors to the conservative side.

Köylü went on to add that

[In terms of the activities], many of them are [in] conservative cities and we, especially in universities or in trade unions ... make face to face communication with conservative people. But in terms of institutionally ... having a dialogue with conservative NGOs or conservative structures, we don't have to come to institutional [levels of] dialogue. But we have an open doors policy. We always [have] an open call, and we always ... invite them and we give the ball to them ... we have that kind of a Turkish idiom. You give the ball to them and wait for them to pass the ball to us."

When asked if they would be open to this approach, he replied,

Of course, of course ... Being opposed to religion is something like being a fundamentalist for me ... Religion is what people live. If it changes in a good way it becomes a good religion or it becomes good people who are living religion in a good way [w]hen it comes to including LGBTIs ... in the understanding of religion or whatever. So we are not opposed to ... religion. It would be a very antagonistic thing to deal with issues ... [I]t wouldn't be, pragmatically good, it wouldn't be ethically good ... it's a Cold War understanding, for me, to be against religion.

Along with these NGO leaders, I also interviewed Murat Renay about this topic. Renay founded *GZone Magazine*, which is an online-based LGBTI lifestyle publication in Turkey. In one of our conversations, I asked Renay if the magazine publishes on issues of Islam related to LGBTI rights. For Renay, one of the challenges for the magazine has been backlash from some conservative elements of society. There are many who view same-sex rights as against the nature of Islam, and thus have a problem with such publications, and are also critical of any demands for LGBTI rights in the country. Sadly, this situation is not limited to Turkey; many throughout the world, use what are in their minds religious arguments for the prohibition of LGBTI rights. Related to this, there are also discussions in the literature about LGBTI activists working to shape the perception of those in the LGBTI community among those who may identify as conservative Muslims. Thus, I was interested to see if he used his magazine to shape how religious conservatives in the country view the LGBTI community. When I asked Renay whether he devotes any of the magazine content towards speaking to the conservative religious community in Turkey, he replied that yes, they did have strategies to deal with conservatives in the Justice and Development Party and in the public. Namely, Renay seemed to believe that his magazine would be able to increase visibility through shared experiences with others who have also been discriminated against in Turkey. As an example, Renay says, "[T]here are some women in burka [who] are best friends of LGBT people and you'll never know because she is a minority ... she was a minority because of her burka and gays are a minority so they became friends ... it's really

complicated, in Turkey, in terms of conservativeness, but it's complicated in every [part] in Turkey ... So, it will be hard but to be more
visible can be a solution." Moreover, it is also important to note that
they have also published stories related to Islam. For example, when a
noted religious figure backs LGBTI rights, they would publish that
information or speak with them.

As shown in this chapter, while activists are not necessarily opposed
to using Islam to promote LGBTI rights, they are not as well versed in
the faith. Instead, they focus more on other activism strategies, which
include socioeconomic rights, lobbying, educational workshops, protests, and running in elections. It seems that activists are open to a
variety of approaches but do believe that those allies who are religious
should be more active in working from the perspective of Islam
towards LGBTI advocacy; it is not that they don't want to address
Islam, but many felt they were not the most qualified to do so. In later
chapters, I will examine the other types of work they do, and in the
conclusion, I will expand upon the importance of working within the
"insider" model, namely, finding those from within the Islamic community who can speak to other religious individuals about the compatibility of Islam and LGBTI rights.

2 | The History of Human Rights Abuses against the LGBTI Community in Turkey

[T]he social psychology of this increasing state violence as well as trends to the society [when it] comes to freedom of expression, and then ... right to association, right to assembly, it's said themselves are increasing the hatred and violence attacks from the society as well from the law enforcement agencies towards [the] trans community because they see trans people ... [and] especially trans women, as open targets.

Janset Kalan

In order to understand LGBTI rights-based activism in Turkey, I believe that it is imperative to first understand the levels of violence and discrimination against LGBTI members in the country. Therefore, in this chapter, I shall examine the history of human rights abuses faced by the LGBTI community in Turkey and more recent actions that suggest the situation continues to be one of difficulty and danger for those who identify as LGBTI. I will discuss the various sorts of abuses facing LGBTI individuals, discussing various cases of murder, torture, and physical assault, along with other forms of harassment. As we shall see, discrimination against LGBTI people extends back decades. We must keep in mind that the incidents discussed below are just the reported cases of abuse; there may indeed exist many more instances of hate crimes against the LGBTI gone unreported due to fears of retaliation or retribution.

These crimes against the LGBTI community have been well documented, and span various activities. For example, in some cases, harassment took the form of posters put up by hardline organizations, groups such as the Muslim Defense Youth, which said: "If you see those carrying out the People of Lot's dirty work, kill the doer and the done!" (Akyol, 2015). In other cases, harassment exists through employment discrimination and attacks and killings of transgendered individuals. But as we shall see, the state often does little to endorse a culture of equality within Turkey, has few legal protections in place for

29

those who identify as LGBTI, and does not go nearly far enough in investigating these hate crimes or in holding perpetrators accountable for their actions. Despite the organizational efforts of human rights activists – and their ability to establish events related to challenging homophobia, such violations of rights continue to occur.

Before delving into the different forms of oppression that the LGBTI community has faced from police, the military, government, and members of civil society, I want to spend some time first presenting the way that members of the ruling government view the LGBTI community and homosexuality in general. Because, as I shall argue, their positions toward homosexuality have been a large explanatory factor in the sorts of policies that the government under the Justice and Development Party (AKP) has pushed, and also what they have not been willing to support in terms of LGBTI rights. I purposely chose to focus primarily on the history under the AKP since their attitudes have both been contrary to LGBTI rights and because their time in power (from 2002–present) largely coincides with the rise of the LGBTI activism in Turkey. Understanding how ruling officials perceive same-sex individuals will help reveal how they have been able to act in ways that minimizes the rights of the LGBTI. When looking at the case of Turkey, and more specifically the tenure of the Justice and Development Party, one finds a pattern of public statements against same-sex rights, along with a history of human rights violations committed against sexual minorities. While backlash against the LGBTI community has come from seculars, as well as some within the religious communities, a great amount of hatred towards the LGBTI in Turkey is a result of the AKP, an Islamist-based party that has been in power in Turkey since 2002. From around the time of the AKP entering into office, and throughout their years in office, it is evident that the leaders of the party have not only done little for the promotion of same-sex rights in Turkey but there actually exists ample evidence to suggest that their ruling period has actually made matters much worse for the LGBTI in Turkish society. It has even been argued that the human rights violations against the LGBTI community "is often promoted by the highest level of the Justice and Development Party (AKP) government, led by Erdoğan, which has done nothing but obstruct attempts at enhancing LGBT rights" (Idiz, 2014b).

President Recep Tayyip Erdoğan and the party's position towards the LGBTI are evident when one examines his (and others') statements and actions as they pertain to same-sex rights in the past decade or so. Beginning in 2003, shortly after the AKP came to power in Turkey, a spokesperson for Erdoğan was quoted as saying that "homosexuals cannot be members" of the ruling party: "They can establish their own" (Özalp, 2003, in Amnesty International, 2011). This sort of comment goes directly in the face of inclusivity of all members of Turkish society, as it suggests that certain people are not good enough for the party, and arguably, not good enough to be in the government (or even in Turkey itself). This was not the only homophobic statement uttered by a member of the AKP party. In 2008, it was reported in *Milliyet* that Burhan Kuzu, who was a parliament member of the AKP at the time, said, "Gays have made requests during the negotiations on constitutional changes. Are we going to respond to their requests? It is not possible in the current conditions. The public is not ready for this" (*Milliyet*, 2008, in Amnesty International, 2011: 9). Others within the party followed with their own comments against the lesbian, gay, bisexual, transgender, and intersex community. Not long after Kuzu's statement, others made similar remarks about Turkish society, also saying that they too did not see the country as ready for the establishment of LGBTI rights (Amnesty International, 2011).

In 2010, Aliye Kavaf, who held the position of minister of state for women and family, said about homosexuality, "I believe homosexuality is a biological disorder, an illness and should be treated" (Amnesty International, 2011: 5). Kavaf went on to add, "Therefore I do not have a positive opinion of gay marriage." Kavaf also talked about not having any agenda with regard to LGBTI rights and also that no such "demand" for one is there (*Hurriyet Daily News*, 2010, in COWI, 2010: 11). Then, "[i]n a 2011 speech on terrorism, former Minister of the Interior Idris Naim Sahin spoke disparagingly of "an environment in which there are all sorts of immorality, indecency and inhuman situations – from pork meat to … homosexuality" (Kaos GL, LGBTI News Turkey, and IGLHRC, 2015: 7). And "[i]n 2012, Ankara mayor and member of the ruling Justice and Development Party Melih Gökçek spoke of homosexuality as contrary to Turkish culture." Speaking on this issue, Gökçek stated,

Each society has its own moral values. Especially for our Turkish society, it is not possible for us to be together with the gay culture in Europe. It is also not possible to approve of this. How we have been brought up, our brand of morality, our views are a little different. I hope to God that in Turkey there will not be a gay and there should not be." (Kaos GL, LGBTI News Turkey, and IGLHRC, 2015: 7–8)

Then, in 2013, Türkan Dağoğlu, Istanbul MP and deputy president of the Committee on Health, Family, Labor, and Social Affairs was quoted as saying "that 'LGBT' is a behavior that is outside the bounds of normality" (Kaos GL, LGBTI News Turkey, and IGLHRC, 2015: 8). Following this, on May 29, 2013, a parliamentary discussion on the issue of LGBTI rights occurred in Turkey. It was here that Dağoğlu of the Justice and Development Party spoke out against LGBTI equality. As Engin (2015) notes, Dağoğlu "began her speech by questioning what it means to have an LGBT identity, asking whether it is a biological deficiency, a sociological appearance, or a psychological problem. Dağoğlu stated that "women marrying women, or men marrying men is not a right, on the contrary it is a proposal that converts accepted sexual understandings that smooths the path of degeneracy of society" (846). Dağoğlu went on to say, "[r]esearches on this topic has been done previously in both in the US in 1972, and by the European psychological association in 1992. They found that what we consider an LGBT status is not normal behavior." As if these problematic statements were not enough to show how Dağoğlu feels about LGBTI, she then expressed how she views LGBTI rights as a negative for society as a whole, saying:

[A]ffiliates of the JDP [AKP], regularly express valuing humans simply because they are humans, treating everyone equal under the law, loving every creature because of the creator. Social measures that are taken are not for a specific sexual orientation, it is for the benefit of all humanity. Nonetheless, these attributes cannot be used as a door opening to lifestyles that our society disapproves of or as an encouragement for the sort of behavior that triggers the degeneration of the population, and cannot be assessed as a criterion for democracy." (Engin, 2015: 847)

Having a ruling government party in which the leaders utter such statements does nothing to suggest a willingness to provide all people in Turkey with complete equality in society. Yet, these are the conditions that the LGBTI community face today; they have to worry about what their political leaders will say about them, whether they view them as equal or see them as a "problem" in Turkey. However, the hatred towards homosexuality is not merely confined to statements made inside Turkey. In 2013, for example, among some of the things said by government officials include a case where Erdoğan, when visiting the Netherlands, was highly critical of the Dutch government's decision to grant a lesbian couple custody of a Turkish boy (who was a Dutch citizen) after his biological mother was found to have mistreated the child. Erdoğan, speaking on this issue, made very troubling statements about homosexuality, saying that homosexuality was not biological, but rather a "sexual preference" that individuals have. In addition, he also went on to say that homosexuality "is contrary to the culture of Islam" (Idiz, 2014b). Erdoğan then seemed to equate homosexuality with instability, because he criticized the government's decision to grant the couple custody of the child by saying that the child should have been given to "secure hands," and also "[i]f we say 'a six-month [-old] child cannot make such a decision so it is the judiciary that decides,' then this could lead us to a big mistake" (Idiz, 2014b).

As Nigar Goksel (2014) argues,

In the past few years, the ruling Justice and Development Party (AKP) has incrementally stepped up its propagation of a conservative agenda, with a focus on protecting traditional-family-based lifestyles, values, and morals. From interfering with the co-ed living arrangements of students to depicting homosexuality as a sickness, representatives of the ruling party have provided ample reasons for concern for segments of the society that prioritise individual choice over the traditional gender norms of the country.[1]

Turkish leaders have continued to make homophobic statements as late as early 2016. For example, as Engin (2015) notes:

[I]n June 2015, Efkan Ala, the former minister of Internal Affairs and a current Justice and Development Party (JDP) candidate for the parliament[,] openly opposed gay marriage, stating that gay marriage is the destruction of humanity. He also criticized the Peace and Democracy Party (PDP) for promoting transgender and homosexual candidates for office. He stated, 'For God's sake, look at these candidates that the PDP put forth. I can't even bring myself to say it. They have put forth candidates that our citizen cannot accept.' He then argued that our society's morality and tradition rejects men marrying men and women marrying women.

Then, LGBTI News Turkey cited a Kaos GL report in which Ayşe Doğan, an MP within the AKP, was quoted as saying "There is no need to change our commission's agenda by including a different subculture, with artificial sexual tendencies that are not in line with human nature and our society's customs and traditions. Here, we discuss values in professional life as ladies and men. There is no point in bringing up [a] different group's private life and their private gender identities in bedroom. Everybody knows that this can be one of the biggest threats to our society" (Kaos GL, 2016, quoted in LGBTI News Turkey, 2016). Then, as Sedef Çakmak explains, during the 2015 elections, AKP leaders spoke against the People's Democratic Party (HDP) because they had a candidate who was a homosexual on their electoral list (Research Turkey, 2015). Erdoğan himself criticized the HDP, saying, "[W]e are not the ones with a homosexual candidate" (Fishman, 2015). This sentiment was echoed by Turkish prime minister Ahmet Davutoglu, who said, "Gays caused the destruction of the (Biblical) tribe of Lot, and the HDP presents [a gay] candidate" (Fishman, 2015). Furthermore,

[d]uring the election season, Zorlu Performing Arts center cancelled an evening with the Boston Gay Men's Chorus after conservative newspapers slammed the theater for sponsoring the program. Yet Istanbul's Boğaziçi University opened its doors to the choir, on June 27, a day before the planned Pride march, leading one pro-AKP university rector, M. Ihsan Karaman, of Istanbul's Medeniyet University, to state on Twitter, "Our universities are not the place to legitimize perverted tendencies and acts. (Fishman, 2015)

Later in May 2016, Erdoğan attempted to criticize the "West" for their support of LGBTI rights (along with animal rights) instead of helping the Syrian refugees, as he saw it. Erdoğan spoke out against the United States and others for what he believed was a lack of concern for helping Syrian refugee. In his critique, he made anti-LGBTI comments, saying, "Shame on those who in the West divert their sensitivity to the so-called freedoms, rights, and law shown in the debate over gay marriage away from Syrian women, children, and innocents in need of aid" (Anadolu Agency, 2016).

Because of such comments and attitudes by some of the political leaders in Turkey, there exists a strong belief that AKP rule – and particularly their attention to more conservative interpretations of Islam – has had a real negative effect on the LGBTI rights movement and on how people in Turkey view the LGBTI community. Ulas Pekin, who manages Sugar Café, a gay bar in Istanbul, was quoted in an interview as saying that "[f]or 13 years when the AKP ruled in Turkey, the perception about LGBTI groups among decision-makers has changed negatively, seen as 'morally indecent' and abnormal people. But, the secular character of the Turkish Republic and the social influence of liberal segments of the society help us in our struggles for survival" (Tokyay, 2015). Pekin went on to say that "[h]owever it would not be an easy endeavor to openly live and have fun in the social sphere as a gay in some Anatolian cities due to the deeply rooted religious conservatism" (Tokyay, 2015).

The history of such comments made by leaders in the country has made life a challenge, with LGBTI individuals feeling unsafe.[2] As I shall show in the following section, these hostile attitudes towards same-sex individuals and same-sex rights is not merely just rhetoric; these comments are part of a larger problem in Turkey, one in which LGBTI individuals face human rights abuses throughout the different aspects of society. While I will not illustrate every single crime committed, I shall point out just some of the cases in which LGBTI members of society have faced discrimination. This will include an examination of cases of murder, firing from jobs, transgender discrimination, etc.

Activists argue that the state has failed to offer protections to the LGBTI community. And because of this, they argue that this inaction "has amounted to a tacit legal endorsement of acts of violence and discrimination" (Kaos GL, LGBTI News Turkey, and IGLHRC, 2014). This inaction in various elements of Turkish society clearly extends to today, where the LGBTI community continues to face discrimination and a lack of legal protections. Furthermore, it seems as if there is little the government is doing to work to correct these problems. For example, in November of 2014, Mahmut Tanal, who is on the Parliamentary Human Rights Commission, and a member of the Republican People's Party, inquired about what the government was doing with regard to sexual minority rights. The Presidency of Education Directorate answered the inquiry, which is tied to the Ministry of Justice. The response was less than encouraging, saying, "[T]here is no work on the protection and recognition of lesbian, gay, bisexual and trans citizens' human rights run by our Ministry. For Ministry personnel at any level, including those working in local bodies, we have not implemented any work so far in order to raise awareness on the issue" (Köylü, 2014). Thus, human rights organizations were furious at the government's lack of attention to same-sex rights issues. It is within this context that I examine how NGOs and LGBTI rights activists are fighting against hatred and injustice. Namely, I hope to answer the question of what sorts of rights-based strategies these rights activists are employing in order to counter such hostility from the government.

Violent Crimes against the LGBTI Community in Turkey

When looking at recent crimes against the LGBTI community, it becomes evident as to why so many in the LGBTI community continue to live in a state of fear. For decades, government authorities have been unwilling to act aggressively to either protect the LGBTI community or have been minimally responsive – to say the least – in following up on a number of murders and other violent crimes that were specifically committed against these individuals. Let's take a look at just some of the cases of abuse against the LGBTI community, and how the government and other Turkish authorities dealt with such crimes.

Arguably the most-noted case that human rights organizations point to as evidence that Turkish officials have not done what is necessary to investigate hate crimes against the LGBTI community is the 2008 murder of Ahmet Yıldız. It is believed that Yıldız was killed outside of his apartment after someone may have been following him out of his residence and as Yıldız was heading towards his car. It was suspected that this was an "honor killing" (a killing committed by a member of Yıldız's family in order to protect the "honor" of the family for what was viewed as an "shame" that Yıldız was openly gay). Part of the reason that many suspect a family member committed this crime was that, prior to his killing, Yıldız felt that members of this family would not approve of him being gay (Ataman, 2011). He even received death threats from his family. He went to report what happened to authorities, even going to the prosecutor's office in Üsküdar, where Yıldız not only filed a complaint but also looked for authorities to provide physical protection (Amnesty International, 2011). However, it is believed that the authorities did not immediately look into Yıldız's complaint about being threatened. According to Amnesty International (2011), "the state prosecutor had transferred the complaint to another office on the grounds that it fell within the jurisdiction of the neighbouring Sarıyer district, where it was not followed up. Activists regard the actions of the authorities – in erroneously transferring the complaint although it did lie within the first prosecutor's jurisdiction – and failing to investigate it, as a symptom of the authorities' reluctance to confront homophobic violence" (29). Furthermore, while authorities finally decided to actually investigate what happened that day, it became evident that they made a number of mistakes in their analysis of the crime. For example, according to Yıldız's partner İbo, there were two cars present during the killing, although only one was investigated.

Furthermore, the authorities were also accused of failing to take appropriate action against the main suspect, the father, until much later. For example,

despite the fact that it had previously been alleged that Ahmet Yıldız's family had been making threats against him, and the fact that a car belonging to a friend of his father was identified at the scene, no attempt was made to interview the father until October 2008, when an arrest warrant was issued more than three months after the murder had taken place. By this time Ahmet Yıldız's father could not be found. Telephone records indicate that by this time he may have travelled to Iraq. (Amnesty International, 2011: 29)

It actually took three years, following a new judge hearing the case, for an arrest warrant to be issued, and for the court to order authorities to investigate the threats that Yıldız was receiving prior to his murder (Amnesty International, 2011). However, as of 2016, Ahmet Yıldız's father is still reported to be at large (Amnesty International, 2016).

Such a murder, and the subsequent police response to a killing of an LGBTI individual, is unfortunately not merely a thing of the past in Turkey. Between 2010 and 2014 alone, human rights organizations have documented a minimum of forty-one murders committed against the LGBTI community because of their sexual identity, with twelve killings of LGBTI individuals based on their sexual identity in the year 2013. However, along with these cases, there were also many more attempted murders, actions that involved violators using torture, acts of rape, lynchings, and other forms of violence against LGBTI individuals (Kaos GL, LGBTI News Turkey, and IGLHRC, 2015). Yet, so many of the crimes are either ignored or severely under-investigated, which has left people fearing for their safety in Turkey.

Employment Discrimination

As discussed in Chapter 3 on Turkish law as it relates to LGBTI human rights abuses, LGBTI individuals are frequently the targets of employment discrimination. This often shows itself in the case of non-hires (which can go unnoticed given the difficulty in tracking data related to LGBTI status and hiring). Still, a number of those within the LGBTI community who have been interviewed in various human rights reports have felt that there has indeed been employment discrimination against them on account of their sexual orientation or gender identity (Amnesty International, 2011). Plus, through various documented cases, evidence suggests that people from the LGBTI community are either not getting a job or have being fired from a position due to their sexual orientation. For example, there was a highly publicized case in 2004 that illustrates this point. An Amnesty International (2011) report states:

[T]he High Discipline Board of the Ministry of the Interior on 20 April 2004 took the decision to dismiss a police officer after hearing evidence that he had engaged in anal sex with a man. The decision was justified on the basis of Article 125 E-g of the Civil Servants Law (no. 657) that provides for persons to be dismissed if found "to act in an immoral and dishonourable way which is not compatible with the position of a civil servant." The administrative court, to which the police officer had appealed, found that the dismissal did not contravene applicable law and confirmed the decision of the High Discipline Board. The decision of the local administrative court was later confirmed by the Council of State, the highest administrative appeal court, exhausting domestic remedies. In addition to this case and another similar but unrelated case involving a police officer, the same article of the Civil Servants Law was used to dismiss a teacher who[,] according to the decision of the High Discipline Board of the Ministry of Education in 2009, was found to have entered into a "homosexual relationship." Again the local administrative court did not find the decision to be in violation of law and rejected the appeal against dismissal. (23)

This issue of employment discrimination is not isolated to government or state-related positions but extends to other sectors as well.

Take the field of education. There does not exist material in schools that educates students on LGBTI issues. LGBTI children themselves often face discrimination and bullying by others (COWI, 2010). In addition, in a

LGBT-survey carried out by Lambdaistanbul, 14 percent of the LGBT respondents reported having experienced discrimination in schools, a figure which should be seen in the light of the fact that most LGBT youth hide their sexual orientation or gender identity in schools. Another consequence of the social pressure is that some LGBT persons choose not start or finish their education[,] a choice that – in particular for transgender persons – is facilitated by the fact that it is almost impossible to find employment afterwards. (COWI, 2010: 14)

This discrimination not only affects the children, but also LGBTI individuals who work as educators. In terms of Turkish law, in Article 27 of the Law on Elementary and High School Teacher's Promotion and Discipline Number 1702, teachers can be fired from their posts if they are found to have behaved in a way that is viewed as "impure." As Öz (2010) explains,

teachers whose [behaviors] are accepted as impure on two conditions, shall be unseated. In the first condition, if the teacher's [behaviors] are accepted as impure against the students in the school, s/he shall be unseated. In the second condition, if the teacher's [behaviors] are accepted as impure and can not fit the teaching profession outside the school (in relation to anyone), s/he shall be unseated. In other terms, impure [behavior] by the teacher at any time – even in private – can result in his/her dismissal. Since LGBT persons' sexual orientation or gender identity is easily accepted as "immoral" or "impure," there is a pressure of such discipline punishment on LGBT teachers. (29[3])

Other Forms of Discrimination against LGBTI Individuals in Turkey

Along with violent crimes and employment discrimination against the LGBTI community, one can look at a variety of other aspects of life as it relates to residing in Turkey and find that the state and state law discriminates against the LGBTI community on many other fronts. For example, with regards to the topic of family-related issues, in Turkey, transgender individuals have to go through a number of legal hoops in order to change their name (Öz, 2010), which poses additional challenges for many transgender individuals with regards to employment, among other things. In addition, if a same-sex couple would like to adopt a child, it is not recognized (whereas single-parent adoption, or second-parent adoption is in cases) (Öz, 2010: 24). A same-sex couple also cannot carry out assisted reproduction legally in Turkey. As Öz (2010) explains,

[a]ssisted reproduction is allowed only for married couples and available for only married couples in Turkey according to Reproduction Assistance Treatment Centers Regulation dated 19 November 1996, Number 22822. Although there is no rule for access to these services by LGBT persons, it is impossible for LGBT persons to access these services because unmarried couples are not allowed to have assisted reproduction. Also a single and/or lesbian mother can not be assisted in reproduction because of the same reason. According to the regulation, if the person is known to be in a lesbian or gay relationship (although there is no regulation on this) it seems impossible to access assisted reproduction. There is also no law for transgender persons to store their own sperm/fertile eggs for future use. (24)

Moreover, LGBTI individuals are also barred from donating blood (since they are asked if they have ever had a homosexual encounter) (Öz, 2010). Thus, these types of rights that are provided to heterosexuals are not granted to homosexuals. They cannot and do not have access to living an equal life with others in Turkey. These individuals not only face violent threats against their lives, but the state does not see them as equal.

Violations of Free Speech Rights for the LGBTI Community

Legally, Article 26(1) of the Turkish constitution guarantees individuals the right to freedom of speech. Here, theoretically at least, the law is in accordance with international human rights law. However, the reality in Turkey is far different. Not only is Erdoğan restricting the freedom of speech through his authoritarianism (such as suing and or jailing journalists), attempting to arrest prominent opposition voices, limit what is posted online, etc., but there also exists a separation between stated law and actual practiced law when it comes to the freedom of speech for the LGBTI community and NGOs advocating LGBTI rights. However, as noted in a joint report conducted by the Turkish organizations Social Policies, Gender Identity and Sexual Orientation Studies Association (SPOD), and Kaos GL, in cooperation with the International Gay and Lesbian Human Rights Commission (IGLHRC) (2012), the problem is that the Turkish government, while guaranteeing free speech, makes no specific reference to LGBTI rights. Because of this, the state, on several occasions, has attempted to stifle any such speech rights.

There are several known cases where the state has abused the right to freedom of speech for LGBTI organizations and or individuals. Below are just a few of those cases. In 2006, the Turkish LGBTI rights organization Kaos GL was investigated by the state because of a LGBTI magazine that they published. The prosecutor's office took offense to one of the issues, where they claim "immoral" art was depicted. Because of this, they asked the court to seize all of the copies of the magazine issue. The prosecutor attempted to act in this fashion under Article 28 of the Turkish Constitution, which does give the state power to limit free press if the speech "'tend(s) to incite offense' or if it contains 'material which contravenes the indivisible integrity of the state'" (SPoD, Kaos GL, and IGLHRC, 2012: 10). And, "[o]n ... [July 21st 2006] ... the 12th Criminal Court of Peace granted the application of the Public Prosecutor, without mentioning the legal grounds for that decision. It only stated that 'some articles and pictures' from the magazine interfered with 'the protection of public morals'" (although it never mentioned the legal reasons behind their action) (Öz, 2010). After going through the domestic courts (which supported the lower-level decision), the organization applied to have the case heard at the European Court of Human Rights (ECHR) (Öz, 2010). In its submissions to the Strasbourg court, the Turkish Government argued that "freedom of expression is the cornerstone of a democratic society. However, as is stated in Article 10/2 of the Convention the exercise of this right may be subjected to some restrictions" (SpoD, Kaos GL, and IGLHRC, 2012: 10; for a timeline of the events of the case, see Öz (2010). Both Article 10/2 and other laws such as 26/2 provide the state latitude with regard to guaranteeing freedom of speech (Öz, 2010).

As mentioned earlier, SpoD, Kaos GL, and the IGLHRC wrote a Shadow Report for the 106th session of the United Nations Human Rights Committee. The report, entitled *Human Rights Violations of Lesbian, Gay, Bisexual, and Transgender (LGBT) People in Turkey: A Shadow Report*, documents other limitations of free speech by the Turkish state with regards to LGBTI rights. Namely,

[i]n July 2009, the Prime Minister's Council of Protection of Children from Harmful Publications decided that the book named "Üçüncü Sınıf Kadın" (Third Class Woman), by the author, Anıl Alacaoğlu, should be distributed in a sealed envelope carrying a warning that it cannot be sold to underage

persons (Case Number B.02.0.MNK-572–02/01242). The reason given for the Court's decision was that the book contained "gay relationships which are not normal according to Turkish customs" and "could harm the sexual health of children." (SPoD, Kaos GL, and IGLHRC, 2012; Jafari, 2013)

Also in 2009, the Public Prosecutor's Office in Istanbul (Press Division) investigated a book published by Kaos GL Association and Sel Publications because, in their eyes, the book discussed lesbian issues, which they viewed as "'an unnatural sexual relation' and 'obscene'" (SPoD, Kaos GL, and IGLHRC, 2012: 11). Other cases include the government temporarily closing certain websites that promote LGBTI content (until court ordered access is given), as well as a case in June 2012 in which the "High Court ruled that oral and anal sex in movies should increase the penalty against the accused for selling CDs with sexual content. High Court convicted S.K. to one-year of imprisonment for selling movies with sexual content. However, the penalty was then increased because the movies contained displays of oral and anal sex" (SPoD, Kaos GL, and IGLHRC, 2012: 11). S. K. did object (and the case went all the way to Turkey's High Court). Here, "[e]xpressing that it is the responsibility of criminal court of first instance to define the quality of the crime, [the] high court sent the file back" (SPoD, Kaos GL, and IGLHRC, 2012: 11–12). However, cases of free speech violation against the LGBTI community and LGBTI content have continued in recent years. For example, in a more recent Periodic Review Report examining various issues on free speech violations in Turkey, different NGOs have noted that

[f]reedom of speech in support of diverse sexualities faces regular challenges. For instance, Turkish courts have censored and blocked gay social networking applications based on Law No. 5651 on Regulating Broadcasting in the Internet and Fighting against Crimes Committed through Internet Broadcasting. In August of 2013, one of the Penal Chambers of the Supreme Court of Appeals in Istanbul ordered a publishing house to stand trial for translating and publishing a novel with "homosexual content," citing Article 226 of the country's Criminal Code on "indecency." In a similar vein, Turkey's Supreme Board of Radio and Television fined a TV network for "promoting homosexuality" by airing a music video in which two females behaved in a manner that could suggest they were in a romantic relationship." (Kaos GL, LGBTI News Turkey, and IGLHRC, 2014: 4)

Media Restrictions

The Turkish government has also restricted media as it relates to same-sex rights issues. A number of different media outlets were the targets of a government crackdown because of what the state viewed to be offensive content. For example, in 2009, the Turkish government banned two LGBTI community websites. The sites hadigayri.com and gabile.com were both closed by the Telecommunication Directorate in Turkey (*Hurriyet Daily News*, 2009). The officials gave no reason as to why they shut down the sites, although this did come after failed attempts at closing online communication networks of human rights organizations such as Kaos GL and Lambda Istanbul (*Hurriyet Daily News*, 2009). Combined, the sites had 225,000 members. Turkey has also banned LGBTI apps and sites that they believed were offensive. For example, in 2013, the 14th Criminal Court in Istanbul (Day, 2013) banned the app Grindr from use in Turkey.[4] Then, in 2014, the government also banned the website Gay.com (Tokyay, 2015), as the government deemed the content offensive. These were not the only sites banned; the government has went out of its way to stifle any community that it deems as "threatening" to Turkish and Islamic culture. Human rights activists have criticized these actions. Ömer Akpınar, the media coordinator for Kaos GL, was quoted as saying, "The [Grindr] ruling is another act of repression against LGBT people in Turkey." Akpınar went on to add, "According to the law, being LGBT is not a crime, but there is no recognition of LGBTs. And we have no anti-discrimination bill to protect LGBTs" (Pittman, 2013). The founder of Grindr, Joel Simkhai, spoke out against this restriction, saying, "Oppression starts with the strangling of free speech and just like the burning of books in the past, today it's done by cutting off people's access to technology." He went on to say that "[f]reedom to communicate is a basic right and Grindr is exploring all options to resolve this matter including a legal appeal."

In addition, the Supreme Board of Radio and Television

RTÜK, the state agency responsible for monitoring and regulating radio and television content, is heavily involved in censoring content. The cable broadcast of *Sex and the City 2*, for example, was blocked due to [what RTÜK saw as] its "twisted and immoral" depiction of a gay wedding. In 2011 the Telecommunications Communication Presidency (TIB) prohibited Turkish

Internet-hosting providers from using the word "gay" along with 137 other potentially inflammatory words, in domain names and websites, according to Freedom House. TIB has also shut down LGBT Internet forums. (Beck, 2013)

Then, in early 2015, RTÜK issued a fine to Genç TV for playing a video by the Swedish musical artist Elliphant entitled "One More." RTÜK took issue with the video because of a scene in which two women kiss. However, this was not the only broadcast to be fined; they also went after Power TV for playing a video by Pitbull for a scene in which there is, as the board called it, "passionate fondling of a woman's half naked body" (SDGLN, 2015). The reason for fining Genç TV in particular was because of the "homosexual" nature of the content in the Elliphant music video. When discussing their reasons for the fines, the "RTÜK cited the controversial remarks on homosexuality made by Cem Keçe, head of the Turkish Sexual Health Institute. Keçe claims that homosexuality is not genetic, but is a defect 'against human nature' and the result of 'parenting mistakes.' Thus, Keçe argues, showing anything beyond heterosexuality on TV could affect gender identity in people who are questioning their sexuality" (SDGLN, 2015). The issues of course with these fines are many; the government – through the RTÜK – aims to have extensive control over free speech in Turkey by trying to monitor what is being said or show on television, radio, and the Internet. But along with this, the government is also trying to define, under its own terms, what is viewed as "appropriate" sexuality and what is not. This is not only dangerous, as it continues to paint the LGBTI community as "not normal" with regard to sexuality, but it further alienates and discriminates against a community in which many have already been attacked, threatened, and ostracized for being LGBTI.

Along with regulating and controlling Internet and media content, various media outlets that are either directly backed by the government or supportive of Erdoğan and the AKP have also used their broadcasts and/or publications to speak harshly and discriminatorily towards the LGBTI community. This was clearly evident during the lead up to the 2015 parliamentary elections. As a response to the campaign of LGBTI parliamentary candidates such as Barış Sulu, for example, some of the news outlets published articles with very degrading titles. For example, *Yeni Akit* published an article about the HDP and Sulu entitled "HDP Receives Homos with Open Arms" (*Hurriyet Daily News*, 2015a).

Yeni Akit is not the only news outlet that has written such problematic statements with regard to the LGBTI community; human rights organizations have also criticized actions by other daily publications, namely *Star, Sabah,* and *Milli Gazete,* along with a television broadcast company, Rehber TV (*Hurriyet Daily News,* 2015a). It is for this reason that individuals such as Sulu and human rights activists have called for laws on hate speech in Turkey (*Hurriyet Daily News,* 2015a). Unfortunately, little has been done to ease activist concerns on these matters.

Gay-Only Prisons

In 2014, the Turkish government began a project that would build prisons that would only house gay inmates. (Hurtas, 2015) There has not yet been a set decision by the state as to whether they will operate such a prison.[5] While the government has argued that the prison is meant to "protect" the gay inmates, the concern by LGBT rights activists is that such a facility would actually bring about further discrimination, with some even calling this project "a medieval-age practice" (Agence France Press, 2014). For example, Murat Köylü of Kaos GL was quoted as saying that "[i]nstead of creating public areas where people from all sexual orientations can live together, the government has once again chosen to ostracise homosexuals." He went on to say that "This will lead to the profiling of gay prisoners, as well as their families and the prison itself. How will the government be able to protect those prisoners who are not openly gay?" (Agence France Press, 2014). While the Turkish government stated in 2014 that there were a total of seventy-nine LGBT prisoners in the country, this number is most likely low, since there may be many more LGBT prisoners who have not made their sexual orientation public (Agence France Press, 2014). Because of their frustration with this proposed new jail, on January 6, 2015, eighteen different organizations made a combined statement against the new planned prison, saying that not only would inmates face stigmatization but that this prison would also make their sexual identities known to family, friends, and others. There is also a concern that being in this jail would hurt their future job prospects as any future employer would know their sexual orientation by knowing in which jail they were held (Hurtas, 2015).

Many activists don't want this new jail to be built and operational; they just want LGBTI individuals to be given proper prison conditions so that issues such as harassment and assaults don't take place. As Hurtas (2015) argues, this can be done. Namely, "[t]he Justice Ministry could alternatively consider the objections of the LGBT organizations and move to upgrade all prisons with special LGBT wards, penalize harassment and violence against LGBT individuals by inmates and prison staff alike and immediately end the practice of 'protective' solitary confinement." Hurtas (2015) goes on to argue that "[t]o the LGBT community, spending the money in the new prison's budget for a special hospital or a school would be much better."

In fact, this issue of existing prison conditions (and treatment) for LGBTI individuals in Turkey is a significant point of concern for many who have went through the system, as well as human rights activists who have researched and reported on the jails. Not only are they upset with this idea of "segregating" LGBTI individuals with separate prisons but there are also problems in existing jails themselves. There have been a number of cases of LGBTI inmates who, after facing assault by other inmates, have been placed in solitary confinement. Here is just one documented account of the experiences of an LGBTI individual in Turkey named Rosida Koyuncu, whose experience, recorded by Sibel Hurtas (2015) in the Al-Monitor piece "Turkey's 'Pink Prison'," highlights the levels of discrimination that LGBTI people face in Turkish prisons. Koyuncu states:

When I first went to prison, I didn't reveal my sexual orientation. But prison administration soon found out I was a homosexual after a quick investigation showed that I had participated in LGBT demonstrations. They wanted to send me for a general medical checkup. I resisted, because the checkup involves an anal examination. Then they forced me to go to a psychiatrist, because in their view, homosexuality is a disease, and I had to have a medical report for it. The report would have allowed them to put me in solitary confinement, but the psychiatrist refused to release the report.

My fellow inmates knew of my sexual orientation, but had no objections. Yet, soon the prison administration moved me to another ward. They put me together with an elderly imam, who treated me with respect. Then I was moved again, to another ward. The inmates there knew my sexual orientation and began to ostracize and insult me for trivial reasons. Eventually one of them attacked me and beat me up. I was subjected to harsh insults and swearing. I couldn't take it any longer and was forced to accept the solitary confinement the prison administration had wanted to impose on me from the very beginning. I spent five months in solitary.

During my stint in jail, I was also [sexually] harassed by prison guards who knew I was a homosexual. They would touch my genitals during searches, for instance. They did it either to harass me or they were secret homosexuals themselves. I don't know.

I've been released but I remain on trial. I will probably go back to jail after the next hearing, on Jan. 23. And because I have no other choice, I'll be back in solitary confinement.

While the report does not state whether Koyuncu was indeed placed back in solitary confinement, the fear of being put back in such holding conditions is quite real. Prison authorities attempt to justify solitary confinement by saying that the practice is intended for those with disease (which they could spread to other inmates) or as a punishment for bad behavior while in general population. As human rights courts (such as the ECHR) have found (based on a 2012 case where an individual was in solitary confinement for eight months), placing someone in solitary confinement because of sexual orientation is against the law, and the actions are not protecting the individual from assault but are due to the fact that one is of a certain sexual orientation (Hurtas, 2015).

LGBTI Refugees in Turkey

The dire situation facing the LGBTI community in Turkey is not limited to Turkish citizens but also extends to LGBTI refugees that may have crossed the border into Turkey seeking protection from violence in their respective home countries. As is well-documented in the literature, refugees have often already suffered so much, well before entering the new host country. So many refugees have had to flee their homes for fear of being harassed, attacked, or killed. Refugees have had to do so quickly, leaving most of their belongings and, in many cases, members of their family behind. Refugees often are separated from their families, who may or may not have been hurt. Then, they have to find a way to leave their country – which is often very dangerous (as there may be a civil war or state violence or state oppression towards the group to which the refugees belong). If they are able to flee safely, they then have to go through border patrol into the new country. If they make it this far, then they have to begin a new life, often with little in terms of material possessions. In addition, many face health issues, specifically psychological issues such as post-traumatic stress disorder (PTSD), as well as the additional challenges of being in a new environment (which may often include language barriers, amongst other things). Yet, despite all that they have been through in their home country, upon arrival into Turkey they find a situation that is not welcoming. In fact, "[m]any arrive in Turkey to confront new violence and harassment by local communities and other refugees. While awaiting the determination of their refugee status, they avoid the police, are afraid to leave their homes, and have very limited access to social support, employment, and medical care. (ORAM, 2011).

Part of the problem with regard to why refugees and asylum seekers in general feel that sufficient support is not offered in Turkey is because of the way that Turkey approaches these people coming into the country. While Turkey has signed and ratified the 1951 Refugee Convention, as well as the 1967 Protocol, "Turkey extends protection … only to persons originating in Europe" (Helsinki Citizens' Assembly and ORAM, 2011: 2). Thus, while Turkey won't accept these individuals permanently, they are allowed to remain in the country until refugee organizations, such as the United Nations High Commissioner for Refugees (UNHCR), completes their resettlement process (Helsinki Citizens' Assembly and ORAM, 2011).[6]

As noted above, what makes matters worse is that the entire process from entering the country until getting permanently resettled takes a very long time. As the Helsinki Citizens' Assembly and ORAM (2011) explain,

> To receive "temporary asylum status," one must apply to Turkey's Minister of Interior (MOI). This status allows asylum seekers to live legally in Turkey while the UNHCR evaluates their refugee claims. Turkey's reception system for asylum seekers is characterized by a policy of dispersal. During the processing, asylum seekers are assigned to live in one of the approximately 50 pre-designated "satellite cities," located primarily in the country's interior. Asylum seekers are required to live in their satellite cities until they depart from Turkey, whether for resettlement or upon being deported. Police permission is required to leave one's satellite city for any reason whatsoever. (2)

In the meantime, asylum seekers and refugees have to think about things such as ensuring their safe living conditions, all the while also hoping for permanent resettlement. Turkey has not guaranteed sufficient housing or healthcare for large numbers of asylum seekers. In addition, unless they successfully receive an exemption, so many of the asylum seekers have to actually pay for a "resident permit" out of their own pockets. Furthermore, without access to many employment opportunities, those seeking protections often have to live, waiting, in horrible social and economic conditions. This can be particularly difficult for LGBTI refugees. For example, as Helsinki Citizens' Assembly and ORAM (2011) note from interviews with many LGBTI asylum seekers,

Refugees reported being denied or evicted from apartments when their gender identity or sexual orientation was discovered. Most were unsuccessful securing work often because of their LGBT status. The few who did find employment reported being terminated – often violently – when their sexual orientation or gender identity was discovered. Since virtually all those interviewed were unable to support themselves independently, many turned to local charities or government agencies for social assistance. A significant number described being humiliated by service providers and some reported being denied services altogether on the basis of their LGBT status. The few who attended adult education promptly dropped out after being ostracized by other refugees attending the classes. Unsurprisingly, many interviewees reported deep feelings of isolation and depression while waiting for their refugee claims to be evaluated. (8)

Thus, given the difficulties that refugees have dealt with in their home state, as well as the limited laws that Turkey has for refugees and asylum seekers, these asylum seekers entering into Turkey who identify as LGBTI often face additional challenges when seeking safety. First of all, as mentioned, many of the LGBTI asylum seekers leave the originating country due to discrimination that they faced; they have to flee for their lives because they have been targeted at home. However, when the host country does not have legal mechanisms in place to recognize sexual orientation and gender identity as categories of protection, then the situation continues to be dangerous. This is the case in Turkey, where legal safeguards for LGBTI are virtually nonexistent. As various human rights organizations in Turkey have pointed out, "LGBT refugees in Turkey enjoy very limited access to social support, employment and medical care. There are worrying omissions where police are called upon to investigate violence and harassment against these individuals. Most persons reported consistent, often violent harassment from local community members" (SPoD, Kaos GL, and IGLHRC, 2012: 7). Öz (2010) explains the process and conditions facing LGBTI refugees upon entering into Turkey, saying that

LGBT individuals are among the most vulnerable asylum seekers and refugees in Turkey today. Having escaped persecution in their countries of origin, they arrive in Turkey to confront significant new challenges to their safety, security and protection. Required to live in small towns in Turkey's interior, they wait a year or more to be recognised as refugees by the United Nations High Commissioner for Refugees (UNHCR) and then to be "resettled" in third countries. During the wait, they often fear leaving their homes due to targeted violence from local communities. They enjoy very limited access to social support, employment and medical care. Conspicuous gaps exist in the level of response by local police to their complaints of violence and harassment. (25)

There are a number of ways in which LGBTI refugees and asylum seekers are unable to access a full set of rights offered to other non-LGBTI refugees and asylum seekers in Turkey. For example, one of the issues facing asylum seekers looking for protection in Turkey are the limitations they face with regard to where they will be placed to live. Amnesty International (2011) explains that there exists a major problem with the living assignments: "[A]sylum-seekers and refugees are required to reside in one of a number of Anatolian towns or cities in central and eastern provinces while they remain in Turkey. These locations are often more socially conservative than Ankara, Istanbul and Izmir where LGBT civil society groups offer assistance and solidarity, and as such are often unwelcoming to asylum-seekers and refugees with different sexual orientations and gender identities" (26).

In addition to the negative treatment and safety issues LGBTI asylum seekers and/or refugees face, their time in Turkey is further complicated because of Turkish law. Given that all aspects of Turkish law also bind these individuals, this means that every controversial law and interpretation of the law (that has been used to suppress LGBTI rights) would also apply to LGBTI asylum seekers and refugees (SPoD, Kaos GL, and IGLHRC, 2012). On top of all of this, these individuals have to deal with all of the difficulties of finding employment, as well as the uncertainty of remaining the country or being deported (SPoD, Kaos GL, and IGLHRC, 2012). Here, the state has even more control over refugees and asylum seekers, which could lead to further negative implications for the LGBTI community. As SPoD, Kaos GL, & IGLHRC (2012) explain in a shadow report to the United Nations, in Turkey "[t]he State reserves the authority to extend the administrative custody period up to 6 months and exclude any regulation regarding access of the civil society to detention and deportation centres. This extended custody and isolation from civil society make it impossible to determine the human rights violations, torture and maltreatment LGBT individuals suffer in such centres" (8). This is dangerous for all refugees, but because of the heightened discrimination that the LGBTI community faces in Turkey and in other places, the worry for abuse against them is intensified.

These sorts of concerns are not merely hypothetical; they are all too real for LGBTI asylum seekers in Turkey. Here are some cases that Turkish human rights organizations documented. For example,

On 16 December 2011[, in the] evening, a gay refugee was attacked by three citizens in Kayseri. At evening time when he was on his way to home, he found that 3 men were following him. The three men approached him and blocked his way. They spoke violently in Turkish and showed him their genitals. He tried to escape with all of his power, but they would not allow him to leave. They took his coat and then one of the men started to hit him. After he could finally escape one of them continued to follow him along the street for 50 meters until finally giving up ... The next day he went to the local police station in Kayseri, and reported the incident to the police. Police told him that they would check the local cameras and follow-up him later. UNHCR was also informed about the incident. (SPoD, Kaos GL, and IGLHRC, 2012: 12)

The NGOs also document another case of abuse of a LGBTI refugee, saying that

when [a transgender individual] was going to home one night, two young men threatened her with a knife and rubbed her. She had decided to report the incident to the police and went to the police station to document the incident. However, the police officers told her that in order for her to make a report she must bring a witness. When the woman returned with a witness, the police still did not investigate or prosecute anyone for the attack made against her. Instead, the police told her to call 155, the general police in Turkey, if she had a problem. (SPoD, Kaos GL, and IGLHRC, 2012: 12)

Unfortunately, there are other cases of LGBTI refugees not necessary protections (see SPoD, Kaos GL, and IGLHRC, 2012: 12), and yet, without legal protections, asylum seekers and refugees are under continued risk during their movement into Turkey as they look for safety from persecution elsewhere.

In 2015, J. Lester Feder wrote an important piece in Buzzfeed entitled "This Is What It's Like to Be an LGBT Syrian Fleeing for Your Life," in which he documents the lives of LGBTI individuals who left Syria on account of the war and who were looking for shelter and full protections in countries such as Turkey. What these asylum seekers and refugees found was a situation that was far from a safe and secure environment for them. They found an environment in which they experienced harassment and alienation. For example, he followed the story of a person named "M." M was a Syrian refugee from Damascus. Before fleeing Syria, M drew the anger of some who ended up interrogating her and then capturing her. She explained that her captors asked her "You are not covered – and why is your hair short?" Then, as Feder (2015) explains, they physically hit her and also "demanded she recite a verse from the Quran to prove she is a Muslim, and she was lucky they picked one that she learned as a child." They went on to say to her, "'Why are you imitating men?' 'All this entitles you to execution.'" Although one of the captors had an order to kill her for *mistarjili* (one who is a woman but acting like a man), she was spared but told to leave because of the threat to her security. Feder (2015) notes that while it was difficult to get independent verification given the difficulty of access to reliable information in areas controlled by the rebels in Syria, he also points out that

her story is far from unique. In September and October, BuzzFeed News interviewed more than 15 LGBT refugees in Turkey from several nearby countries who had fled everything from Islamist militias to sexual assault to death threats from family members. Many had been pushed out of more than one country, caught up in anti-LGBT crackdowns that have rippled across the Middle East in recent years. M's disappointment in the resettlement system overseen by UNHCR was nearly universal.

Because the United Nations High Commissioner for Refugees views the LGBTI refugees as a highly vulnerable group, they attempt to resettle LGBTI refugees in countries with much more supportive rights systems for same-sex individuals. However, given the high number of overall refugees, in combination with understaffing and overworked aid workers, it becomes difficult to resettle LGBTI refugees quickly.

Unfortunately, "LGBT refugees will usually have to wait about two years for a ticket out of Turkey, said Selin Unal, spokesman for UNHCR's Turkey office: one year for UNHCR to decide if they're eligible and a second for another country to grant them a visa and fly them over" (Feder, 2015). Plus, each stage of the resettlement process to the United States, for example, can take a long time. There might be months where refugees do not hear something about their status. Of course, this is very concerning for all refugees. What makes the situation much even more difficult for LGBTI refugees are the worsening conditions in Turkey, even in traditionally safer cities such as Istanbul (Feder, 2015). Actions such as the police violence during the 2015 LGBTI Pride March have led many to feel that Turkey itself is no longer a place where LGBTI rights will be respected. Plus, there is a concern that longer wait times leave this group much more at risk for hate crime. Many of the refugees have been attacked by from within their own communities on account of being LGBTI (Feder, 2015). Thus, refugees not only have to deal with the series of difficulties but for LGBTI individuals, the security concerns are intensified.

This feeling of insecurity has sadly become more and more of a concern. On August 4, 2016, it was reported that a gay Syrian refugee by the name of Muhammad Wisam Sankari was brutalized and beheaded in Istanbul. According to Kaos GL (Tar, 2016b), "Sankari left his house in Aksaray on the night of 23 July. He was found dead in Yenikapi on 25 July. He was beheaded and his body mutilated beyond identification. Wisam's killers have not been caught. Wisam, who was previously threatened, kidnapped by a crowded group of men, and raped, was trying to go to another country as a refugee because his life was in danger." In an interview with Kaos GL, Sankari's friend Rayan spoke about the dangers that they felt, saying,

We were staying in a different house before and we had to leave that house just because we are gay. People around would constantly stare at us. We did not do anything immoral? About five months ago, a group kidnapped Wisam in Fatih. They took him to a forest, beat him and raped him. They were going to kill him but Wisam saved himself by jumping at the road. We complained to the Police Headquarters but nothing happened. (Tar, 2016b)

Another friend, Diya, discussed the fear that they live with, saying,

I am so scared. I feel like everyone is staring at me on the street. I was kidnapped twice before. They let me go in Cerkezkoy and I barely got home one time. I went to the UN for my identification but they did not even respond to that. No one cares about us. They just talk. I get threats over the phone. I speak calmly so something does not happen. It does not matter if you are Syrian or Turkish, if you are gay you are everyone's target. They want sex from you and when you don't they just tag along. I don't have identification, who would protect me? Who is next? (Tar, 2016b)

Human Rights Abuses against Transgendered Individuals

While I have discussed the plight of LGBTI individuals as a whole, I believe that time should also be devoted to specifically examining the human rights violations committed against the transgendered community. The transgender community in Turkey is a particularly marginalized group, and they often face additional challenges because of state and local-level discrimination against them; the situation for transgender individuals in Turkey is quite horrendous. In fact, the level of discrimination and violence against the transgender community in Turkey is unrivaled in Europe: it has been argued that because Turkey ranks as having one of the highest trangender murder rates (with a minium of thirty-six transgender murders between January 2008 to September 2014 alone), it is viewed as being "the most dangerous place to be a transgender person in Europe" (Carter, 2015). As one individual by the name of Oyku Ay said about conditions in Turkey, "Abuse, assault, hate murders. These are what we're dealing with" (Köksal, 2015).

Öz (2010) notes just some of the other murders of transgender individuals. For example, "On 18 December 2008 a transgender woman was killed in Gebze. On 10 March 2009, prominent transgender rights activist Ebru Soykan was stabbed numerous times and killed in her home in Istanbul. Police arrested Birol Can Korkmaz for the murder. Soykan had made numerous complaints to the police and the prosecutor that Korkmaz had beaten her on several occasions and asked for protection" (Öz, 2010: 19). Human rights organizations were in fact highly critical of the prosecutor's office for its inaction. More murders followed: "On 29 March 2009 a transgender woman named Eda Yıldırım was killed in Bursa. On 26 June 2009 a transgender woman named Hadise was killed in Istanbul" (Öz, 2010: 19). Furthermore,

[o]n 16 February 2010 a transgender woman called Aycan Yener was killed in her apartment in the Fatih area of Istanbul. Yener's legal identification

name was Fevzi. Her throat was slit, and she was stabbed 17 times. Assailants also stabbed her roommate, Seyhan Özmemiş, aged 32, who survived. According to Turkish media, witnesses reportedly observed three people fleeing the scene, but no one has been arrested. On 8 February, Derya Y., a 35-year old transgender woman, was killed in her home in the Altındağ district of Antalya. Police found Derya Y. in her bedroom with her throat cut and 27 multiple knife stab wounds to her face and body. (Öz, 2010: 19)

On May 3, 2015, protesters came out to demonstrate more recent hate crimes against transgender individuals. It has been reported that on May 2, 2015, a transgender individual (known by friends as Gülşen) was stabbed. The assailant was a client. However, that was not the only attack on a transgender individual that night, for "[o]n the same night, unknown assailants in Istanbul shot another transgender person." Then, in the town of Izmir, an individual who goes by "Rüya" was stabbed. And yet another incident took place in Kocaeli (Doğan News Agency, 2015). Human rights groups documented a number of additional cases of attacks against transgender individuals: "The activists say there were at least five attacks against LGBT Turks in a week ... [the] spring [of 2015] alone. Two more assaults, including an alleged rape in July, pushed the United Nations High Commission for Human Rights to express 'deep concern' about LGBT rights in Turkey" (Köksal, 2015). Then, in late November 2015, "[t]here was another transphobic hate crime ... in Maltepe, Istanbul. The victim was a young trans woman who was 33 years old. Nilay, the victim of transphobic murder[,] was stabbed several times and strangled with a bathrobe cord at her own house by a client" (Pembe Hayat, 2015a). According to Nilay's friend,

The attack took place yesterday after 3pm. Our mutual friend Emel talked to Nilay on phone around 3 pm. Nilay said that her client was about to arrive and then she hung up. Later, we tried to call her again but couldn't reach her. Emel got suspicious at night and went to her home. She kept knocking on the door but there was no answer. They called for a locksmith and found Nilay's dead body.

I saw the house myself, too. Everything was scattered. There was blood. The girl's body was stabbed everywhere. In the end when she was in death agony, he strangled her with the belt of a bathrobe, and left her there with the knife he used. (Pembe Hayat, 2015b)[7]

On December 2, 2015, a transgender woman by the name of Alev was stabbed to death in the Haramidere part of Istanbul. There have been a total of four transgender murders in Turkey in 2015 alone (Pembe Hayat, 2015a). Then, on August 8, 2016,

[Hande] Kader [who was an activist and sex worker] was last seen getting into a car with a client in the city's Harbiye district in late July. Her charred body was found in the posh Zekeriyaköy district of Istanbul on Aug. 8. Authorities did not comment on the circumstances of her death but the 22-year-old was believed to be heavily mutilated before her corpse was set on fire, possibly to avoid identification of the perpetrator or perpetrators. (*Daily Sabah*, 2016)

It was also reported that she was "finally identified by prosthetics at the city morgue" (Jones, 2016). Kader was also an outspoken voice for LGBTI rights in Turkey. These murders have shocked the LGBTI community, and they have demanded justice for these crimes. It is quite clear in fact that the transgender community is living in a high state of concern and alert, or as one Turkish transgendered woman by the name of Niler Albayrak has labeled it, "an empire of fear" (Köksal, 2015).

Along with the murders of transgender individuals, those who identify as transgendered also frequently face employment discrimination, as well as other sorts of discrimination in the public sphere. In fact, even with legal and public opinion advancements in Turkey on the issue of same-sex rights, "life still remains very difficult for transgender persons in Turkey. They continue to be banned from employment, refused service at shops and restaurants, thrown off public transportation and face violent attacks from the police and the public, along with relatives out to 'cleanse the family honor'" (Idiz, 2014b). Furthermore, police, government officials, and individuals in civil society not only dismiss the rights of transgendered individuals but also have actually caused significant harm through their actions, policies, or indifference to the community.

These sorts of crimes against the transgender community go back years, and are often committed by both civil society members and the state. One of the most noted realms of abuse that the LGBTI community has faced has come from the Turkish police force. Transgendered individuals have often been the targets of injustice by police in the country. It has been so bad that in some cities, transgendered individuals could not walk down the street without a real risk of being harassed or arrested by the police. Amnesty International (2011) notes that

[t]he police stations in the Beyoğlu area of Istanbul and the Alsancak area of İzmir have been particularly notorious for the torture and other ill-treatment suffered by transgender women picked up by police officers on the street. In a rare example of a prosecution for such abuse, one police officer, Süleyman Ulusoy, nicknamed Hortum Süleyman (Suleiman the hose) was indicted for ill-treatment against nine transgender women during his tenure as head of the Beyoğlu police between 1996 and 1997. However, the prosecution was discontinued before its conclusion under the terms of an amnesty. (12)

Human rights organizations have spoken with transgendered individuals about any wrongdoing that they may have suffered.

While there are a number of other cases of abuses against the transgender community,[8] I will briefly mention a few to further illustrate the sorts of abuse that LGBTI individuals and activists have faced at the hands of police. In 2010, for example, there was an incident between police and members of the LGBTI human rights group Pembe Hayat (Pink Life). Police pulled over a car with four Pembe Hayat members inside. During the police stop, the officers wanted the individuals in the car to get out but did not tell them for what reason. The individuals in the car did not get out but did give the officers their identification. Then they called their organization, and other members came to the scene. During the incident that night, it was reported that "the police used disproportionate force against those who had come to the scene, using pepper spray and beating them with batons ... [T]hey also sprayed pepper gas in to the car, forcing the five transgender activists to come out. In addition, some of the police officers were said to have attempted to incite local residents into making complaints about the transgender activists" (Amnesty International, 2011: 14). The activists soon reported the incident and filed a complaint against the police officers. However, this was dismissed. Furthermore, the prosecutor actually decided to begin an investigation into the actions of the activists (although this case was also dismissed (Amnesty International, 2011). Others instances of police abuse that have been reported relate to public treatment of transgendered individuals. Using laws that can be easily abused, given broad interpretations of what constitutes traffic violations, the police are able to further harass transgender individuals. For example, police have arrested transgender individuals for merely walking the street.

Through their investigations of LGBTI rights abused in Turkey, Amnesty International (2011) came across a document illustrating police discrimination against the transgender community. This

internal document issued by a district police authority in İzmir in 2006 seen by Amnesty International authorizes police officers to stop and search any "transvestite" seen on the street without any indication that a crime had been committed, indicating a systematic practice of harassment. The document identifies strategies to be taken "in the context of our work to prevent inconvenience caused by people identified as transvestites." It continues, "due to our recent work the area has been 'cleaned' of such people but transvestites, women involved in prostitution, glue sniffers and 'psychopaths' are still present in the area." It authorizes police units to stop and search all "transvestites" along with women involved in prostitution, glue sniffers, homeless people and "psychopaths" before being taken into custody as required. The activists told Amnesty International that fines were issued routinely when transgender women were taken into custody. (15)

These fines vary in amount and have actually been given to an individual more than once a day. Furthermore, police seem to specifically target transgendered individuals by looking for them in busy markets or in locations away from their homes (Amnesty International, 2011). Because of this, those in the transgender community are not only afraid of more fines (which, because of low incomes, can be even more economically burdensome) but police behavior has also resulted in fear of travel because of concerns of transgendered people being at a high risk of receiving a fine or being harassed (Amnesty International, 2011). While some have tried to fight the fines in court, many more just refuse to pay them, whereas others choose not to challenge the citations. However, ignoring the fines can have additional negative consequences; not paying the fines can make getting credit or establishing a bank account difficult, and there is the risk of having a noted place of address for fear of authorities coming due to the unpaid fines (Amnesty International, 2011). With all of the attention on the cases of abuse that the transgendered community has faced, the hope would be that violence against them would end. Sadly, this has been far from reality.

Along with threats of physical violence and harassment, transgender individuals also have problems in other aspects of their everyday life, such as finding housing. Earlier, I spoke of cases where transgendered individuals have been attacked at their homes. But with regards to housing, depending on the city they live in, authorities may discriminate against where transgender individuals can or cannot move. This sort of treatment seems to be specifically targeting this group. Amnesty International (2011) has documented the housing discrimination that transgendered individuals have reported facing:

[I]n Istanbul, for example, the city with the largest population of transgender women in Turkey, successive operations by the authorities to "clean up" neighborhoods resulted in transgender women being forced out of particular areas. In many cases those forced from their houses had previously migrated to Istanbul due to the transphobia in their hometowns and cities across Turkey which made it impossible for them to live there. The most notorious event, ahead of the UN Habitat II conference in Istanbul in 1996, saw transgender women being beaten in their homes and arrested in the process of forcing the women out of Ülker Sokak in Cihangir where many transgender women lived. (20)

Police often enter into the homes of transgender individuals with the goal of either intimidating them or getting them to leave their current residence if where they lived was not satisfactory to the officers. Transgender individuals have been unofficially restricted from living in certain parts of cities, and if they do so, are harassed (Amnesty International, 2011). In some cases, the police will use the excuse of targeting prostitution in order to abuse transgendered individuals. In the instances where the police have perceived transgender individuals to be prostitutes (even those that were clearly not), this allowed the police to carry out an illegal search (Amnesty International, 2011). Moreover, following a raid, police have the ability to ban reentry into the place of residence for months, leaving the person who occupied the apartment now looking for another place to live (Amnesty International, 2011). In Turkey, prostitution is something strongly looked down upon by the conservative AKP government, and thus the state has been much more critical of the practice, as well as towards those engaged in it. As Engin (2016) writes: "[S]tate control over prostitution has become much stricter. The current legislators consider prostitution immoral and sinful behavior because according to Islamic religion, sex outside of marriage is forbidden. As a result, policymakers often

portray those who participate in sex work as individuals who degener-
ate societal and traditional family values."

But, even if someone is willing to risk this sort of abuse that occurs in
Turkey, there are other ways in which they are not even given the
opportunity to live where they choose. For example, if someone is
looking to rent a place of residence, landlords can (and often do)
discriminate against someone who is transgendered. Many
transgender individuals have stated that in order to rent an apartment,
they needed to have someone who is not transgender sign the lease.
Moreover, renting poses other challenges. For example, if someone is
renting an apartment, their lives are also subject to any development
initiatives that are taking place with the building or in the neighborhood. For example, there is a part of Istanbul called Tarlabaşı where
many of the older buildings have been planned to be demolished in
order to build newer, more expensive living quarters. Many of the
transgender community live in this part of Istanbul. But because of
these new development projects, those who live in the old buildings
have had to leave; they had to then go looking for another place of
residence. But because many of those living in these buildings were
renters (and not owners), they were not only expected to leave but they
also failed to receive any sort of financial compensation, nor any other
reasonable place to live (namely, places that are within their price
range). Tenants were also not kept up to date with any building
developments (Amnesty International, 2011), which could lead to
surprises when they are told – all of a sudden – that they needed
to move.

Plus, with the increase in demand for Istanbul housing comes more
problems for the transgender community to secure adequate housing.
As Carter (2015) explains, "[A]s Istanbul has grown as an international destination so too have its property prices, and the centrally
located Tarlabasi neighbourhood has faced gentrification and redevel-
opment projects which have forced out poorer communities." It is for
this reason that so many transgender individuals living in Istanbul have
decided to leave and move elsewhere to cities such as Izmir (Carter,
2015). The problem thus continues for the transgender community.
Not only do they face poverty, which leads to many of them being
pushed out of their homes and communities and forced to other cities,
this new environment is also usually much less accepting of the transgender community compared to Tarlabasi, for example (Carter, 2015).

Gender Confirmation Surgery Discrimination

One other important issue that has plagued the transgender community in Turkey has been the process for a person to undergo gender-affirming surgery. As of right now, gender confirmation surgery is a difficult process for those who identify as transgender. Legally, the procedure is highly problematic. While it is technically legal in Turkey, there are a number of requirements that must be met in order for someone to undergo gender-affirming surgery. Some of them include a minimum age (of eighteen); a personal application to the court for gender reassignment surgery; the individual should not be married; they should have what is seen as a "natural tendency to transexuality" (Öz, 2010: 44); and they have to make clear that the gender-affirming surgery is needed for their health, etc.(Öz, 2010: 44). Along with these stated requirements, one of the most controversial requirements to undergo gender confirmation surgery is that in order to do so, one must first be sterilized. This has caused outrage by activists, as they have pointed out the inhumanity associated with the process of gender confirmation surgery in Turkey. Plus, early in 2015, the ECHR also deemed this practice of mandatory sterilization counter to the human rights of an individual (Banco, 2015).

The reason that the ECHR spoke on this issue is because a case was brought to the court where an individual was challenging Turkey's Article 40, and more specifically the section where the government requires sterilization as part of the gender confirmation surgery process. The details and history of the case were as follows: There was an applicant who identified as a man, and wanted to thus get registered as a man in Turkey. Thus, in 2005, this person (known as "Y. Y.") started the process through the Turkish courts, beginning first at the Court of First Instance. Then, in the following year, according to existing Turkish law, the individual received two psychological reports, both that said that the individual would continue to identify as a male. The issue arose in May of that year with a report that noted this person still could reproduce. Following this, "the court ruled that the applicant does not fulfill the requirements of the Article 40" since the article requires a person who wants to go through gender confirmation surgery give up their reproductive rights. The applicant challenged the ruling at the Court of Appeals, but their 2007 ruling upheld the previous decision. It was then in 2008 that the applicant filed the case at the ECHR and where "he underlined that the relevant requirement of the law can only be fulfilled by a surgery, leaving himself in an inconclusive situation." Here, "[a]lthough it was proven by the medical reports that the applicant identifies as a man and his physiology does not fit his gender identity, it was not enough for the court. The applicant claims that his right to privacy, designated in the Article 8 of the European Convention on Human Rights, is violated" (TGEU, 2015). Because the man was still able to reproduce, his request for confirmation surgery was denied (TGEU, 2015).

On March 3, 2015, The ECHR reached a verdict on the issue. They found – unanimously – that Article 40 is "a violation of Article 8 (right to respect for private and family life) of the European Convention on Human Rights" (European Court of Human Rights, 2015). Specifically,

[t]he Court could not understand why an inability to procreate would have to be established – for a person wishing to change gender – before the physical sex change process could be undertaken. It did not see how, except by undergoing sterilisation, the applicant could have satisfied the requirement of permanent infertility. In any event, the Court did not find it necessary to rule on the question of the applicant's access to medical treatment which would have enabled him to satisfy that requirement. The Court took the view that the principle of respect for the applicant's physical integrity precluded any obligation for him to undergo treatment aimed at permanent sterilisation. (European Court of Human Rights, 2015: 3–4)

They challenged the idea that in a liberal democracy, a government could become involved in one's private life for such matters. Thus, by not allowing the person to get gender confirmation surgery, this went against one's right to privacy (European Court of Human Rights, 2015).

It should also be noted that while the case was being heard at the European Court, the applicant submitted another application at the Mersin District Court for the approval to get the gender affirmation surgery. This time,

[o]n 21 May 2013 that court granted the application and authorised the requested surgery, finding it established that Y. Y. was transsexual, that protection of the applicant's mental health required a change of gender, and that witness testimony had shown that the applicant lived as a man in

every respect and suffered from the situation, such that the conditions laid down in Article 40 § 2 of the Civil Code were met and the request should be granted." (European Court of Human Rights, 2015)

It should be noted that as of early 2016, there started a movement to have Article 40 removed from the Turkish Civil Code (Şimşek, 2016).

However, even with the recent ruling that Article 40 was against the domestic rights of the individual and international human rights treaties, those looking to have surgery face additional challenges. Namely, the wait to be approved can often take years, and for some, even decades. Furthermore, the surgery is very costly in Turkey. As Banco (2015) explains, "The process is daunting, especially for people who do not have the money or guidance to navigate the law. As a result, many are resorting to unsafe and unregulated medical practices to speed up the transition process." Banco (2015), writing on this issue, found through interviews

that the laws in Turkey are creating a new, harmful and misguided trend. Men who want to speed up the process of transitioning to a woman now board small ships off the coast of Izmir in southwestern Turkey ... and head for international waters far from Turkish law and oversight to undergo castration. The operations, performed at sea, are expensive, illegal and very dangerous – and people who undergo them then return to land with the hope that the government will have no other choice but to give them a pink ID card.

However, many view this alternative as dangerous, and therefore activists and lawyers often advise against this option for those looking to do go through gender confirmation surgery. For example, Suleyman Sennur, an attorney who deals with gender confirmation surgery laws, was quoted as saying that "[t]his kind of thing actually pushes the process back, not forward. If an individual gets a procedure like this done off the books, then I need to go and convince doctors to write a note saying the patient had the procedure done legally" (Banco, 2015). In addition, the legal process is highly complex and financially costly (with fees being in the low thousands of dollars in cases) (Banco, 2015). If they decide against going through with the legal processes, there are many dangers associated with nonregulated procedures. Even if one is able to have the surgery done, they still may face discrimination post-surgery. For example, some who want to change their names after surgery may have a difficult time doing so (Banco, 2015).

Because of the discrimination and violence towards the transgendered community in Turkey, there are many worries about its future, whether it is their physical safety, emotional well-being, opportunities for jobs, education, or elected positions. Overall, many who are transgendered do not feel safe in the country. They often cannot live where they want, and they have a very hard time finding a job. Because they cannot get work, other benefits such as social security may not become available. Also, many LGBTI – and specifically transgendered persons – are also without health insurance. While health insurance can be provided with employment, since many are discriminated against in the workplace, the loss of a job means the loss of other benefits as well. For many transgendered individuals, the only health insurance option is through the private sector (Öz, 2010), which is unaffordable for those who do not have access to work or to jobs that pay enough to afford the insurance (Amnesty International, 2011). Moreover, even if some LGBTI individuals do have public health insurance, the reality on the ground and its risks of discrimination against LGBTI persons means they may fear actually using their insurance, as they don't know if authorities will actually treat them (Amnesty International, 2011: 24).

Not only are all of these horrific rights abuses being carried out against transgendered individuals in Turkey, but what makes all of this worse is that there is very little said about these abuses in the media. Part of the issue is that transgender rights are still not viewed as equal rights compared to other international rights. Now, this is not to say that international human rights law does not treat transgender rights as equal, but there is a belief that transgender issues are not represented as much as lesbian, gay, and bisexual rights. Moreover, as others have mentioned, and as I shall discuss toward the end of the book, part of the issue is that much of the attention on Turkey has centered on authoritarian actions of Erdoğan, the ongoing conflicts in southeastern Turkey and Syria, and the refugee crisis. This is not to say that these topics do not matter; they are of course of serious concern. However, what is happening is that because the dominant conversations are centered on these issues, there is very little being spoken about with regard to lesbian, gay, bisexual, and transgender rights. It is for this reason that the work of transgender human rights organizations, as well as those media outlets that do cover abuses against the group, is so important. As we shall discuss, one of the most critical issues is the need to raise awareness about the plight of those in the transgender community, all the while working on increasing visibility for the transgender (and also the wider LGBI) community. It is imperative that the stories about them are told, that human rights abuses are documented, and that the world knows about the sorts of violence that the transgender community in Turkey are facing.

3 | The Lack of Legal Protections for the LGBTI Community in Turkish Law

If you push hard enough, you can get an appointment with [members of parliament]. You can talk about your demands face to face. So, we pushed hard enough to get ... to that point. And we went there and we talked about our demands.

Cihan Hüroğlu

As I discussed in the previous chapter, Erdoğan and the AKP party have a recent history of suppressing any serious commitment to and movement for LGBTI rights within Turkey. But in addition to this, they have furthermore extended their attitudes toward the LGBTI community and LGBTI rights through the use of domestic and international law. While this chapter will primarily center on the way domestic law is used to suppress LGBTI rights, let's momentarily look at Turkey's actions at the international level as they pertain to LGBTI rights. The United Nations is one of the most important international organizations with regard to international and human rights law. Over the years, the organization has become one of the central places for the creation of human rights declarations, covenants, treaties, international courts, etc. Within the United Nations, there has been a recent push by some states to guarantee the rights of LGBTI communities.

However, a number of states have pushed back on the issue of LGBTI rights at the international organization, attempting to make arguments based on religion or culture. It is for this reason that much less progress has been made on LGBTI rights in the United Nations than in the European Union legal system (Swiebel, 2009). Sadly, Turkey falls within the camp of those state governments unwilling to express their support for LGBTI rights in international law. When looking at the attempts by some states' politicians to advocate for LGBTI legislation, it becomes evident that Turkish leaders are not among them, as they have not wanted to sign declarations or treaties aimed toward providing much-needed rights for lesbian, gay, bisexual, transgender, and intersex rights. To give an example, under its periodic review for the Human Rights Council, Turkey has not been following international demands for implementing domestic laws that directly provide LGBTI rights. In addition,

[i]n December 2010 Turkey also failed to register a vote during the historic adoption by the United Nations General Assembly of the Resolution that condemns extrajudicial, summary or arbitrary executions and references those targeted due to their sexual orientation. Underlining Turkey's failure to support the protection of the rights of lesbian, gay, bisexual and trans-gender individuals at the international level, Turkey did not support a joint statement issued in March 2011 by Colombia with the support of 85 states at the United Nations Human Rights Council on ending acts of violence and related human rights violations based on sexual orientation and gender identity. (Amnesty International, 2011: 9)

Furthermore, LGBTI human rights organizations in Turkey have submitted a number of Periodic Review Reports on Turkey's conditions for the LGBTI to the Human Rights Council. One such report was issued in November 2014 by Turkish nongovernmental organizations Kaos GL Association and LGBTI News Turkey, as well as the International Gay and Lesbian Human Rights Commission (IGLHRC). In their report, they noted numerous human rights violations against members of the LGBTI community. Other reports focusing on Turkey around the same time period contain similar conclusions. For example, "[a]ccording to the European Commission's 2013 Turkey Progress Report, advocacy of hatred amounting to incitement of violence and physical attacks against gay and lesbian individuals increased from 2012 to 2013. The Report cites 12 murders of LGBT people in 2013 alone, as well as a number of attempted acts of lynching, and instances of torture, rape, ill-treatment, domestic violence, and harassment of LGBT persons" (Kaos GL, LGBTI News Turkey, and IGLHRC, 2014: 3). As I shall argue, Turkish leaders and judges have found ways to approach the law in a way that does not offer equal rights to the LGBTI community. Let us now look at the different domestic laws (whether through the Turkish Constitution or the criminal law) that are often viewed by some as being used to repress LGBTI rights.

Article 10

Article 10 of the Turkish Constitution stipulates that individuals are equal in Turkey, and because of this, are entitled to the same rights under Turkish law. The specific language of Article 10 reads: "Everyone is equal before the law without distinction as to language, race, colour, sex, political opinion, philosophical belief, religion and sect, or any such grounds." Later additions to Article 10 also speak on gender equality, noting that "men and women have equal rights" and that "[t]he State has the obligation to ensure that this equality exists in practice." The Turkish government references Article 10 when it is attempting to show that it provides equal rights to all within the country. However, as has been noted, not everyone in Turkey is treated equally. The problem with Article 10 is that it makes no mention of LGBTI individuals as a category for equality (Öz, 2010). Without the specific reference, the Turkish government can act as if the LGBTI are not deserving of the same protections provided to all other individuals.

Activists have raised objections to the missing language within Article 10. For example, Kaos GL spoke out on the issue of Article 10 and the importance of ensuring that language protecting sexual minorities exists, saying in 2012 that

[t]he existing constitution does not recognize LGBT reality. Thus Kaos GL has been constantly expressing its summarized demand about Article 10. LGBTs are real and a part of the Turkish society and will be a party to the New Civil Constitution as well. Fundamental rights and freedoms shall not be restricted owing to abstract and arbitrary reasons (which differ from time to time, from person to person) such as "public morality," "national security," "public order" and "public health." Such expressions shall not be placed on the constitution and the lines of the constitutional amendments should be clearly drawn. (Akpinar, 2012)

It is for this reason that NGO recommendations often include a point that Article 10 be amended to specifically mention LGBTI individuals and their right to be seen as equals under Turkish law, and from that, to be protected as such by the state. However, attempts to revise Article 10 in 2012 were not supported during the process of constitutional changes that took place that year, and this continues to be an issue that the AKP-led government does not seem willing to revisit. Because of the unwillingness of the AKP to include a revision to Article 10, they are creating an environment where the LGBTI community cannot point to the law as a protected group, which unfortunately could lead to further discrimination, whether it is in terms of employment, education, etc. The fear is that employers or others in a position of power can suggest that LGBTI individuals are not protected because of a lack of a specific reference within this article.[1] The Equal Rights Association for Western Balkans and Turkey (2017) argues that "[i]n practice, LGBTs are not protected by this law [Article 10]."

Article 90

Article 90 of the Turkish Constitution is interesting in part because it recognizes the importance of international law within Turkish domestic law. While this in and of itself is worth noting, what is particularly important to note about Article 90 is that it states that "[t]he ratification of treaties concluded with foreign states and international organisations on behalf of the Republic of Turkey shall be subject to adoption by the Grand National Assembly of Turkey by a law approving the ratification" (Turkish Constitution). Now, there are caveats to Article 90. For example, language within the article states that the government does not have to act upon those international treaties domestically if the treaty will cause the Turkish government to expend financial resources to implement said treaty. Furthermore, the treaty is not in effect if it goes against either individual rights, or property rights (Turkish Constitution).

The reason that mentioning Article 90 and the caveats to the law is important is that

[i]n March 2012 Turkey became the first country to ratify the Council of Europe Convention on preventing and combating violence against women and domestic violence, which explicitly includes sexual orientation and gender identity as categories of non-discrimination under Art. 4(3). The protection of the rights to freedom of expression and association and the prohibition of discrimination based on sexual orientation are covered by Articles 2(1), 3 and 26 of the International Covenant on Civil and Political Rights and Articles 3, 8, 10, 14 of the European Convention on Human Rights, which Turkey has ratified. (Hashimi, 2016)

Thus, because of their ratification of the Council on Europe Convention, many argue that Turkey has a legal obligation to adhere to the international treaty, even over any domestic law, so long as it does not incur costs or infringe on individual rights (or individual property rights) (Hashimi, 2016). Yet, despite their ratification of said law, the Turkish government continues to ignore these legal requirements, both in terms of writing similar law into their own constitution and actually applying the law domestically. One example of Turkey violating such international laws is the case of the government confiscating copies of an LGBT magazine put out by Kaos GL. Authorities took these copies because of what they believed was sexually explicit imagery. On November 22, 2016, the ECHR found that this action was a violation of Article 10 of the European Convention of Human Rights. The commentary related to this case stated that the state is unable to advocate the "protection of public morals" position generally against free expression (IJRC, 2016).

Article 29

Article 29 of the Turkish Criminal Code is centered on punishments for crimes committed in anger or hostility because of an "unjust action." The article specifically reads that "[a] person committing an offense with effect of anger or asperity caused by an unjust act is sentenced to imprisonment from eighteen years to twenty-four years instead of heavy life imprisonment, and to imprisonment from twelve years to eighteen years instead of life imprisonment" (Kaos GL, LGBTI News Turkey, and GLHRC, 2015: 3). This is another article that has been heavily criticized by activists who view the language as ambiguous and legally problematic, and one which others have used justify their hate-filled actions against the LGBTI community. In fact, the law does not specifically state (or offer concrete and in-depth clarification regarding) what "unjust action" or "unjust provoca-tion" actually refers to, which in turn has allowed a great deal of flexibility in interpretation and has led to judges being more lenient with those who have attacked LGBTI individuals (Kaos GL, LGBTI News Turkey, and IGLHRC, 2015). As professor Yasemin Inceoglu of Galatasaray University points out, this in turn has a detrimental affect on the culture, saying, "When an individual commits a crime on the basis of the victim's sexual orientation, Turkish Courts pass [a] reduced sentence on the ground of 'unjust provocation.' Thereby, the impunity culture becomes widespread and further encourages such acts" (quoted in Tokyay, 2015).

What is also problematic with Article 29 as it relates to LGBTI rights is that some have attempted to use the article to make a case that in a crime against a member of the LGBTI community, the mere fact of being gay or transgender can itself be a "provocation." Criminals have argued that they were "provoked" by the individual who happened to be gay or transgendered. This has added another layer of concern for the LGBTI community. These sorts of legal arguments are not hypothetical; there have been multiple cases of individuals trying to reference Article 29 as a way to reduce their criminal sentences. Unfortunately, it has worked. For example, in "February 26, 2014, a man who killed a trans woman was given an "unjust provocation" sentence reduction from life to 18 years. According to the verdict, the "unjust act" was the victim's "being a transvestite" (Kaos GL, LGBTI News Turkey, and IGLHRC, 2014: 3). With these sorts of rulings, it is difficult to believe that the LGBTI can be safe in Turkey, especially when the judicial system leaves ways for people to try to justify their horrendous crimes against LGBTI people (Kaos GL, LGBTI News Turkey, and IGLHRC, 2015).

Article 122

Similar to Article 10, Article 122 of the Criminal Code prohibits discrimination of individuals in Turkey with regard to access to services, employment, and the ability to buy or sell property. However, while such protections are in place, activists have called into question as to whether these protections in Article 122 apply to LGBTI individuals. The reason that some believe Article 122 either does not apply to those who identify as LGBTI, or that the government could easily dismiss the LGBTI from receiving these rights, is because there is no specific mention of the LGBTI as a social group that should not be discriminated against. The article states:

Any person who makes discrimination between individuals because of their racial, lingual, religious, sexual, political, philosophical belief or opinion, or for being supporters of different sects and therefore;

a) Prevents sale, transfer of movable or immovable property, or performance of a service, or benefiting from a service, or bounds employment or unemployment of a person to above listed reasons;
b) Refuses to deliver nutriments or to render a public service;

c) Prevents a person to perform an ordinary economical activity, is sentenced to imprisonment from six months to one year or imposed punitive fine (Turkish Criminal Code).

As we see, many types of groups are mentioned. However, an LGBTI category is not listed here. Because of this, the state (or other actors who may discriminate against LGBTI) could argue that since they are not a specified and protected category with regard to the article, that the law does not provide them such rights (Öz, 2010). The spirit of the article seems to clearly try to eliminate group discrimination. Because of this, one could easily argue that LGBTI community, as a group, would receive the same protections (Öz, 2010). But sadly, the situation is not so for the LGBTI community in Turkey (Öz, 2010). As Cetin (2016) explains,

[T]he most recent changes to the Turkish Criminal Code in March 2014 failed to incorporate the terms "ethnic affiliation" or "sexual orientation and identity" into the catalogue of criteria. Because of this, it is only with difficulty that Roma, Kurdish and LGBTI persons can plead for their rights in the face of discrimination or hate crimes. For instance, the dismissal of a gay teacher was justified with reference to public social morals and his sexual orientation could be represented as "contrary to social values." Similar strategies can be used to assign guilt to trans sex workers as well. In a reverse move, transphobic violent criminals use such value judgments to escape punishment. The terms "morality" and "social order" are firmly rooted in the Constitution and are often applied against LGBTI persons in court cases. The lack of an explicit mention of sexual orientation as a basis for the prohibited discrimination grants the courts broad discretionary powers, which they often use against LGBTI persons.

Again, similar to other parts of Turkish law, failing to include inclusive language within Article 122 leads one to believe that the government does not view everyone as equal. Those in the LGBTI community do not have a place in the law where they can point to for protection, which only increases their vulnerability in Turkish society.

Article 40 of Turkish Civil Code

As mentioned in the previous chapter on human rights abuses against transgender individuals, those who suggest that the Turkish government is supporting LGBTI rights also point to Article 40 of the Turkish

Civil Code. This article is another part of the law used against the LGBTI community, since it "stipulates that a court permission must be obtained in order to undergo gender reassignment surgery. According to the article, the permission can only be given if the person is over 18 and unmarried, and has the official medical board reports to prove that the operation is psychologically needed and that the ability to reproduce is permanently lost" (TGEU, 2015). So while it does allow for gender confirmation surgery, the individual does not have the freedom to do so themselves without judicial approval. Another quite limiting and demeaning aspect of Turkish law with regard to gender confirmation surgery is the psychological tests that one has to go through in order to be given medical approval with regards to the operation. There have been cases where individuals were not given the necessary court permission in order to begin gender affirmation surgery. Thus, the Turkish government's numerous legal hurdles before someone can get gender confirmation surgery suggests that they don't view transgender rights as being at the same level with other human rights. One such case is that of *Y. Y. v. Turkey*, where the state did not grant permission for Y. Y. to undergo gender confirmation surgery. After looking at this case, on March 10, 2015, the ECHR found, unanimously, that the state was in violation of the law when they did not grant authorization for the surgery (IJRC, 2015).

Article 56

One of the other more controversial interpretations of Turkish law has to do with Article 56 of the Turkish Civil Code. Article 56 states that "no association can be formed for an object contrary to laws and ethics." The vagueness in the meaning of Article 56 – namely, the part related to "contrary to laws and ethics," has allowed groups upset with providing same-sex rights in Turkey to reference the article as a way to go after the LGBTI community and their supporters. An example of this was cited in the "Periodic Review of Turkey" in the United Nations Human Rights Council. The report states that "[i]n November 2013, the governing administration of Turkey's Van province – in eastern Turkey – threatened to file a lawsuit to shut down the Youth and Ecology Association, a student environmentalist group, citing Article 2(27) of the group's charter, which states that it will 'work on the rights of people with different sexual orientations.' The Directorate claimed that the clause violates Article 56 of the Turkish Civil Code" (Kaos GL, LGBTI News Turkey, and IGLHRC, 2014: 4). The arguments made by the Directorate were that nonheterosexual sexual orientations directly violated the civil code (Kaos GL, LGBTI News Turkey, and IGLHRC, 2014). Because the government has not come out and defined "ethics," and with their history of unwillingness to clearly establish a law that specifically references the rights of the LGBTI community, this often poses trouble for LGBTI groups.

In Turkey, the Directory of Associations is the organization to which other organizations must apply to if they want official state recognition. The Directory of Associations has a presence throughout different cities, and organizations operating in a city would apply to their related Directory of Associations. As Öz (2010: 7) explains, "The Directory of Associations is affiliated with city governorships and the Ministry of Interior Affairs in a hierarchical way." However, in Turkey, if the Directory of Associations has an issue with a particular organization, they have the ability to go to the prosecutor's office (of the specific city) and make a claim. They would do this if they believe that said organization is violating some aspect of Turkish law and/or ethics. From here, the prosecutor's office takes over, investigating as to whether or not the organization has in fact violated Turkish law or ethics. Then, if the prosecutor agrees that they believe some ethic or law was broken, they can then file a case in the Civil Court of First Instance. If the prosecutor disagrees that the organization violated ethics or broke the law, then the case ends there, with a prosecutor denial (Öz, 2010: 7–8). Nevertheless, it must be noted that even if the prosecutor's office denies that any ethics were violated, the Directory of Associations is legally able to go to the High Court to appeal (Öz, 2010).

In the case of Turkey, four different Directory of Associations tried to close down five LGBTI human rights organizations, arguing that these groups were violating public morality. The five LGBTI human rights nongovernmental organizations were: Kaos GL Association (Ankara; decided in 2005); Gökkuşağı LGBTT Derneği (Rainbow LGBTT Association; Bursa; decided in 2006); Pembe Hayat LGBTT Derneği (Pink Life LGBTT Association; Ankara; decided in 2006); Lambda Istanbul LGBTT Association (Beyoğlu/Istanbul; decided in 2009); and Black Pink Triangle İzmir LGBTT Association (İzmir; decided in 2010)

(Öz, 2010).[2] The authorities went through the processed outlined above, but these attempts were denied (Öz, 2010) (in the case of Lambda Istanbul, the initial ruling by the local court was to close down the organization. However, Turkey's Supreme Court overturned this ruling (Lambda Istanbul, 2015)).

Again, what is important to remember when discussing the interpretations of the laws (and in this case, Article 56) is not necessarily what is clearly stated, but rather, what is not mentioned. For example, this article does not directly criminalize homosexual sexual orientations. However, "the lack of explicit legal protection based on sexual orientation and gender identity has allowed government officials to apply their own interpretation of 'ethics' in order to violate or limit the fundamental rights of LGBT individuals" (Pink Life LGBTT Solidarity Association and Kaos GL, 2015). What is missing is clarification on such laws to specifically state what is meant by "ethics" or "morals." What is necessary is language within these articles to state unequivocally that these laws in no way allow human rights abuses and discrimination against sexual minorities. If there are statements, or clarifying legal points that are established alongside these articles and laws, then there exists a legal statute for which human rights activists can point to when making their argument that discrimination against the LGBTI community exists. But as long as such laws are open to interpretation, this gives the government an open avenue in which to persecute the LGBTI community. As Öz (2010) explains, "[W]henever an LGBT organisation has been established in Turkey, the Directory of Associations has requested the closure of the organisations. Although the prosecutor offices and the courts ruled in the favour of the organisations, the authorities went on filing charges against the newly opened organisations. All the organisations faced the same process" (7–8). Öz (2010) continues by saying that "[i]n all cases the authorities applied Article 56 of the Civil Code and in most cases applied Article 41 of the Constitution. The authorities claim that LGBT organizations are against morality and ethics and ruin the structure of the family" (8).

Article 216 of the Turkish Penal Code

The Turkish Penal Code sets out punishments for various crimes committed in Turkey. In the Penal Code, Article 216 provides protections against discrimination, specifically by criminalizing actions intended to incite hatred (Öz and IGLHRC, 2011). While there are no direct anti-hate crimes laws, those who discriminate based on one's race, religion, religious sect, ethnicity, or social class can be penalized (Öz and IGLHRC, 2011). Although Article 216 is important and provides the necessary attention against discrimination, it does not include protections for the LGBTI community in Turkey, as it makes no reference to sexual orientation as a category of discrimination. Because of the failure to specifically include a reference to the LGBTI community, "it is not clear that LGBT groups can apply the article when they face hate speech or not" (Öz, 2010: 18).

Furthermore, as others have argued, not only does Article 216 fail to mention sexual orientation as a category for hate crimes but there have been noted cases of hate crimes against the LGBTI community that have gone unpunished within the Turkish court system. For example, Öz and the International Gay and Lesbian Human Rights Commission (2011) cite a specific case that was brought to the courts through Article 216. Namely,

On Sunday 6th August 2006, The Rainbow Association of Bursa called for a pro-LGBT demonstration. Before the group could hold the march, however, approximately five hundred counter-demonstrators gathered around the association's headquarters. They chanted and threw stones, forcing the activists to seek shelter inside the building, where they remained for hours. Following this incident, the police cancelled Rainbow Association's planned demonstration[,] stating that they would be incapable of protecting the group. In February 2007, a criminal case was filed against Fevzinur Dundar, the individual who had led the counter-demonstrators. The charges were brought under Article 216. However, although Mr. Dündar's homophobic comments had been recorded in the media, he was acquitted on the basis that the Bursa Criminal Court of First Instance could not find sufficient evidence to support the charges. (2)

It is incidents like this that have led many to fear for their safety, all the while questioning the state's commitment to offering safeguards against discrimination for the LGBTI community and effective punishments for cases when human rights violations do occur. Thus, in terms of policy recommendations for the protection of the LGBTI community, amongst other suggestions raised, activists have called for the clarification of Article 216 to ensure that it indeed also protects members of the LGBTI community from hate crimes (Öz and

IGLHRC, 2011). This is a necessary and needed clarification that will surely have a positive effect and not only in terms of punishing hate crimes. Moreover, clarifying this article may also help those in the LGBTI community feel safer and more protected, compared to fears raised about the lack of government response to these issues today.

Article 226

Article 226 of the Turkish Penal Code relates to issues of indecency and the penalties surrounding related crimes. In Article 226, the Penal Code states that individuals cannot do things such as expose children to indecent images or language, as well as publicize such images. Article 226 also speaks to issues of child pornography. So, Article 226 is very important in the fight against child abuse and for children's human rights. However, despite the good behind this article, there are also sections that have been used to discriminate against the gay, lesbian, bisexual, transgender, and intersex community in Turkey. One of the most discussed sections of Article 226 is in relation to parts of point 4. The entire section of Article 226 (4) states: "Any person who produces products containing audio-visual or written material demonstrating abnormal sexual intercourse by using sex, or with animals, or body of a death person, and engages in import sale, transportation storage of the same and presents such material to other's use, is punished with imprisonment from one year to four years" (Turkish Criminal Code, 2004).

The part of the Article that has stirred controversy is the language related to "abnormal sexual intercourse." It has been argued that on the surface, this might seem to be speaking about things like sex with animals or with dead bodies. However, as Idiz (2014b) explains, "[T]his vague reference has been used frequently in the past by prosecutors and judges against transgender persons, thus establishing a string of legal precedents." For example, there was a case of a member of the LGBTI community being brought to court on charges of selling gay pornography. They were charged under Article 226. As a result of this, "[t]he judge filed an application with the Constitutional Court after accepting the defense's argument that using Article 226 against transgender persons was unconstitutional" (Idiz, 2014b). Furthermore, "[a]fter studying the application, the Constitutional Court decided it was admissible. The Constitutional Court has in recent months provided a series of rulings, based on reforms enacted over the past few years within the context of Turkey's application for membership in the European Union, which upholds rights and freedoms" (Idiz, 2014b).

Article 125E(g)

Article 125E(g) of Turkey's Law on Civil Servants gives the government the power to terminate employment of an individual working for the state if said employee is seen "to act in a shameful and embarrassing way unfit for the position of a civil servant." The government has used the law to discriminate against the LGBTI community. Authorities have used this law to target those in the LGBTI community, since, as established elsewhere, some members of the government view homosexuality as shameful, embarrassing, and a "sin." Thus, members of the LGBTI community are often afraid to reveal their sexual orientation and/or gender identity, since they know that they can (and often are) targets of government and employee discrimination (Amnesty International, 2011; Kaos GL, LGBT News Turkey, and IGLHRC, 2015). As human rights organizations in Turkey have noted, "In 2012, that clause was used to dismiss a police officer due to his perceived gender identity" (Kaos GL, LGBT News Turkey, & GLHRC, 2015). The National Police fired F. B., a fellow officer, after investigating the individual's gender (SPoD, 2013).

Law Number 5651

Law number 5651, on "Regulating Broadcasting in the Internet and Fighting against Crimes Committed through Internet Broadcasting," is also referred to as "The Internet Law." In place since May 2007, the Turkish government has used the law to control publishing content online and to ban sites that the state finds offensive. A YouTube video with an anti-Mustafa Kemal Ataturk message (which included "scenes disparaging the Turkish Flag") led the government to first pass this law (Akdeniz, 2010).

Here, the government, and more specifically, lawyers at the Telecommunications Communication Presidency (TIB) (Schechter, 2011) have a wide net with which to monitor publications and step in and ban content that goes against other Turkish laws. While the initial idea of the law was for good, as it was used to go after sites that had child pornography, the Turkish government has also pursued information and sites that are not illegal but that they find threatening. They tie Law number 5651 to the Turkish Constitution, and interpret the law in a very broad way to justify crackdowns on media. For example, "[t]he explanatory note of the Law referred to article 41 of the Turkish Constitution states that, 'the state shall take the necessary measures and establish the necessary organisation to ensure the peace and welfare of the family, especially where the protection of the mother and children is involved.' The Parliament essentially explained that they had a duty to protect 'our families, children, and the youth'" (Akdeniz, 2010: 6–7). So, in the name of protecting individuals and families, they have also found a way to suppress anything that is outside of what the government deems appropriate.[3]

This law, in combination with others in the country (such as Article 226) has been particularly troubling for the LGBTI community. The Turkish state has used this law, and their calls for "Safe Internet Service" (Schechter, 2011) to ban any homosexual content that they find online. There have been several documented applications of this law, in conjunction with Article 226, against the LGBTI community. For example, as Akdeniz (2010) explains, from May 2007, until December 2009,

access to approximately 3700 websites have been blocked under Law No. 5651. This includes access to a considerable number of foreign websites – including prominent sites such as YouTube, Geocities, DailyMotion, and Google – that have been blocked in Turkey under the provisions of this law, by court orders and administrative blocking orders issued by the Telecommunications Communication Presidency (TIB). Similarly, websites in Turkish, or addressing Turkey related issues have been subjected to blocking orders since Law No. 5651 came into force. This is particularly prevalent in news sites dealing with south-eastern Turkey, such as Özgür Gündem, Keditör, and Günlük Gazetesi. However, Gabile.com and Hadigayri.com, which combine to form the largest online gay community in Turkey with approximately 225,000 users, were also blocked. Furthermore, access to popular web 2.0 based services such as Myspace.com, Last.fm, and Justin. tv have been blocked on the basis of intellectual property infringement. (Akdeniz, 2010)

Akdeniz (2010) of the OSCE has argued that these sorts of activities could be a violation of Article 10 of the European Court of Human

Rights if the motivations of the government for closing or banning sites
are due to politics.

Furthermore, as documented in an NGO universal periodic review
report,

[i]n August of 2013, one of the Penal Chambers of the Supreme Court of
Appeals in Istanbul ordered a publishing house to stand trial for translating
and publishing a novel with "homosexual content," citing Article 226 of the
country's Criminal Code on "indecency." In a similar vein, Turkey's
Supreme Board of Radio and Television fined a TV network for "promoting
homosexuality" by airing a music video in which two females behaved in a
manner that could suggest they were in a romantic relationship. (Kaos GL,
LGBTI News Turkey, and IGLHRC, 2015)

Military Law

Along with the many constitutional and Criminal Code articles that
seem to allow for an interpretation that could hurt the rights of the
LGBTI community, military law in Turkey is also used to discriminate
against the community. Baba, writing in 2011, argues that "[t]he
atmosphere of tolerance behind the walls that was inherited from the
Ottoman times was observable until 1980. However, the military coup
of 1980 devastated the life of many gender and sex non-complying
individuals and subjected them to state violence. The highly heterosexist attitudes of the military continues to this day." The biggest issue
with regards to military law as it relates to homosexuality has to do
with the fact that in military law, homosexuality is viewed as a "psychological" sickness (Ozer, 2013). The Turkish military has upheld this
policy since the introduction of the American Psychology Association's
Diagnostic and Statistical Manual of Mental Disorders (DSM) in 1968
(Kaos GL, LGBT News Turkey, and IGLHRC, 2015). However, in
1973, after an analysis of various theories in the field on the issue of
homosexuality (Drescher, 2015), and a vote among members of the
APA conference in 1973 (with 5,854 psychiatrists voting to take out
homosexuality from the manual (3,810 voted to keep it in) (Burton,
2015), "homosexuality" as a diagnosis was removed from the *DSM*
(Drescher, 2015).[4] But it is important to note that this wasn't a complete removal of homosexuality, but rather more of a compromise,
instead, "replacing it, in effect, with 'sexual orientation disturbance'
for people 'in conflict with' their sexual orientation" (Burton, 2015).

The new language of "Sexual Orientation Disturbance" (SOD) led to other problems, since "the new diagnosis legitimized the practice of sexual conversion therapies" (Drescher, 2015). Then, in the *DSM-III*, they took out SOD and added "Ego Dystonic Homosexuality." Realizing this was also problematic, and as a result of compromises, it was not until 1987 that homosexuality as a disease was completely removed from the *DSM* (Drescher, 2015). Subsequent iterations of the *DSM* still kept this position, and the language was only more recently changed. It was in *DSM-5* (2012) in which "Gender Identity Disorder" (GID) was removed, which many believe is a good development with regards to "removing stigma against transgender people based on false stereotypes about gender identity and expression, as well as the word 'disorder'" (Heffernan, 2012). However, despite the shift away from thinking of homosexuality and sexual orientation as a disease within the APA, the military in Turkey continues to maintain the position as found in the 1969 *DSM*.

Furthermore, all Turkish males (from the ages of 18–41 are expected to serve in the military. However, homosexuals cannot serve in the military, although this is only after the individuals undergo an intense process of interviews with hospital workers and military officials (Kaos GL, LGBT News Turkey, and IGLHRC, 2015). Furthermore, the law withholds their objection to military service, violating Turkey's obligations under the European Convention on Human Rights. Objectors are forced to "prove" their homosexuality in examinations defined by Human Rights Watch as "humiliating and degrading." In addition, the military for quite some time actually "required intimate photographic evidence or family testimonials from anyone seeking exemption [from military service] because of sexuality" (Jamieson and Akyavas, 2015). Family members can be asked questions about a person's military service (or the lack thereof), and in some cases, the military, in looking for their "proof" that someone is a homosexual, may call family members to inquire about someone's sexual orientation (Amnesty International, 2011), which can lead to further emotional stress, as well as possible physical danger. There were also instances where individuals had to "submit to an unscientific rectal exam, and to submit photos of themselves having gay sex before being discharged because of their sexual orientation" (Brydum, 2015).

These sort of activities clearly show a military unsympathetic to and not understanding of the challenges that LGBTI individuals face, and thus, make any rights equality for the LGBTI community more difficult to attain because of their policies and behaviors against this group. As noted in interviews conducted by Amnesty International (2011), "Gay men who spoke to Amnesty International in early 2011 stated that they were subjected to threats and abuse from commanding officers and from fellow conscripts and in some instances that they were subjected to homophobic violence by army conscripts due to their sexual orientation" (17). Because of such violence or violent threats, a number of people have tried to circumvent any military service (Amnesty International, 2011). In late 2015, the military changed their regulations so that an individual did not need to prove that they are gay in front of a doctor (Gurcan, 2015). The new policy is similar to the "don't ask, don't tell" US military policy (Brydum, 2015). But even with the change in military procedure with regard to LGBTI individuals, Byrdum (2015) argues that

a self-declared gay identity is still grounds for dismissal for military school students, commissioned, and noncommissioned officers. Such a dismissal, denoted by an "unfit report" that effectively outs the service member, can lead to severe social, professional, and religious isolation and cultural rejection, notes Al-Monitor. A study conducted this year by the Al-Monitor reporter who authored the article found that 96.3 percent of current Turkish military officers did not believe gay people should be allowed to serve in the military.

Even if the candidate is exempt from serving in the military, they continue to face many challenges in their everyday life from this decision. What often happens is that "the local authorities are informed of the decision. If the man is from a village or small town where individuals are likely to be known by public officials, this may result in details of his refusal to perform military service or sexual orientation being made public – and putting him at risk of homophobic abuse or violence" (Amnesty International, 2011: 18). There are other instances where a person at one point may have tried to get military exemption, but the application was refused. However, the information that they applied may still be available, thus opening them up to further potential physical abuse (Amnesty International, 2011: 18). Furthermore, this process continues to encroach upon their privacy. Moreover, employers may do the same thing: if they see that an individual did not serve in the military, their sexual orientation and/or gender identity may be used against them with regard to employment discrimination (Kaos GL, LGBT News Turkey, and IGLHRC, 2015). They are able to know this information since anyone that completes their military service is provided a certificate verifying their time in the military. But if an employer sees an exemption certificate in its place, it may use this to discriminate against the LGBTI individual (Amnesty International, 2011).

Law of Misdemeanors and Traffic Law

Human rights organizations in Turkey have pointed out that "Turkey's Law on Misdemeanours" is regularly used to discriminate against transgender persons. For example, transgendered individuals in Istanbul report being stopped by the police while merely walking around or working, and being told that they violate the Law on Misdemeanours by "disturb[ing] the environment" (Kaos GL, LGBT News Turkey, and IGLHRC, 2015: 9). Others have been found to violate traffic law; some transgendered individuals have been arrested because of what the police say is "obstructing traffic," whereas others have been arrested on charges of "breach of the peace" (Amnesty International, 2011: 14). The situation regarding arbitrary arrests of the transgendered community in Turkey became even worse

after Istanbul Chief Police Officer Huseyin Capkin introduced a bonus system that gives officers "points" for the number of fines they assess. Because the Law prosecutes misdemeanours and not "crimes", police enforce the law, without any judicial oversight. The law's vague and extensive language thus allows the police to act with impunity while targeting marginalized members of the population. In May 2013, a proposal for government to investigate the problems faced by Turkey's LGBT population was voted down by Parliament. (Kaos GL, LGBT News Turkey, and IGLHRC, 2015: 9)

Thus, the Turkish police use very subjective interpretations of the law as an excuse to arrest and detain transgendered individuals, and then, as I discussed earlier, they implement significant fines against them (Amnesty International, 2011). To make matters worse, no reliable system of oversight into police behavior against the transgendered community exists (Amnesty International, 2011).

COWI (2010) cites a LGBT Rights Platform (2009) publication in which they document such abuses by police. They tell of one incident in 2008 regarding police brutality against a transgender individual.

[A] transgender woman (S. L.) was insulted and beaten by four plain-clothed police officers by using truncheons when she was walking on the road at night in Marmaris in Muğla on 12 January 2008. She was also given the punishment of an administrative fine worth 58 TL by the police officers on the basis of the Code on Misdemeanour (*Kabahatler Kanunu*) Article 37th which orders an administrative fine to people who disturb other people around in order to sell goods or a service. She went to the state hospital and took a forensic medical report after the attack. While she was walking on the same road at the same time the next day, she was insulted and beaten again by two of the four police officers who attacked her the previous night. She applied to the Office of the Public Prosecutor in Marmaris (*Marmaris Cumhuriyet Başsavcılığı*) the next day and made an official accusation against the four police officers and demanded that they would receive punishment. There are witnesses and forensic medical reports regarding this case. She also submitted some photographs, which showed physical harm over her body, to the Office of the Public Prosecutor in Marmaris. M. D., who was also a transgender woman and a friend of S. L ., saw that her friend was beaten by the police officers by using truncheons on 12 January 2008 and asked the police officers why they were doing it by going to the place of the crime. She was also beaten and given the punishment of an administrative fine. She also made an official accusation against the police officers. (10)

It is for reasons like this that the transgender community in Turkey, and particularly those working in the sex trade industry, have been especially careful when dealing with police officers. Working in prostitution can be especially difficult, as some have been treated quite poorly by violent officers, and others have also been discriminated against, even if not being hit physically. For example, "[w]hile licensed prostitution is legal in Turkey and state-registered brothels undergo a strict registration process, [some transgendered sex workers work] off the books, since the state does not accept transitioning women or gay men into their brothels" (Mortada, 2015). In addition,

[t]he police routinely perform raids on brothels in an attempt to eliminate prostitution all together. Recently, numerous closures of legal brothels in the red light districts of Turkey have occurred without legal justification. By eliminating safe spaces for sex workers without providing any long-term solutions to help them obtain other forms of employment, government policies further add to their stigmatization and marginalization. Stricter prostitution legislation and criminalization also negatively influences trans-gender sex workers. (Engin, 2016)

Because of the threats that transgender prostitutes face from the state and others parts of society, they have developed ways to further protect themselves against those who might pose problems for their activities and/or threats to their safety. Mortada (2015) wrote a story on how the transgender community in Istanbul has been using a language called Lubunca to conduct their business. Lubunca is slang language that was first used towards the end of the Ottoman Empire. There is not much research on the early uses of the language, although "Lubunca was found in spaces where men engaged in sex work, such as bathhouses" (Mortada, 2015). So while there is a longer history of Lubunca in Turkey, the slang language seemed to increase in usage in the 1980s and 1990s, particularly among sex workers. Nikolas Kontovas notes that "[e]ventually, the spaces where Lubunca was used expanded into unregistered brothels and their neighborhoods, where male and trans sex workers interacted with minority communities like the city's Roma and Greeks or musicians and other artistic groups. 'There is lots of Romani. A lot of the vocabulary [of Lubunca] overlaps with Romani'" (quoted in Mortada, 2015).[5]

2012 Constitutional Update and 2012 Veto of Same-Sex Rights Legislation

In 2012, Recep Tayyip Erdoğan and the ruling AKP party in Turkey moved to introduce changes to the constitution. This came following significant constitutional reforms following a 2010 referendum, which, amongst other things, expanded Turkey's High Court to seventeen judges, most of which were then to be appointed by the president. Among the more recent attempts to establish legislation for the protection of same-sex rights in Turkey came in 2012 and 2013, when two major parties in Turkey, the Republican People's Party (CHP), as well as the Peace and Democracy Party (BDP), introduced calls for same-sex rights legislation.

This came on the heels of prior attempts at nondiscrimination legislation in 2011 (which eventually left out specific mention of gender identity, as well as sexual orientation, as categories for which discrimination would be illegal) (Amnesty International, 2011: 9–10). As Bozkurt (2012) explains, "The [2012] proposal was introduced during debates on the principle of equality as part of the ongoing meetings on drafting of the 'Fundamental Rights and Freedoms' chapter of the

Constitution by the Parliament Constitution Reconciliation Commission." Bozkurt goes on to say that "CHP's İzmir deputy Rıza Türmen and the BDP's Diyarbakır deputy Altan Tan asked for constitutional protection of gay rights along with the inclusion of notions of 'sexual orientation' and 'gender identity,' within the article covering protection equality among people." With regards to the importance of this legislation, a member of the BDP was quoted as saying that "[i]t is the duty of a state to eliminate practices and legal rules which stem from cultural or societal prejudices which are based on the supremacy of a gender" (Bozkurt, 2012).

During the process of changing the constitution, same-sex rights activists called for the government to include language specifically protecting the rights of sexual minorities. However, the government purposely refused to include any such language to support same-sex rights in Turkey's new constitution. Again, as discussed earlier, some tried to press for the inclusion of language to protect sexual minorities' right to not be discriminated against. However, speaking about this issue in 2012, AKP Party Deputy Mustapa Sentop was quoted as saying that "[w]e don't find it right to have an expression concerning gays in any part of the constitution" (Akpinar, 2012; Bozkurt, 2012). Yet, despite attempts by some political parties and human rights activists to push forward this agenda, the AKP party vetoed the legislation, which would have granted these protections for individuals in Turkey (Bozkurt, 2012).

However, it is not that the AKP has avoided enacting all forms of antidiscrimination laws, rather, it is just that they choose not to include specific antidiscrimination protections for the LGBTI community. For example, "[i]n March 2012, Turkey passed the Law to Protect Family and Prevent Violence against Women. While one may commend the effort of the Government of Turkey in passing this law, the law leaves important terms undefined. It contains no definition of either 'gender-based discrimination' or 'gender-based violence.' Moreover, there is no reference to the terms 'gender,' 'gender identity,' or 'sexual orientation' in this or any other Turkish law" (Kaos GL, LGBTI News Turkey, and GLHRC, 2015: 9). In addition to the 2012 "Law to Protect Family and Prevent Violence against Women," the AKP passed additional and specific pieces of legislation related to combatting discrimination and hate crimes through their "2014 Sixth Democratization Package" of laws. However, similar to the 2012 legislation, these more recent laws also do not reference sexual orientation, nor do they mention gender identity (Kaos GL, LGBTI News Turkey, and IGLHRC, 2015: 8–9). There was a case where a transgender women was discriminated against because of their LGBTI identity, yet the persons behind the physical attacks were never arrested, and some have argued that the police have not done enough to pursue justice for the victim (ILGA, 2013; Kaos GL, LGBTI News Turkey, and IGLHRC, 2014). While we cannot know for certain the specific difference that including LGBTI as a protected group within this 2012 law would have made in this or other instances, and while the law does state that it protects all women, there is indeed a belief that having these specific references to the LGBTI community would not only help in prioritizing LGBTI rights but this law would have also allowed activists and lawyers to be able to reference this law when arguing for stronger punishments of crimes and supporting LGBTI victims.

2013 "Democratization" Legislation

In December of 2013, the AKP government proposed what has been dubbed the "democratization package." While these reforms looked to penalize discrimination in a wide range of categories, what was missing is the reference to hate crimes with regard to sexual orientation (Ozer, 2013). Organizations such as the European Commission (2013) wrote that – at the time – there existed a bit more openness on previously suppressed issues such as the rights of the Kurdish minorities, the Armenians, and LGBTI rights. However, at the same time, they also noted that "further progress is held back by various persisting factors. The political climate is still marked by polarisation and lacks a spirit of compromise. The government has tended to rely exclusively on its parliamentary majority to pass laws and decisions, including on socially sensitive issues, without sufficient consultation and dialogue with stakeholders" (2). Plus, it can easily be argued that Erdoğan and the AKP have taken Turkey down an increasingly authoritarian direction since 2013, with attempts to quell protests, quiet anyone associated with Fethullah Gulen and the Hizmet movement, including journalists and news outlets critical of the Turkish government (even more so after the July 2016 failed military coup), as well as the Kurds in the south, who continue to face mass discrimination and criminal actions committed by the Turkish military. Again, activists were concerned that by not including sexual orientation as a hate crime category, it would only allow people who have committed such crimes to argue "unjust provocation" (Ajansı, 2013) (as discussed earlier in the chapter). In one case, an individual who killed a transgender individual was given a sentence of eighteen years instead of a life sentence for using this argument. The hope would be that having a sexual minorities category of hate crimes protection would instill much harsher penalties for such violations.

2016 Equality Agency Discrimination

In 2016, different political parties within the government began working on a draft for a Human Rights and Equality Agency that would be tasked with responding to human rights abuses committed in the country. Putting aside the hypocrisy of the AKP for a moment (given that the government under Erdoğan has been responsible for overseeing crimes in the Kurdish region of the country), the AKP-led government rejected calls by the CHP and the HDP to ensure that sexual orientation, as well as gender identity, would be included under the equality agency. However, while "[t]he draft prepared by the Turkish government bans discrimination based on gender, race, color, language, religion, belief, philosophical or political view, ethnicity, wealth, birth, marital status, disability or age[,]" it fails to protect LGBTI individuals (Kaos GL, 2016a). According to reports, in responding to questions about the sexual orientation category and the AKP's unwillingness to support the inclusion of this category, Vice Prime Minister Lutfi Elvan suggested that Europe is dealing with similar questions about sexual orientation rights inclusions. He was quoted as saying that "[i]n Europe, too, there is a serious debate about it. When we consider the Constitution and international conventions we ratified, we thought that it would be inappropriate to add such a term in this [draft]. We have to embrace the whole society and act according to this approach" (Kaos GL, 2016). However, others such as GHP MP Mahmut Tanal demanded that a reference to the LGBTI and sexual identity be in the draft of the document. Tanal was quoted as saying,

They [the AKP] said that there is a digestion problem regarding especially sexual orientation. But there is as such a reality and there are also international conventions we ratified and recommendations. Not accepting this phenomenon while following recommendations in general and trying to solve it by dismissal means continuation of the problem. As you know, this [LGBTI rights] is not something that has no support in the public opinion. (Kaos GL, 2016)

Along with the CHP's attempt to get sexual orientation in the draft, other officials, such as members of the People's Democratic Party (HDP)[6] tried to do the same. For example,

HDP MPs Ayse Acar Basaran, Burcu Celik Ozkan and Ayhan Bilgen proposed the addition of "sexual orientation and gender identity" on the draft article regulating discrimination ban in public employment, which was also rejected by the government. The MPs stated that the AKP does not even bother to listen to any proposals by other parties and civil society, and that the draft is being prepared in a rush without a human rights perspective. (Kaos GL, 2016)

These statements are not out of the norm concerning conduct of AKP officials. As has been discussed earlier, there is a history of discrimination by AKP leaders against LGBTI rights. Their unwillingness to add a LGBTI and gender identity component to the recent Equality Agenda is just the latest in a series of discriminatory actions by AKP members of the government.

Conclusion

By not passing specific LGBTI protections, along with articles of the constitution that condemn "immoral" behavior (which is often used by the state against homosexuality and the LGBTI community), specific legal protections facing the LGBTI are almost nonexistent. It is for this reason that many human rights NGOs and other activists have worked to advocate change of existing laws. For example, in many of the reports on the rights abuses in Turkey, NGOs recommend stark changes to the existing laws. For example, they call for Article 29 to be amended to specifically note that being a member of the LGBTI community is not grounds for provoking one's behavior. They also call for reform to Article 216 as it is currently stated (SPoD, Kaos GL, and IGLHRC, 2012). In fact, a comprehensive reworking of all of these laws in order to include specific LGBTI friendly language is necessary, and is the only way that Turkey can truly move to have a society that does not discriminate against the LGBTI. As long as subjective interpretations of existing laws are even possible, then the state, or criminal defendants, can sadly try to use them in order to justify horrific rights abuses.

Given the multiple ways that the existing laws are used to discriminate against the LGTBI community, it is absolutely necessary that one avenue for change with regards to increased protections of LGBTI rights must come from alterations in local and national laws. Continued discriminatory laws (or the lack of laws recognizing the LGBTI community) will continue to have a harmful effect on long-term work toward equality. As Murat Cekic says, "We cannot seriously talk about improvements until LGBT rights are given legal protection. As a result, chronic problems persist. Furthermore, LGBT people have to put serious pressure not only on political parties, but unions and civil servants" (*Turkish Weekly*, 2014). Organizations such as the European Union (in their report on LGBT rights in Turkey) have continued to call for the necessity of legal improvements for the LGBT community in Turkey, something that the Turkish government has repeatedly failed to do.

Now, this is not to say that the LGBTI has no legal recourse if violations occur against them. For example, Article 5 of the Turkish Constitution does guarantee equality and justice, saying that

[t]he fundamental aims and duties of the state are[:] to safeguard the independence and integrity of the Turkish Nation, the indivisibility of the country, the Republic and democracy; to ensure the welfare, peace, and happiness of the individual and society; to strive for the removal of political, social and economic obstacles which restrict the fundamental rights and freedoms of the individual in a manner incompatible with the principles of justice and of the social state governed by the rule of law; and to provide the conditions required for the development of the individual's material and spiritual existence.

As mentioned earlier, Article 10 does say that "[a]ll individuals are equal without any discrimination before the law, irrespective of language, race, colour, sex, political opinion, philosophical belief, religion and sect, or any such considerations." Given the failure to specifically include sexual minorities as a specific category, the LGBTI community and their supporters in Turkey still attempt to cite this article to show that they deserve equal treatment.

Along with domestic constitutional law, since Turkey is a party to the ECHR they are expected to adhere to all rights set forth through the ECHR; the European Convention on Human Rights stipulates that countries party to the Convention must uphold the rights set out within the document. Article 1 states that "[t]he High Contracting Parties shall secure to everyone within their jurisdiction the rights and freedoms defined in Section 1 of this convention." Among other things, the ECHR includes protections for sexual minorities. For example, Article 14 states that "[t]he enjoyment of the rights and freedoms set forth in this Convention shall be secured without discrimination on any ground such as sex, race, colour, language, religion, political or other opinion, national or social origin, association with a national minority, property, birth or other status." But it does not seem that ruling lawmakers in Turkey are willing to include the same protections in domestic law as exist in European Union law.

4 | LGBTI Advocacy Methods and Approaches
Looking at the Wider Field

A sustainable relationship between local governments and LGBTI initative[s] [is] the most important thing right now on my agenda.

Boysan Yakar

In this chapter, I shall review the academic and policy literature as it pertains to an NGO and activist strategies on issues of same-sex rights. In this discussion, I will focus on common LGBTI rights tactics and approaches used by activists. Of course, as activists note, "[g]lobally, the LGBT experience of promoting and achieving change and understanding with policy makers and the general population is that progress is extremely slow. Those living in environments particularly hostile to LGBT people often meet refusal and obstinacy from public representatives when they try to claim a space in civil society – by holding public assemblies, participating in public policy formulation, having their relationships recognised, etc." (Carroll, 2010: 5). Furthermore, because of the difficulties of even bringing up the topic of LGBTI rights in many countries, the research on these rights is still in relatively early stages,[1] and one can argue that this is even more so with regard to the work on this topic in the Middle East and Turkey (Engin, 2015), particularly as the LGBTI rights advocacy movements are still relatively new there compared to other LGBTI movements elsewhere.[2]

Yet, despite the difficulties and dangers of this work, thanks to the tireless efforts of LGBTI activists, it is clear that there have been many successes of LGBTI rights movements around the world. Take the case of the United States. In the past few decades, activists have been able to increase public visibility for the LGBTI community on television, in music, in sports, and many other aspects of public society. In addition, because of this activism, the LGBTI community has also received better medical treatment, more rights for adoption, the right to marry, among other issues. However, there continues to be discrimination against

LGBTI individuals in America. As Rimmerman (2014) writes, "[b]ut for all of the so-called progress, lesbians and gay men remain second-class citizens in vital ways. For example, though in May 2013 the Boy Scouts of America ended its long-term policy of preventing openly gay youths from participating in any of its organizational activities, this major policy change, effective in January 2014, was passed only after considerable acrimony and internal organization debate" (4). Then, in 2017, US President Donald Trump called for a ban on transgender individuals serving in the military.

Considering these examples, there are many other places in the United States where change continues to be difficult. For example, very few gay and lesbian individuals serve in elected positions, and even fewer transgendered individuals hold public office, in America. There still exists discrimination as it pertains to equal marital rights (despite the Supreme Court ruling). Just giving one example, in 2015, Kim Davis, who was the clerk for Rowan County in Kentucky, refused to grant a marriage license for a same-sex couple. She was one of three clerks in the state who declined to give the licenses to couples in same-sex relationships (Gutierrez and Schuppe, 2015).

What makes matters even more difficult for the LGBTI community is that "If evicted from their homes, expelled from their schools, fired from their jobs, or refused public lodging, they usually are not able to seek legal redress" (Rimmerman, 2014: 4). In addition, the LGBTI continue to face discrimination in other parts of their everyday life. For example, in Indiana, members of the Indiana State Senate passed what they called a "Religious Freedom Restoration Act" (Senate Bill 568), which would have made it legal for an individual businessperson to deny services (such as baking a wedding cake) for LGBTI individuals based on their religious beliefs. While this bill was signed by then-governor Mike Pence in late March 2015 (Cohn, 2015), in April 2015 Pence then signed another law on "religious freedom" in Indiana in which "[t]he revised law explicitly bars a business from denying services to someone on the basis of categories that include sexual orientation and gender identity (Terkel, 2015).

As we can see, there is still so much that needs to be done in the United States – and elsewhere – with regard to the rights of LGBTI individuals. The question that those interested in the topic, as well as people who are willing to fight for LGBTI rights, often ask centers around what strategies have been most effective in increasing visibility, rights, and overall support for LGBTI issues. This is a very important question, particularly for those who are looking to work on improving LGBTI conditions. There are various places to possibly begin from and concentrate on. Rimmerman (2014), looking at LGBTI activism in the United States, raises two questions: "Should policy and cultural change reflect a top-down model, or should it be inspired by grassroots organizing in local communities throughout the United States? And should the goal be a more assimilationist, rights-based approach to political and social change, or should movement activists embrace a more liberationist, revolutionary model, one that might embrace a full range of progressive causes[?]" (5). Whether the change is much quicker (liberationist) or gradual (assimilationist) is at the heart of a lot of debate among scholars and activists.

As I (and many others have argued), it is also important to keep in mind that one has to be careful to suggest that what works in one country will automatically lead to similar gains elsewhere; there are often subtle complexities that might lead a policy approach to work well in Country A but not in Country B. However, activists can examine what has worked elsewhere, try this strategy in their own contexts, report the results, and then, if successful, continue with the tactic. If it is not successful, they can either alter the approach or try a new strategy. This sort of work has been used throughout human rights social movements (Keck and Sikkink, 1998), and is a good way for individuals to share experiences and overall strategies. Plus, even though each specific strategy might be tailored to a specific case, one would expect there to be great similarities with regard to the types of strategies employed. For example, when we talk about increasing visibility (something that I shall discuss in more detail shortly), the exact method of raising awareness may be unique to each case, although the overall goal of greater recognition of the LGBTI community continues to remain the same.

An important conversation among LGBTI activists and the LGBTI rights-based movement has been whether to embrace the "assimilationist" or "liberationist" approaches to human rights reform. This debate on the best strategy for LGBTI rights has taken place within activist circles for many years. It could also be argued that these umbrellas speak to movement differences in general: for any issue, some have preferred activities that might introduce more immediate change, whereas others have advocated that it be better to work gradually towards rewriting the current conditions within a society or system. Rimmerman (2014) describes the two "camps" and what each sort of strategy might look like. He notes that "[t]he assimilationist approach typically embraces a rights-based perspective, works within the broader framework of pluralist democracy – one situated within classical liberalism – and fights for a seat at the table. In doing so, the assimilationists celebrate the 'work within the system,' or 'let us in,' insider approach to political activism" (5). He goes on to say that "[a]ssimilationists are more likely to accept that change will have to be incremental and to understand that slow, gradual progress is built into the very structure of the US framework of government" (5). In non-US cases, the assimilationist position would recognize the structural barriers to immediate change within a society and attempt to work with that preexisting system, with the goal of altering the status quo over time. The insider tactic includes lobbying, and private, closed-door negotiations, all within the political system (Gordon, 2011).

A different activist strategy is often referred to as the "liberationist" approach. Those who adopt this perspective are quite critical of the idea that through merely getting "a seat at the table" will any sort of real change come. In fact, "[f]or many liberationists, what is required is a shift in emphasis from a purely political strategy to one that embraces both structural political and cultural change, often through 'outsider' political strategies" (Rimmerman, 2014). Strategies here are not centered on working within channels of lobbying candidates or officials but are much more grassroots focused and include activities such as canvassing, protests, rallies, and litigation (Gordon, 2011). Thus liberationists are looking to reform or greatly overhaul the existing societal framework as it pertains to LGBTI rights (Rimmerman, 2014). What is also important to note is that in many cases, an NGO could actually be carrying out some work that is assimilationist, whereas other activities within the organization may seem to fall under the umbrella of liberationism. As I shall show in the next chapter, Turkish NGOs are using both assimilationist as well as liberationist strategies in their LGBTI rights work. Often, organizations work on many activities, and these activities can either be seen to have more immediate or more long-term success depending on the specific approach.

How to Change Public Opinion on LGBTI Rights Issues?

One of the most-asked questions with regards to LGBTI rights advocacy is the question of how activism work can effectively change public opinion on LGBTI issues. In societies in which LGBTI communities are not accepted as equals, whether it is in the law or in daily interactions, it can be quite an uphill battle to alter opinions towards acceptance of such rights. However, time and time again, we see that even in the most LGBTI-oppressive societies, such movements can be effective. The academic literature has shown that there do exist strategies that can help change public opinion. One of the most effective ways to change public attitudes on the LGBTI community is through what is referred to as "contact" or direct engagement between individuals. It is believed that "[c]ontact allows individuals to confront stereotypes or beliefs they may have long held with the realities of the targeted group" (Deese and Dawson, 2013). There are a number of published works that show contact between a member of the LGBTI community and someone who is not from that community tends to lead to a change (towards acceptance) of LGBTI rights.[3] These studies have been done in many contexts, whether in the general public, at universities (Deese and Dawson, 2013), etc.

Another strand within this research of changing public opinion centers on the specific activity of promoting messages of support and rights for the LGBTI community. This can be done through phone calls or through other forms of outreach to the non-LGBTI community. Many scholars have looked at how canvassing (going door to door, for example) and speaking with individuals about LGBTI rights may alter public opinion on the LGBTI community. Much of the discussion on this question focuses on who the "messenger" is when the canvassing is conducted. Scholars have argued that what tends to work better with regards to changing public opinion is not sending a canvasser from the LGBTI community to have conversation with someone who is not LGBTI but providing a message in support of same-sex marriage from someone who is of the same identity as those who are hearing the opinion.

Harrison and Michelson (2015b) published a piece in the *Washington Post* 's *Monkey Cage* entitled "How to Change Minds about Same-Sex Marriage." In the piece, they argued that if an individual is trying to change another person's opinion about an issue such as religion, for example, then it is best to send someone from the same religion as those hearing the message. In a 2012 experiment, Harrison and Michelson (2015a), found that "[r]eligious individuals exposed to the quotation attributed to a reverend were 11 percentage points more likely to say that they supported same-sex marriage, and 10 percentage points more likely to say that they approved of gay men and lesbians being parents." If you are looking to change the minds of sports fans with regard to their position on LGBT rights, Harrison and Michelson argue that it would be best if you use a professional sports player (from a favorite team, for example). With this strategy, they found that the level of support for same-sex marriage rights increased greatly when the message backing same-sex marriage came from a former Green Bay Packer and Hall of Famer LeRoy Butler (a player known and well-liked by those hearing the message) compared to someone in the entertainment business. In their study, they compared Butler with hip hop artist Jay-Z and found that "[s]upport among Packers fans who were shown a statement of support from Butler was 14 percentage points higher than fans shown the same statement attributed to Jay-Z." Also interesting, they found that to those who were not sports fans, having Butler's name next to the statement of support had no effect. They did a similar study where they used a Baltimore player as the source, compared to an anonymous person, and found that this yielded the same type of result, with over a ten percent increase in those supporting same-sex marriage.

Let's look at another example to see how this type of strategy can work. Take the case of the referendum on same-sex marriage that took place in Ireland in 2015. Harrison and Michelson (2015b) point out that

[d]ays before the vote, an elderly Irish couple, Brighid and Paddy Whyte, married 50 years this coming September, posted a video on YouTube urging a yes vote. They reached out to their fellow Irish as Catholics and as people who wanted to make the world a better place for their grandchildren. The video went viral, reportedly inspiring many conversations – and was a perfect example of the power of using in-group messengers. The strategy used by supporters in Ireland was modeled on work in the United States by Freedom to Marry, who based their successful campaigns in 2012 on internal research on how to connect with people and change their minds.

Many other Irish Catholic clergy said that they were voting "yes" on the referendum. For example, there existed "a group of priests who have bucked Church leadership to voice support for the amendment. Speaking to BuzzFeed, The Reverend Tony Flannery, founder of the reform-minded Irish Association of Catholic Priests, estimated that 25 percent of the country's clergy would vote "yes" (Kaplan, 2015). While it is difficult to know exactly how many Catholics voted in favor of the amendment, it is important to note that many of the clergy were speaking about the importance of LGBTI rights among their followers and church goers, were working in other advocacy mediums (such as public speeches), and some were also writing op-eds (Kaplan, 2015).

Again, this seems to support the idea that having an individual who might strongly identify with the contact group offering the message will be likely to yield much better results than if the message is anonymous. This differs from having someone who is LGBTI deliver the message to a group who is not LGBTI, as this may actually have a less-positive effect than having someone who is not LGBTI or a person who does not disclose their sexual orientation (Harrison and Michelson, 2015b). Therefore, given the various findings to support this idea that having an "in-group messenger" works well, in my research, I wanted to examine whether groups in Turkey were using Islamic advocacy to promote LGBTI rights. While the next chapter looks at overall strategies that the Turkish activists and NGO leaders used to promote same-sex rights, I have devoted a section to look more specifically at their use of Islamic-based advocacy.

Various Strategies Employed by LGBTI Rights Movements

In this section, I will discuss additional tactics used by NGOs in LGBTI rights advocacy. NGOs working on LGBTI rights have embraced a series of approaches in their efforts to bridge any inequality gaps. The work has taken a number of forms, and as we shall see in the next chapter, Turkish LGBTI rights-based activists are using many of the varied approaches in the field. This includes a human rights framework the concentrates on agenda setting, pushes for changes in international human rights law, the fostering of domestic and international linkages, advocacy in terms of media and issue reporting, visibility politics, advocacy for the assurance of health services, and access to employment, among other approaches.

One of the most-noted and preferred ways that NGOs approach LGBTI rights is through a framework of human rights (Mertus, 2007; Mincheva, 2012), that is, approaching LGBTI rights within the language and varied institutions of human rights. As Mertus (2007) notes, "Many advocacy groups turn to human rights language and adopt human rights strategies because doing so enhances their ability to become more significant players in international relations and to advance their cause in their home countries and regions" (1037). Referencing human rights is useful because it not only raises awareness on that particular rights violations (whether it is healthcare, employment discrimination, etc.) but it also allows NGOs to speak from "the moral high ground," and also helps build linkages with other rights advocates in the country, region, and then world (Mertus, 2007). But it should be noted that in some cases, groups might not look to use identity markers for their rights advocacy (Mertus, 2007). Again, this depends on the strategies groups believe will be most effective, or it could be based on what they themselves prefer to do in their advocacy.

There are a couple of different ways that activists can use a human rights framework. One is the documentation and publicizing of the conditions and rights abuses facing members of the LGBTI community. Often times, the LGBTI community is not only highly marginalized, but there is almost no attention given to them, which includes little in the way of reporting the suffering and discrimination that they face. People in the community often are afraid, and with stigmas in society, these individuals may be hesitant to report crimes committed for fear of additional abuse (Sheill, 2009). This makes it difficult to know just how deep the problem goes. This is why so much of the LGBTI rights-based work is on reporting abuses domestically as well as through international channels. While activists may try to do this using traditional and existing media outlets for the dissemination of information and stories, these organizations have also established their own outlets for the sharing of said information. Activists themselves can monitor state behavior and speak on any abuses through papers or through testimony at international organizations (Mertus, 2007). In addition, they also work on promoting rights, fighting to include said rights in the human rights lexicon. This can include, but is not limited to, calls for the inclusion of "the right to sexuality" (Mertus, 2007: 1039) as attachments to existing domestic and international documents (such as state constitutions, or United Nations documents) or through a new convention or treaty.

Swiebel (2009) argues that there is often a process that NGOs go through to be able to influence policy at international organizations. These are the ability to:

(1) gain access to the organization;
(2) define – or "frame" – the problem in such terms that the international organization they approach can be expected to contribute to its solution; in other words, they must produce a vision with some legitimacy;
(3) see that the problem is really taken on board by the organization; that is, it is put on the agenda;
(4) develop specific demands, that is, break down the issue into edible bites and deposit each chunk in the appropriate pigeonhole;
(5) and finally, of course, organize the necessary political support to see their demands go through the internal decision-making process and reach the outcome they desire.

(20–21)

This is a key component of social movement theory (Swiebel, 2009) and the ways that actors can effectively alter policy.

Some of the work includes fighting for socioeconomic rights. For example, LGBTI community members are often discriminated against when it comes to health services. Individuals that have come out saying they are LGBTI and/or that live in a country in which the policies are written with favoritism toward "traditional family" structures may miss out on much-needed medical support. This can often include both the young and the elderly members of the LGBTI community (Concannon, 2009). This can also be seen among the transgender community, for example, where they are not given the proper medical resources because of gender discrimination. There have also been cases where doctors are hesitant or unwilling to treat members of the transgender community. As discussed earlier in the book, another looming challenge is the inability to receive safe gender reassignment surgery. So, a way to bridge this gap is to provide health services to those in need. As we shall see, this can be by pushing the national government to allow equal access to health services.

Human rights organizations also believe that increased activity for the LGBTI community through elections has a positive effect on society and thus are involved in the electoral process. There are many reasons as to why working through elections might be beneficial. Increased representation of underrepresented groups (such as women in govern-ment, for example) "does not necessarily imply that women vote together or vote to protect the specific interests of their sex. However, it does mean that their faces and voices are present in a lawmaking body, and, therefore, present in decision-makers' minds" (Reynolds, 2013). In addition, having more members of politically marginalized groups in government can also change the attitudes of others in the government and in society as a whole (Reynolds, 2013). Focusing on elections, whether it is through the promotion of LGBTI candidates running for office, or on working with non-LGBTI politicians to ensure that they guarantee they will fight for the rights of sexual minorities, all of this can be very effective strategy for the protection of LGBTI rights in Turkey. Plus, this raises the visibility of the LGBTI community in a society. As Golebiowska and Thomsen (1999) write:

There are several reasons to expect the electoral success of lesbian and gay candidates to have salutatory consequences for the welfare of the broader lesbian and gay community. First, merely increasing the public's exposure to gay men and lesbians through the high-profile visibility of openly lesbian and gay candidates and officials should contribute to the breakdown of negative stereotypes and prejudices, thereby reducing their pernicious consequences in the form of discrimination, hate crimes, and political and social intolerance of gays and lesbians ... In addition ... increasing electoral success of lesbian and gay candidates is likely to translate into stronger legal protections of lesbian and gay rights and, ultimately, into greater tolerance of gays and lesbians in areas beyond the political sphere. Finally, openly gay and lesbian public officials may provide role models for lesbian and gay youth, a popu-lation that appears to be particularly vulnerable to the consequences of membership in this stigmatized group. (193)

Having LGBTI candidates running for elections has been an integral part of the overall activist strategy for decades. However, deciding to take this approach has often depended on a host of factors within a country. There are cases where potential candidates are threatened, so that they don't run for office. Sadly, "politicians around the world are increasingly using 'gay issues' as a wedge issue in election campaigns. Homophobia is a potent weapon for candidates from Zimbabwe to Malaysia to the United States. As such issue dominate national cam-paigns, the need to represent the community at risk becomes more urgent" (Reynolds, 2013). So many individuals decide to run for office despite challenges with regards to winning, funding, or threats to their personal safety. They have done so, campaigning at various levels, whether in local mayor elections, in municipal elections, or at the national level. However, compared to countries in the "West," there have been few open LGBTI officials in Turkey and the Middle East and even less when looking at the highest levels of government (Reynolds, 2013). Yet, as I shall show, elections continue to be a fundamental strategy for LGBTI activists in Turkey. Even those organizations that do not officially back political candidates have offered their support for LGBTI candidates running in elections.

Along with elections, educating the public about the LGBTI community, and the rights abuses they face is another important strategy for activists. Often times, the majority of the public is unaware of the harsh conditions that this group faces. The state – which may be the perpetrator of its own abuses – is often unwilling to admit their abuses. Plus, the media may not provide ample time for stories on LGBTI abuses. It therefore becomes essential for activists to raise awareness through their own platforms. They can do this through the establishment of independent media outlets and also through canvassing communities. So, here, protests, public demonstrations, and the distribution of pamphlets and other literature are vital for achieving this goal of public awareness. They might also attempt to work with community members and professionals through education and training workshops (Carroll, 2010). We are also seeing the use of social media and Internet technology for the creation of websites that can serve to educate people about LGBTI rights.

An additional strategy that has been used is the approach to challenge existing law within local or national settings. For example, activists have worked hard to challenge existing laws that might, for example, bar homosexuals from serving in the military, laws that might not grant them children rights, work rights, or benefits for them and their partners. In the United States, for example, there have been a few very important Supreme Court decisions that have positively affected same sex rights. In 2003, "'Lawrence v. Texas' ... struck down laws making gay sex a crime" (Liptak, 2015). And In 2013, the "'United States v. Windsor'... struck down a federal law denying benefits to married same-sex couples" (Liptak, 2015). These sorts of legal appeals are happening throughout the world. As we mentioned, in the case of Turkey, individuals have not only taken LGBTI related cases to the Turkish high courts but they have also appealed to the ECHR.

The level of success with regards to changing national laws (such as the Constitution) often centers on the type of political opportunity structures that exist within the society. This can be at the international level (within international organizations) (Kollman and Waites, 2009) or at the national level. There are many factors at play here. What positions does the ruling government take? What is public opinion like? What other socioeconomic or political factors within society need to be taken into consideration to better understand public attitudes? Are there security concerns? What is the relationship between the police and the state, and the police and civil society? The conditions on the ground are important factors to better evaluate the challenges that LGBTI rights-based activists face.

One of the more recent pushes from within the LGBTI activism community has also been to change national laws on the issue of same-sex marriage. As Lahey (2010) notes,

In 2000 same-sex couples could not legally marry anywhere in the world. By 2005, the right to marry had been established through legislation in the Netherlands (2001) and Belgium (2003), had been won in court battles across Canada (2001–2005), and was followed by national Canadian and Spanish legislation (2005). By 2010, another three countries had extended marriage to same-sex couples, two more bills were pending, two countries had made it available in selected regions, four recognized marriages performed elsewhere, and another twenty had enacted registered unions. By the end of the decade, 35 countries had extended substantial marital or spousal rights to same-sex couples. (380)

Argentina, through a Senate vote, became the first county in Latin America to legalize same-sex marriage (Barrionuevo, 2010). Before that, places like Mexico City, Uruguay, Colombia, and Ecuador had all given recognition to civil unions (Barrionuevo, 2010). Then, in 2013, the Brazilian Court Council stated that notaries had to perform ceremonies for same-sex couples when requested (Romero, 2013).

More recently, successful campaigns have led to the US Supreme Court 5–4 ruling in favor of same-sex marriage (Liptak, 2015), as well as in Ireland, where, through a national referendum, the people of the country voted to support same-sex marriage. In July of 2017, Germany also legalized same-sex marriage. Furthermore, at the time of this writing, Australia was preparing for a "Yes" or "No" vote on the question of whether to legalize same-sex marriage. These actions were hard fought, are very important for the overall progress of LGBTI rights in the respective states, and arguably, also for LGBTI individuals throughout the world. This has been a more common strategy by Western-based activists, and they have been able to get results. However, as I shall show in the upcoming chapters, there are many human rights advocates who think pushing for same-sex marriage rights in Turkey would not be productive to the overall movement. This has also been a point of tension between Western-based activists who may want to prioritize this issue, compared to local activists, who, while not opposed to same-sex marriage, are putting their efforts into advocating for other rights that they feel are much more pertinent to the immediate safety of the LGBTI community.

A Strategy of Visibility

Again, from the discussion above, LGBTI activists, and the LGBTI community at large have to decide on what strategies would be most effective in the advocacy of LGBTI rights. Given the complexity of social movements, this is not an easy answer. In fact, depending on the context, the response can (and often does) vary. However, one of the most common tactics has historically been that of visibility, namely, working to become more visible in society, which in turn would hopefully lead to greater acceptance amongst the public, as well as the lawmakers in government. Visibility activism has been said to shape perceptions and attitudes of LGBTI individuals in a number of cases throughout the world. For example, Wilson (2012) argues, "In the historic aftermath of the American public voting to affirm marriage equality, it's clear that the turnaround in majority public opinion comes in large part from ever-increasing LGBT visibility. Just about everyone knows someone who is gay: next-door neighbors, aunties, cousins and celebrities, all making gay folks real and human." In so many cases, visibility politics is clearly at the center of the struggle for LGBTI rights.

But while this strategy has been used in many human rights contexts, and is often a go-to approach for activists, adoption of this strategy rarely happens without some thought and discussion. The reason that the tactic of visibility is often a topic of debate has less to do with the belief in its effectiveness and more to do with activists weighing the value of visibility with the risk associated with promoting a visibility strategy. For example, at the individual level, persons who are deciding whether to make their LGBTI sexual orientation known often have to deal with the difficult question about what their visibility will mean if they come out. Namely, they often reflect on whether their announcement will affect their familial relationships, their employment, and interactions with others who may respond to their sexual orientation in a negative fashion. However, this question of visibility is not confined to the individual. With regards to LGBTI rights-based organizations, Jaspers (2004; 2006; in Currier, 2007) argues that organizations often have to make a choice, or a "strategic dilemma," between becoming visible or holding a position of invisibility with regards to their work; there are times where activists have found that maintaining a position of "invisibility" is more effective for their objectives. Currier (2012), in her work studying LGBTI movements in Namibia and South Africa, points out that

invisibility sometimes emerged as a politically effective option. Invisibility surfaced as a strategic possibility immediately when activists faced hostile counter-protestors; withdrawing from the encounter kept activists safe. In addition, although delaying the launch of a campaign resulted in activists' invisibility, sometimes this was the best option for activists who were debating the merits of different actions. Rushing into action prematurely could generate unwanted consequences, such as negative publicity for the LGBT movement, which faced considerable opposition in both Namibia and South Africa. In these examples, invisibility was a choice that LGBT activists made, albeit a choice that activists wish that they did not have to make, but alternative pathways were even less appealing.

But while some find value in maintaining a position of invisibility, many other activists and human rights organizations have preferred to advocate forms of visibility tactics as an approach to further the LGBTI rights movement, believing that the benefits outweighed any risks.

There are different levels of visibility. For some, this visibility begins at the individual level, with the act of coming out. As Harper (2012) explains, "[c]oming out is important. Visibility is important. Being out and being visible represents an opportunity to educate people on the reality and normality of LGBT lives and the normality of being in a relationship with a person of the same gender. Change comes about through this education. The effect of visibility illustrates the futility of any opposition, fear, prejudice, or intolerance." One of the more recent ways in which activists have been working to increase their visibility of the LGBTI community has been through the use of the Internet, and in particular, social media and the use of digital media platforms. However, as discussed above, the issue of visibility as a strategy is always a risky one, in particular in societies in which publicizing issues such as LGBTI rights is either illegal under national law or seen as being against the "morals" or "ethics" of a society. In addition, one must remember that the dangers do not necessarily subside in countries where there is no discriminatory law and where society is rather accepting of LGBTI rights; sadly, various rights abuses have taken place against LGBTI in the most "open" of societies. Thus, in these various spaces, LGBTI activists have to be very careful, given that governments may try to crack down on their political and social activities and/or may use language that further pushes some in civil society to condemn homosexuality.

Yet, despite all of these fears, activists continue to press forward. As mentioned, one way in which they are doing so is through the use of online, digital, and social media. In fact, various documented cases exist with regard to how activists have worked to promote LGBTI rights online in countries that are not friendly and supportive of the LGBTI community. Because of a lack of ability to promote LGBTI in open, public spaces, they are looking to the Internet as a means of LGBTI rights advocacy. For example, the Daily Beast, in a series on LGBTI rights called Quorum, has a segment where they discuss online activism with Xiaogang Wei (who works on LGBTI issues in China with his site Queer Comrades), and Suzan (who did not reveal her last name), working on LGBTI rights in Egypt and in the larger Middle East and North Africa with her site Ahwaa.org (Mid East Youth).

In the case of Wei, he explained that he founded his site in 2007 and that prior to that year, there was little in terms of LGBT images in the country. He was asked what sort of impact has occurred in China from 2007 to 2014, and he replied that he was approached by an individual a few years ago, who expressed happiness to meet him, saying that she was able to watch the work being done and to be exposed to a community of LGBT individuals. He said that this was important, as it showed that great things were happening, and that those in the LGBT community were not being passive with regards to the situation facing them in China. In addition, he says that "[a]ctually, the whole ... Chinese ... LGBT movement started [on the] Internet ... Before I feel like people ... feel more secure just go online to meet people because also ... don't have a lot of the space for LGBT people." And in the case of LGBT rights in the Middle East, Suzan said that her organization "was meant to fill a space that really didn't exist before. Ahwaa.org was created because the queer issues that the LGBT communities in the Middle East are concerned with are very different from the issues that ... other queer communities around the world are concerned with. So it was formed to create a space for people to really explore the issues that matter to them" (Daily Beast, 2015).

Digital media has opened up new opportunities for LGBTI rights activists. In their edited book entitled *LGBT Identity and Online New Media*, Pullen and Cooper (2010) state that online media is powerful in many ways. For example,

[o]nline new media is a convergent form, which can be related to preceding historical and generic influences of other media, such as radio, television, film, and print. It can also be placed in context with antecedent issues of representation, which for LGBTs have been reductive within various media. In addition, recent contexts of address and stimulation are relevant, such as the opportunity for self disclosure, and its therapeutic potential, within television and documentary form.

They go on to say that "[w]hilst online new media appears to offer increasing democratic scope for LGBTs, it is the journey that we have taken which informs the way ahead, as much as the imagined destination. This equates to a need to understand issues such as the subjectivity of 'queer' identity, the potential of social construction, and the contemporary setting of self reflexivity." Related to this, they argue that online media also offers the ability for "emancipatory politics" in which "[o]nline new media provides an arena for this in the display and potential of intimacy, which in the conditions of late modernity stimulates LGBT identity in new and productive ways. LGBT identity within online new media offers new scope, particularly when it is reflective, contextual, and continuously self aware."

The categories discussed above are just some of the approaches LGBTI activists take. As I shall show in the next chapter, LGBTI rights-based activists in Turkey have fought for LGBTI rights for years, and are continuing the fight, working hard at the individual level, at the national and international levels, and in different forms. They are fighting through traditional media, social media, protests, through workshops and other forms of education, as well as through elections. Let us now turn to the specific work by LGBTI activists in Turkey and the effect that this work has had with regard to increasing the visibility and overall rights for LGBTI people in Turkey.

5 | The Use of Media in Promoting Sexual Minority Rights in Turkey

This new media school is very important for us because by that we don't only educate our correspondents, we, at the same time...educate people to be an independent reader. We give them ... a kind of media literacy.

Murat Köylü

Whether it has been through derogatory statements dismissing homosexuality as a "sin" or "unnatural" (thus ostracizing the LGBTI community); an unwillingness to include sexual orientation as a category of protection in Turkish law; ambiguous interpretations of national law that demonize and offer few protections for those who are LGBTI; or disruptive behavior by police and others, including arbitrary arrests and evictions, individuals within this community have not been given the opportunity to live their lives freely. They have been persecuted, stigmatized, and discriminated against in terms of employment, holding public office, and other aspects of Turkish society.

As a result, human rights activists in Turkey have been working tirelessly to improve the conditions of the LGBTI community. The next few chapters are dedicated to the different strategies that individuals and NGOs use or have used to improve the standing of the LGBTI community in the country. Through examination of the literature, interviews with individual activists, and leaders of LGBTI organizations, such as Kaos GL, Pembe Hayat, Social Policies, Gender Identity and Sexual Orientation Studies Association (SPoD), and LİSTAG, among others, I shall examine how activists use media, politics, education, and other avenues to highlight concerns that the LGBTI community may have, as well as to bring to light rights abuses by the state and members of Turkish society. As I shall show, some, such as Murat Renay, the founder of *GZone Magazine*, are using digital media, in this case a magazine, to focus on LGBTI issues. Others, like Barış Sulu, the first openly gay candidate to run for elections to Turkey's parliament, have decided to run for political office as a way to alter the legal positions that might negatively affect the LGBTI community. Along with Bariş Sulu, some political candidates and politicians outside of the LGBTI community have also shown their public support for the rights of the LGBTI community. Others still are working within government municipalities and through nongovernmental organizations in Turkey. This particular chapter will examine the history of LGBTI rights abuses, and then will specifically address the use of media in LGBTI activism in the country.

History of Same-Sex Rights Activism in Turkey

In order to understand the current conditions facing the LGBTI community in Turkey, as well as how activists are operating in the country as it pertains to fighting for equal rights based on sexual orientation, it is imperative that we first understand the history of same-sex rights activism in Turkey. As we shall see, LGBTI activists have had decades of experience advocating for equal rights in Turkey. Their strategies and goals have varied throughout the years, with some continued constants. A lack of full rights for the LGBTI community throughout the years in Turkey has made the work of these activists all the more important.

While much of the history presented here will be devoted to the work in the 1990s and onwards, it is important to examine the early history of same-sex rights activism in Turkey. While the celebrity of Turkish singers Zeki Muren and Bulent Ersoy brought attention to not only homosexuality (and transgender issues, respectively) but also the reexamination of gender norms in Turkey (Özbay, 2015), some of the earliest activism work for sexual minority rights in Turkey was in the 1970s, in which sexual minorities began to establish communication with one another. One of the first places for more-established activism came from the city of Izmir. It was here that Ibrahim Eren, while employed at the Izmir Environmental and Health Organization, "established therapy/conversation sessions with gays and lesbians of Izmir" (International Lesbian and Gay Association [IGLA], 2009). While the 1980 military coup resulted in the suppression of human rights and free speech and the closing of this organization, Eren and others worked to establish a Radical Green Party as a platform from which they could advocate for sexual minority rights (and although the party was not officially established, many LGBTI individuals become more politically involved through this network of activists). Then, in 1987, after systematic police discrimination towards the transgender community, in which they would harass those who identified as transgendered, and following little media attention on the issue, thirty-seven LGBT activists began a hunger strike. ILGA (2009) speaks of the significance of this event, saying that "[a]lthough no substantial success was achieved from the action, it raised attention both internally and internationally. Some successful figures of the time such as Rifat Ilgaz (author) and Turkan Soray (actress) supported their cause." This strike has been called a "watershed event" by the LGBTI community in Turkey (Çetin, 2015). While the party itself ended up breaking apart, some continued working on LGBTI issues. For example, Sevda Yılmaz, a writer who works under the name of Ali Kemal Yılmaz, then served as the spokesperson behind this protest strike (İnce, 2014). Yılmaz still works on transfeminist issues in Turkey (Güneş, 2014; Baş, 2015).

The early 1990s were important for the LGBTI rights movement in Turkey. Not only did we see the beginnings of LGBTI rights-based organizations but it was also during this period that a stronger push for public advocacy in the form of marches and protests in Turkey took place. For example, in 1993, activists in the country were organizing the first Gay Pride March. However, Turkish authorities put a halt to the march on the grounds that, in their eyes, "society was not ready" for what was happening (COWI, 2010). Yet, despite the intervention by Turkish authorities, LGBTI rights activists continued to press forward with the idea of holding public marches centered on LGBTI rights. Because of their persistence in the years that followed, these activists succeeded in being able to successfully hold such public Pride Marches. While it took a decade, "Since 2003 the marches [were] not ... banned or stopped by the police" (COWI, 2010: 8; until 2015, when all this changed). These victories did not come easily. Even though the police acquiesced, allowing LGBTI marches, "every year the organisers have to negotiate with the police authorities about where the demonstrations are allowed to be held – an issue not only applicable to LGBT-organizations" (COWI, 2010: 8). Again, despite continued problems caused by Turkish authorities, 2015 marked the 23rd year that the Istanbul Pride Week took place (Tokyay, 2015).

The 1990s were a time when activists also began forming more human rights organizations, and NGOs established additional networks centered on LGBTI rights. As previously mentioned, in 1993, those in the LGBTI community and their allies worked to establish an LGBT Pride conference in the city of Istanbul. However, despite organization efforts, the event got called off shortly before it was to commence. According to the governor at the time, this event was not only against the "morals" of society but it was also seen as a disturbance to peace. Following the ban, "[t]he next day, Turkish authorities detained 28 foreign delegates, most of them while they were on their way to participate in a press conference in protest of the ban. They were detained for over 5 hours, threatened with possible strip searches and human immunodeficiency virus (HIV) tests, and deported on a Turkish airline to Germany. The organizers had previously received approval of the event from the Interior Ministry" (ILGA, 2009). However, from this government crackdown rose new LGBT organizations such as Lamba Istanbul (1993), Kaos GL (1994) as well as Lezbiyen Gay Toplulugu, and LEGATO, which was among the very first LGBT student organizations in Turkey (ILGA, 2009). This last organization spread rapidly to have chapters throughout universities in Turkey (ILGA, 2009).

As mentioned, the 1990s were a time when activists began forming more human rights organizations, and NGOs established additional networks centered on LGBTI rights. Some of this can also be attributed to the 1997 "post-modern coup," where the military called for "recommendations" that the government followed. This coup was heavily structured on the principles of secularism, and was highly critical of religious organizations. During this coup, "the military issued a series of 'recommendations,' which the government had no choice but to accept. Prime Minister Necmettin Erbakan, agreed to a compulsory eight-year education programme (to prevent [pupils] from enrolling in religious schools), a headscarf ban at universities, and other measures. Erbakan was then forced to resign" (Al Jazeera, 2016). The military also stressed an increased role for citizens in democratic society.

While the Islamist AKP party came into power in 2002, arguably shifting attention away from LGBTI rights, activists point to the period from 1997 until 2002 as an important time for the development of LGBTI rights organizations. It was with the rise of civil society at this time that LGBTI groups began forming. Throughout this period, LGBTI activism was also centered on community building. It was then that "generally ... people were meeting in each other's homes, getting to know each other, and that's the time where people just wanted to get together ... with others who are facing the same problems. So this is ... the understanding of that time period. But starting with the 2000s, the LGBT movement ... start[ed] to appear more in [the] public sphere" (Sedef Çakmak, City Council Member, Department of Social Equality, Beşiktaş Istanbul).

During the 2000s, the number of LGBTI organizations and public activists increased greatly. While initial membership numbers were much lower than what we see today,[1] the groups were able to make great strides on LGBTI rights, especially with public events such as the Pride Marches. Along with the first LGBTI Pride March in Istanbul that took place in 2003 (Pearce, 2014b), "[t]he first demonstration marking the International Day against Homophobia was held in Ankara in 2008 – the march was jointly organi[z]ed by Kaos Gay and Lesbian Association (Kaos GL) and Pink Life LGBT Association" (COWI, 2010: 8). Along with the International Day against Homophobia, a year later, Kaos GL held another rally, this one also with the purpose of speaking out against homophobia. The day that they organized their events purposely coincided with "the International Day against Homophobia and Transphobia" (COWI, 2010: 8). Then, in 2010, Turkey also witnessed the first separate march for the rights of the transgender community. These sorts of successes have been crucial to the formation of the current LGBTI rights platforms in Turkey.

Activists noted that a very important reason that Turkish civil society opened up at that time (which allowed LGBTI organizations and activism to flourish) had to do with Turkey's desire to enter into the European Union. Attempts at greater ties between Turkey and the European Union led to a shift in civil society within Turkey due to the European Union's demands for greater human rights and democratization within the country. Boysan Yakar, an LGBTI rights activist who worked as the first openly gay advisor to the mayor in the Şişli municipality in Istanbul, mentioned that during this time period it was much easier to form a recognized association. Before then, the Turkish government would restrict groups from organizing, often citing concerns about terrorism or Turkish values-based arguments. As Murat Köylü of Kaos GL also explained,

in 2003, 2004, [and] 2005 the atmosphere and the political agenda of Turkey was much, much different. Those times were the first times of AKP government, and the first days of Turkey's European Union candidacy, and those times [the] AKP was a coalition of different political groups. Of course the political Islamists were one of them but they were labeling themselves as conservative democrats or liberal, conservatives ... and among [the] AKP there were social democrats, liberals, and other Kurdish people, some ... groups from Kurdish movement, and individuals ... Those times Turkey had its reformist era, actually, ... and KAOS GL used that, decided to utilize that momentum in the society and in the political spheres, and started to ... debate... adding sexual orientation and gender identity in the constitution, in the ... legislation.

Yakar believed that it was also around this time, in 2006, for example, where the LGBTI community's visibility in the eyes of the state increased. But if we recall, the government was not sitting by idly as the LGBTI movement was pressing forward. In fact, it was during this period that the government attempted to close Lambda Istanbul and other LGBTI rights organizations. So while LGBTI visibility was on the rise, the government – under the AKP – was still taking a hardline position with LGBTI organizations.

Yet, despite the attempts at shutting down these groups, activists continued their work, often by sharing information about the presence of the LGBTI community with the greater public, as well as fighting to make people aware about issues related to the LGBTI community. As Sedef Çakmak explained,

it was really hard to break their homophobia, transphobia back then. And in media it was ... impossible to see any positive comment about LGBT rights in 2006. You would be seeing lots of negative issues ... that the LGBTs [were] represented in a negative way ... So, back then we were monitoring these media reports, we were doing all of these voluntarily, by the way. We weren't getting any money from the association whatsoever and we [were] monitoring all of these media and we were trying to reach out to journalists, we were organizing ... trainings, I would say for the ... journalists. But ... this was so amateur ... We would just be getting up with the journalists. We will be telling our stories to the journalists and we [were] trying to ... change their perspective.

However, these groups have made large strides in LGBTI activism since the early years. Let us now turn to discuss the more-recent ways that these activists and organizations have fought for equal rights.

In order to understand modern LGBTI rights-based activism, we have to examine recent civil society protest movements in the Middle

East. The uprisings in the Middle East and North Africa in 2010–2011, and the 2013 Gezi Park protests in Turkey, can be viewed as part of yet another period with increased human rights activism, as civil society groups came together in these different countries to challenge authoritarian rule. In the case of Egypt, for example, Muslims and Christians, secularists and Islamists worked together to overthrow the dictator Hosni Mubarak. Now, while the uprisings in North Africa and the Middle East did not spread to Turkey in 2010 and 2011, the country did see its own large-scale mass civilian movements in 2013, which have been labeled the "Taksim Square" and "Gezi Park" protests.

At the time, Turkish leader Recep Tayyip Erdoğan was calling for a series of changes in Turkey related to his push for economic development. However, many of these policies were at the expense of environmental issues (Muedini, 2015). Initially, hundreds of protesters came out to challenge Erdoğan's plans to build a mosque in Gezi Park in Istanbul. However, others quickly joined them, speaking out not only against these development plans but also other issues that included rising authoritarianism, concerns over Erdoğan's attempt at controlling parts of the judiciary, and other matters. Here, those from throughout different parts of Turkish civil society – united in their concerns about the direction Erdoğan was taking the country – called for democratization and a repeal of many anti-environmental actions put forth by the state. In addition, they also used the protests to advocate for a full set of human rights for everyone in Turkey. The protests received further attention after police responded to them with violence, unwilling to allow freedom of speech to be practiced uninterrupted. The police were reported to use tear gas, rubber bullets, and additional acts of violence against some of the protesters. Human rights organizations like Amnesty International (2013) quickly condemned the authorities for their actions against civilians as well as their violations of the right of people to free and peaceful assembly.

Looking at the Gezi Park protests from the perspective of the LGBTI rights movement, many activists argued that the events in 2013 were when the LGBTI community greatly expanded their public activities in the country. The LGBTI movement was quite vocal during the Gezi Park protests against Erdoğan. In fact, it has been argued by many that for the LGBTI community and LGBTI human rights activists, these particular protests not only showed how violent the government is towards the LGBTI community (which in turn may have actually mobilized more individuals to get involved in the movement) but that the activities during this time also helped LGBTI activists build networks across the different communities in Turkey (Feldman, 2014). Activists such as Volkan Yılmaz argue that even though the LGBTI movement was quite large before Gezi Park, "Gezi led to a leap in awareness among the left about LGBTI rights. The movement's voice was heard in more venues and taken more seriously" (Ayyıldız, 2015). As explained to me in our interview, Sedef Çakmak, among others, decided that "right after the Gezi incident . . . we just thought that we should be getting into politics [political parties]." So, among other outcomes, the LGBTI activists mobilized further following Gezi Park protests, moving some of their efforts towards electoral politics.

While I will go into the impact of the 2013 protests in greater detail later on, it is important to step back momentarily and examine the decades-long struggle for equal rights based on sexual orientation in Turkey. While much of the attention to LGBTI rights is recent, in the case of Turkey, the LGBTI rights community has been working diligently on advancing equal rights for quite some time. This becomes evident once one traces the history of LGBTI activism in Turkey. Again, the Turkish-based human rights and specific LGBTI human rights organizations we see operating today were first formed in the 1990s. These initial organizations served a variety of functions early in their activism. We have to keep in mind that although a great portion of their work centered on advocacy, the organizations also provided places where people from the LGBTI community could congregate, support one another, and work together on these rights issues. The organizations also played an important role in the providing of resources. This point is important to mention not only because it shows the diversity of activities that early LGBTI groups offered (and still provide today), but it also reminds us of the negative consequences that face LGBTI individuals when the government attempts to shut down these organizations.[2] They are rarely just suppressing a political voice; the state is going after groups that provide so many critical social services that the government itself has either failed to provide or purposely choses not to offer to LGBTI individuals.

Strategies and Successes of LGBTI Rights-Based Advocacy in Turkey

As discussed in the earlier chapter on the history of same-sex rights, the Turkish government has gone after both LGBTI individuals as well as those advocating for their cause. Yet, despite the attempts to suppress LGBTI rights, human rights groups have been able to make numerous strides with their work. In fact, some, such as Andrew Gardner of Amnesty International, argue that the increased visibility of the LGBT community and LGBT rights has been a result of the work of activists and human rights organizations, saying that "[t]he change, where it has come, has come from civil society and LGBT groups." Gardner added, "In previous years there was a situation where virtually all [LGBT rights groups] faced closure on grounds of public morality. Largely, this isn't happening anymore – there are fewer of these cases now" (Jamieson and Akyavas, 2015). The late Boysan Yakar, who served as an advisor to Hayri İnönü, the mayor of the Şişli district in Istanbul, even argued that the Lambda Istanbul closure case brought more awareness to the plight of the LGBTI community in Turkey. Again, the Lambda Istanbul Closure Case was an attempt by the government in 2008 and 2009 to shut down the LGBTI rights organization Lambda Istanbul (while they initially shut down the organization, Lambda Istanbul won its appeal in 2009) (Amnesty International, 2009). In our interview, Yakar said that the case "help[ed] ... the movement a lot to show all the homophobia and transphobia going around the movement actually. So with the [help] of these candidates, it was one of the very first [times] I ever seen in my life in a city center the independent candidates talking about human rights plus LGBTI rights as well, so we saw for the very first time with our eyes that it's happening in the streets by them." He went on to say that "from 2003 to now [2015], we are marching, we're giving press releases, openly, I mean, in 2006, 7, 8, 9, me and many other friends of mine. We became the faces of the associations, and we began to give releases with our names, real names, and faces. It was an important thing also. The Closure Case helps all the activists to join themselves [as] individuals to fight."

There are many active nongovernmental organizations in Turkey working on LGBTI rights issues. A number of them are specifically devoted to LGBTI issues, whereas others are more general human rights organizations that, in their work, have given attention to the human rights of LGBTI people in the country. While there are dozens of organizations that are actively fighting to improve the lives of LGBTI people in Turkey, there exist a number of very well-known and active organizations that I will discuss in greater detail. As I shall show, these groups are steadfast in their work, despite the risks associated with their activism, and are operating on various fronts, whether it is through social media, politics, education, health services, networking with international groups, etc. Let us know turn to the categories of activism, beginning with attention on the use of media for advancing lesbian, gay, bisexual, transgender, and intersex rights in the country.

Media

Traditional as well as "new" media have both been important tools for LGBTI activism in Turkey. However, traditional media has been viewed as failing to provide adequate covered for LGBTI issues. In fact, the media often framed same-sex issues in a problematic way. As Kaos GL (2005) explains,

In the first period, (early 80's) the homosexual man, the "gay[,]" was something not fully understood. Gays were portrayed as a stereotype. A distinction between a homosexual man and a transgender was not made. Anyone "not normal" was considered to be homosexual. The inside pages of the newspapers often used homosexuals as subjects to news of "murder, perversity and immorality." Homosexuality was shown as an issue to entertain the public. This was also the period when AIDS became known as a disease of homosexuals. AIDS was breaking news, along with homosexuality.

But along with this, over the years, the media has failed to adequately report on rights abuses against sexual minorities. Here are just some examples of how the media has chosen to not report on violations against the LGBTI community. In 1987, police harassment of transgendered individuals in Istanbul was very high. Yet, while the media knew about what was taking place, they "chose not to report it" (Kaos GL, 2005). In 1995, the Istanbul government decided to ban an LGBT conference. It was here that "Lambda Istanbul announced the city government's anti-democratic actions to the free world through the Internet and Reuters. Despite the Turkish media's failure to report these developments, the international media did, and the Turkish Ministries of Internal Affairs and Culture received over-whelming national and international [condemnation]" (Kaos GL, 2005). In 1996, police-forced evacuations of transgendered individuals received little attention from the media, and even with some reports, very few stories approached the issue from the perspective of the transgendered community (Kaos GL, 2005). For example, even when there was coverage about the incidents, the media did not discuss the underlining causes of the oppression that the transgender community was experiencing (Selek, 2001, in Görkemli, 2015).

Part of the negative treatment of the LGBTI community also had (and has) to do with the way that people from this community have been portrayed in both television and film. Saruhan (2013) argues that

despite the positive intention to highlight the transsexual members of society and portray them in a sympathetic way, these films still succumbed to the same stereotypes present in the heteronormative discourse treating prostitution, alienation, [and] psychological and physical violence. The films portray the worst-case scenarios transsexual subjects may face, while failing to empower the transsexual characters or punish violent actions aimed against them. Therefore, the Turkish media and film industry seem to contribute to the prevalence of stereotypes about transsexual subjects, who also may reproduce and reinforce these stereotypes, even though unwillingly.

Just to give an example, in the case of Turkish cinema, there have been few depictions of transgendered individuals in the twentieth century. However, in many of the cases where there are examples, it is usually found in the genre of comedy. Instead of open and honest depictions of characters representing transgendered persons, what has often happened is that a non-transgender character dresses up as someone of the opposite gender for some other non-gender-based purpose. For example, in one of the first depictions of a transgender character in Turkish cinema, in the 1923 film *Leblebici Horhor*, the main character, who is a male, dresses as a women in attempts to help save another character, his girlfriend. Then,

[i]n the following decades, until the 1980s, stories in which men dressed as women were almost unanimously seen in comedies. In the Turkish version of Billy Wilder's timeless classic *Some Like It Hot*, two popular actors, Sadri Alışık and İzzet Günay, dress as women to escape the mafia before falling for the same girl. Perhaps the last example of transvestism used as a source of

comedy came in 1984 with one of the most popular comedies in Turkish cinema, *Şabaniye*, in which the central plot revolves around men dressing as women to hide their identities. (Güler, 2012)

These sorts of representations do not accurately depict the transgender community, and actually make matters worse, since the viewer might incorrectly assume as to the reasons why some are transgender.

Thus, because of the power and influence of media, having someone from the LGBTI community working in traditional media outlets has been very effective for the advancement of LGBTI rights, as it offers a positive image of the LGBTI community to the public. A consistent theme that links various LGBTI rights organizations and individual activists are their goals to increase the visibility of LGBTI community in Turkey. They believe that an increased presence will lead to further discussions about their challenges and rights abuses in Turkey, which will hopefully generate more attention from these outlets, as well as from politicians and the state.

Another way in which the LGBTI community has been able to receive visibility has been through nationally known LGBTI individuals. While a later section spotlights some of the political candidates in the 2014 and 2015 elections, there are also nonpolitical personalities who are doing their part in bringing attention to the plight of the LGBTI community. Take Michelle Demishevich, for exampe. Demishevich was Turkey's first transgender television reporter, working for IMC TV as a reporter for a current affairs show (Mchugh, 2014). She began working for the company in March of 2013 (Tahaoğlu, 2014). Her appointment has been a great success for LGBTI rights in the country. Her presence on television has helped the LGBTI rights movement by increasing visibility for lesbian, gay, bisexual, and transgendered rights. This form of activism is not focused on elections or on publication of news articles per se but is done through the continued presence of a LGBTI trans-gendered individual in front of millions of television viewers. As Demishevich explains,

Activism is not about only marching on the streets with flags. What I call activism is my working as TV reporter when other trans people are only depicted negatively by the media. It is important to show that 'others' are also capable of doing meaningful things. Therefore, I decided to march with my flag in the hand. At work, I am just like everyone. My gender identity is out of question. I love my job." (Mchugh, 2014)

Demishevich's position allowed her to bring increased attention to LGBTI issues, as well as to the transgendered community in Turkey (Kellaway, 2014). In addition, she has also spoken about a hate crime committed against her in 2012 (Mchugh, 2014), sadly something that is not a rare occurrence in Turkey. Her speaking about the issue has helped bring much-needed light to such horrible situations taking place in Turkey and throughout many parts of the world.[3]

Human Rights Advocacy through Digital Media

Given the lack of positive attention to LGBTI in traditional media, the rise of digital media has been able to partially fill this gap left by traditional media outlets. Digital media has not only allowed for more stories to be written about sexual minorities, but the stories have approached the topic with a positive narrative. As Gorkemli (2012) argues "Turkish lesbian and gay activists have utilized the Internet to advance their activism since its inception in 1993" (63), adding that "the Internet built on the sexuality-related legacy of traditional media by enabling something altogether new: It provided the means by which otherwise isolated individuals with nonmainstream gender identities and/or sexual orientations could connect with each other to form communities" (73). This has continued for years, with new approaches to LGBTI advocacy through this medium. For example, in 2001, activists initiated a campaign called "Coming Out of the Internet"[4] where people could not only express their sexual identities, but they could also find others from within the LGBTI community (through an online group named Legato) (Görkemli, 2012, 2015).[5]

Among the best recent examples of the use of digital media is the work of activist Murat Renay. Murat Renay is an internationally known human rights activist and music DJ. In fact, Renay has played in clubs around the world and was also asked to play in Stroudsburg during the Gay Pride Parade in the city. Moreover, he has also been asked to play by LGBTI organizations. He views music as a way to further promote LGBTI rights. However, along with playing music, Renay has been a leading voice with regard to LGBTI rights for years in Turkey. He began his own work by writing a blog called Homo-Hobia, where he documented his personal experiences. He said of this blog, "It's basically a story of a gay person in Turkey, or in general, or all in the world. [Renay is] ... telling the stories starting from the child, to being an adult." However, after developing a strong fan base that called for Renay to write a book, he decided to write two. One is in the form of an autobiography. Renay explained to me that "[i]t's [an] autobiography of a gay guy, a normal gay guy in Turkey or in any part of the world that what can he experience from birth to being an adult and [in addition to Renay's life story,] it [also] has some short stories about tri sexual people, lesbian people, and all of them."

However, Renay's work is not limited to writing books and being a DJ. Among his various activities with regard to same-sex rights advocacy, Renay is also a founding editor of the primarily online Turkish language magazine *Gay Zone Mag*[6] (or *GZone Magazine*), which focuses on gay lifestyle issues (Feldman, 2014). Renay explained to me how the online digital magazine came about, saying that after his work with his own writings, as well as his DJ work, that "all of these [works] are not enough" and that "[w]e started to think with my friends that we should print a gay magazine." He explained (and was aware) that there existed a variety of LGBTI magazines in Turkey, but he found a specific niche for *GZone Magazine*; this online publication would differ from most in Turkey because it would not be focused on politics. Rather, this publication would stress a variety of gay issues in Turkish society. Renay explained the reason for his work with the magazine: "We want people to know that we exist." Renay also said, "We have personalities, identities. We're not just about people's bedrooms" (Feldman, 2014). He also realized that Internet and social media presence is critical for the advancement of LGBTI rights in the country, saying in one of our conversations, "We believe media, social media, is really important. I mean ... it's 2015, it is important even though you may not be a magazine, a Twitter account who is tweeting about LGBT issues is important. We have Twitter accounts, Instagram accounts, Facebook accounts, and we are reaching maybe one hundred thousand people every month." Thus, his magazine is building a strong following in Turkey and elsewhere. It is important to now examine what strategies Renay and his team are using through his magazine to promote LGBTI rights in the Middle East.

The Normalization of LGBTI Life in Turkey

One of the primary objectives of *GZone Magazine*, to Renay, is to use it to normalize the LGBT community in the country. They do this through covering a variety of pop culture issues, such as discussing music, movies, and other lifestyle topics. Many activists often approach the issue of visibility in the context of the government, given that part of their strategy is to affect current laws or government behavior. However, the issue with visibility is that it is often difficult for groups to become known in society and visible to political leaders. Some of this has to do with the lack of attention in the media. For example, Currier (2007) cites Koopmans (2004: 371), who works on LGBT rights in Africa, and speaks about the number of stories that exist in a media cycle, and how this may make it difficult to become visible. Applying this to the situation in Turkey, in my discussions with Renay, it seems that a goal for the magazine was not necessarily to direct it just to the government officials but to help shape perceptions in civil society by being more visible.

One of the normalization strategies that they use is related to their cover; they aim to put celebrities on the front of the magazine not only show that there are famous non-LGBTI individuals supporting LGBTI rights but also as a normalization tactic for LGBTI issues in Turkey. Renay explains that this approach of using celebrities for their magazine is not trying to be done in a way similar to the US outlet *TMZ*, but they do speak "with celebrities about gay issues, [in] every issue" in attempts to show Turkish and international readers that there are people outside of the LGBTI community who are talking about gay issues and are supportive of LGBTI rights. The non-direct political angle that Renay takes with regards to the magazine's content is not to suggest that there is no discussion about politics[7], but, as Renay explained, "[W]e don't always want to reflect the hate crimes ... we don't want to terrorize people ... We do make them as a new story, but as I say we want to create, we want to feel. People like ... good feelings about [the] LGBT [community]."

I asked Renay more about this issue of normalization and whether he thought that this approach of normalizing is the most effective way that activists are fighting for LGBTI rights. In response to this, Renay said that activists are using different tactics for the promotion of these rights:

I'm not sure activists are using that strategy ... They are using it, but ... they are using it in an aggressive way ... to make protests, to do something else. But what is more important for me to be in the Parliament, for example, to be a party that people can vote for and do all that stuff. But they are the local activists, and I respect that, ok. But what we are trying to do, we were invisible, like ten years ago maybe ... [W]e had big singers like Bülent Ersoy[8] [who] is a transvestite ... and also Zeki Muren [who] is really feminine, out male singer[,] but they're both great singers. People respected them, even though they see that ... one is a transsexual and one is a feminine gay man, of course. But they respected them. But other than that no gay, no LGBT visibility[,] has [been] recorded in Turkish history. So ... within the social media, and the gays that protest, LGBT people are soon to be recognized ... people are thinking, look, there are guys like who can be lesbians, gays, or transvestites and it's an identity ... it's a sexual identity, of course, but it's an identity, [a] social identity, also. They start to accept that. So what I believe it is ... as we can be visible, so people will start to accept us, but not [that] they want [this], but at least they will see and that, oh they are visible, there are people like this.

Or, as Renay says, there may be someone who may say, "'Maybe I don't agree with that, but I shall respect that.' And after that, maybe they start to empathize with our feelings. Maybe they thought something like that."

Renay believes that this notion of normalization has been instrumental with regard to the advancement of LGBTI rights in Turkey in recent years. For example, Renay says that about "five years ago, nobody [was] ... talking about gay issues ... in a negative way or a positive way ... nobody was speaking. But now, people are speaking [about LGBTI issues]." Renay goes on to say that the visibility may not always lead to positive statements; regardless, the visibility will nonetheless still push the discussion forward. On this issue of negative statements, he says, "Of course, it also has some, they also have some bad reactions ... people are speaking not positively, of course, but when we are visible, of course, maybe half of the people, fifty percent, will talk very bad things about us, I know. But we must be visible for whatever it takes, we must be visible."

It can be understood that, given the presence of conservative elements (including the government) in Turkey and the greater Middle East, the question of visibility is not without risks in Turkey. It has been well-documented in the human rights literature that the LGBTI communities are under significant stress and discrimination. Again, government leaders in Turkey (with the AKP) have continued to frame homosexuality as a sin. In addition, there are other groups that have called for violence against LGBTI individuals. Thus, individuals such as Renay understand why visibility is needed but also recognize the realistic possibility that negative reactions might arise from the LGBTI community being more visible in a Turkey, because a number of conservatives are critical of recognizing LGBTI rights. Related to this, Renay said that while the LGBTI community was invisible in years past, "after the Gezi protest and everything we, we start to become visible. But being visible has consequences both negative and both positive ... in this period, in this process we will be much, much more visible in every way but it will also bring some, bring out some hate."

Use of Celebrities in Promoting LGBTI Rights

The use of celebrity status as it pertains to awareness about LGBTI rights has been an approach used not only in Turkey but throughout other parts of the world. Celebrities have attempted to bring attention to the plight of LGBTI individuals through campaigning, public conversation, and service announcements. Celebrities with followings have the ability to influence many people who otherwise may have not thought about that particular issue that the celebrity is advocating.

In my second interview with Renay, he iterated this point about celebrity influence as it relates to LGBTI normalization and visibility, saying that "if a celebrity talks about [an issue such as violence against women] ... you get the message." He went on to add that their approach is "nothing different from that." Renay also said that "what we're trying to do is to be visible, to be visible with the famous celebrities and the people and everything to normalize this ... if [celebrity] Sezen Aksu says something about the LGBTs[,] as a straight fan of Sezen Aksu you may think that 'oh, she is saying that so it is okay to say this.'" Renay believes that his magazine can be a platform for celebrities, and with them speaking on LGBTI issues, others who read the magazine, or hear about the story, might better see the LGBTI community as a part of Turkey, as well as see them in a positive light.[9]

However, despite the positive feedback received by using this approach, there continue to be challenges to not only how the celebrities and their messages may be received but also how there may exist different standards for celebrities and noncelebrities in the LGBTI community. In relation to the first point, using the strategy of celebrity activism has at times been met with hatred and criticism. For example, in our first interview Renay explained that

[w]e are using the celebrities ... in this issue there is one of the biggest pop divas of Turkish music [who] will be on the cover and she will talk about LGBT issues. And she has maybe millions of listeners ... we are sending this news to the mainstream media, of course, also ... we are telling them this woman said this about LGBT, [talked] to [a] LGBT magazine and ... mainstream media sometimes publish that. So people will understand that this is a talkable thing, I mean they can talk about this. So this is our first strategy."

In fact, Turkish pop artist Demet Akalın. Akalın – who, as Renay explained, has a very large social media following (over 6.2 million on both Twitter and Instagram as of this writing) – publicized *GZone Magazine* by bringing attention to it through her social media messages. Because of her posts on social media, he says that many people who had not heard of LGBTI were now first being exposed to the community. But with the positive also came the negative; there were hateful comments that were made as well. But Renay was willing to take controversial risks, saying of this situation, "Some people cursed her. Why are you doing this? But, thirteen thousand people liked the picture so it's okay for us. I mean, she's the queen for us, so there is no problem. We may have some ... impact like this but it's okay, we will go on doing this. It's ... maybe controversial too ... [for] some LGBT people and some straight people, but it's okay."[10]

Despite the risks, as well as debate amongst activists associated with this visibility tactic, the approach of using celebrities for their covers – and in their magazine stories – seems to be a very good strategy for the increased visibility of the LGBTI community with regard to *GZone Magazine*; the academic literature shows that celebrities and celebrity behavior can influence individuals from an early age onwards. For example, Gomillion and Giuliano (2011) cite Boon and Lomore's (2001) research on the influence of celebrities, extending it to LGBTI rights: "Boon and Lomore (2001) found that among young adults with strong attachments to celebrities, participants believed that their attitudes, values, and personality characteristics have been influenced by their idols. Although neither Matthews nor Boon and Lomore examined the influence of the media in relation to sexual orientation, their findings suggest that the media could similarly contribute to the development of GLB identity throughout the lifespan" (332).

One of the other issues related to celebrities and either their support for LGBTI rights outside of the community or as members of the LGBTI community themselves is often the dual treatment that society may give them as celebrities who are publically LGBTI compared to noncelebrities who are LGBTI, which infuriates those fighting for the rights of all LGBTI people (Köksal, 2015). For example, "[p]eople in Turkey's LGBT community often point to two of Turkey's most famous entertainers to illustrate what they feel is a dangerous hypocrisy. Zeki Muren was visually equal parts Elton John and Liberace and one of the most beloved singers in Turkish history. Muren was gay, but never spoke publicly about his sexuality. Despite homophobic attitudes, he was awarded Turkey's version of the Order of Canada." Along with Muren, "Pop star Bulent Ersoy, known to her fans as the 'Diva,' first achieved fame in the 1970s and transitioned from male to female before anyone knew to use the word transgender. She performed as a man early in her career and never changed her name after her transition" (Köksal, 2015). However, activists such as Oyku Ay spoke about this double standard, saying that "[t]he Turkish people, they applaud the ones on stage and stone the ones on the street" (Köksal, 2015). So, while using celebrity status is an effective strategy, and although it has helped matters, LGBTI celebrities themselves continue to be treated differently than LGBTI noncelebrities.

Social Media

Within new digital media, social media has developed to become a fundamental tool of LGBTI activists and organizations in Turkey. In fact, social media is one of the central components of the media strategies employed by groups such as Kaos GL, Pembe Hayat, etc. For example, in one of my interviews, I asked Murat Köylü of Kaos GL about their use of social media. Köylü responded:

At the moment, we have three different [media] outputs. ... One is the Kaosgl.org, second is *KAOS GL Journal* [which] is [a] printed web design, and [the] third one is *KAOS GL Q Plus*; it's an academic journal. And Kaosgl.org is of course, is a new media instrument. It's a website and it's integrated with social media, Facebook, Twitter, and other stuff.

Köylü went on to say that

[s]o, this new media school is very important for us because by that we don't only educate our correspondents, we, at the same time ... educate people to be an independent reader. We give them ... a kind of media literacy. I took this same course many years ago as well. And I'm not an expert on new media or media ... issues actually ... With [these] new media schools we ... expand our network, we educate our constituents, we get educated ... because we have correspondents from every city of Turkey[,] and under this kind of siege of political Islam's party in Turkey ... this new media['s] existence is very important. And even there are some ... [things] that they want to get rid of ... We are still coping with the administration in Turkey and that new media is, again, important ... because it ... as the LGBTI movement is international, or even not international, it's a transnational ... movement. The opportunities coming out of this new media technique and political opportunities should be used as ... the transnational...movement [expands]. So, as ... the old media, let's say is much less slower and much less small than new media dissemination. So yes, this is why we ... [give] big importance to this new media outlets, I'd say.

Activists and NGOs have been active on social media platforms such as Twitter, Facebook, and Instagram, promoting LGBTI rights issues. They have argued that the work on social media has been quite effective in advancing the LGBTI rights cause. Buse Kilickaya, who is an internationally known LGBTI rights activist and also the head of Pembe Hayat (Pink Life), credits social media for awareness about the LGBTI rights movement, saying, "The struggle is becoming widespread. There is a wider visibility of our advocacy campaigns and people are much more aware of our problems mainly due to the social media" (Tokyay, 2015).

I also asked Janset Kalan of Pembe Hayat about how the organization uses media (and social media) to advocate for transgender rights. Kalan explained that to the organization, media is viewed as "the fourth power in the power system, in today's society. And Internet is probably the fifth one." Kalan spoke about the importance of media, saying that the

media has a ... very important role in changing minds and municipalit[y leaders' minds,] in providing public awareness [on] an issue, and if [the] media likes to show something negatively, it is very easy for them to do that. And they have a huge influence in the society, especially the televised media and … what we can do with our capacity is we can [focus more] on social media and the written media.

Kalan also said that they also set up their

own media capacity, our own media channels, our own online news bulletins and I think this has been something what we are going as LGBTI movement in Turkey very successfully because there has been a change of language in the mainstream media as well when it comes to LGBTI issues, when it comes to fighting on hate crimes and then it comes to how to represent LGBTI identities in possible interviews and articles in the media.

Kalan went on to add, "In the televised media … there are some subliminal messages which indicate some of the characters are, gay, lesbian, or transgender. And we also succeeded [in the] empowerment of queer actresses and actors and performers to be more visible in the media." For Pembe Hayat, they have been able to use traditional media, and social media to also provide support to transgender actors. Kalan explains that

[t]here are a couple of trans actresses right now. There is one trans actor who was famous before the transition, and right now transitioned, and still wants to continue with his work. And we're giving support and showing solidarity with that actor, also. And there are a couple of trans journalists who can find job[s] in some of the mainstream corporat[ions], I think that this is this is this is something that we can manage, that we can achieve.

Human Rights through Film Documentaries

LGBTI rights activists have also used film to document human rights conditions the LGBTI community faces and to share this information so that conditions can improve. One of the key LGBTI advocacy organizations in Turkey using film documentaries has been LİSTAG (Families and Friends of LGBTIs in Turkey).[11] Although LİSTAG's primary mission is as "a voluntary support and solidarity group for families and friends of lesbian, gay, bisexual, and trans people in Istanbul" (LİSTAG, 2017), the late Boysan Yakar explained to me that some of the most influential work they have done has involved their documentaries. The organization put out documentaries noting the plight of LGBTI members in Turkey. The first film was based on showing how the media portrayed transgender rights. They also created a documentary on the Pride Parade, among other films. One of the most noted was entitled *My Child* (of which Boysan Yakar worked as the assistant director). *My Child* documents statements, thoughts, and feelings of families of LGBTI individuals. The other films were on transgender issues, including one on a march that was banned by football (soccer) supporters. However, Yakar told me that *My Child* was different, and what separated *My Child* from the others was that

[b]efore that mothers were getting releases, but they were not sharing their names and faces. But with the movie, before the movie, they began to come out as family members of the LGBTIs, and ... it [was a big deal] all around Turkey, and the support changed its status. Now it was not only civil society, but many other people were normally adjusted to the LGBTI rights, and with this movie ... they traveled a lot. We traveled a lot, all around the country. With many different social movements, we did many screenings. We did some screenings, very important ones, with [the] UN in [the] [n]orthern part of Turkey ... [where people] are very nationalistic, and masculinity is a thing there. ... It was not really easy ... but ... the UN [was] there, and the police were there to protect the groups to screen the movies. So ... legendary things happened on the way of screening the movie.

Yakar described the effect of LİSTAG on altering the conversation toward LGBTI rights in the country and also on reshaping the way many in Turkey thought about notions of family. Before, there were many stereotypes surrounding LGBTI individuals. Yakar explained the hostility that he received when meeting with political officials, saying "I remember that when we were going to Ankara to meet with MPs from every party, that were pro-Kurdish or were whatever, they were not even shaking our hands. All the things that they have they have in their minds... when you touch [a homosexual], you can become homosexual." With the release of the film, mothers and fathers of LGBTI people would also go around the country and speak to crowds. These conversations were often emotional, as people were crying and sharing stories. Yakar believed that these discussions shaped the way people thought about family in Turkey, saying that "when we took the mothers down there in 2009, 2010, they were crying, drinking teas, and having important[,] long one [hour], two hours long meetings with them, so yeah they did a huge thing. It was important" Yakar said of this work, "It was the most important thing we've done for Turkey."

Earlier I spoke about the importance "in-group messenger" strategy of activism as a way to change hearts and minds on an issue. If we recall, it has been found that individuals are much more receptive to a message if the advocate for that message is someone from their own "in-group." This could be a pastor from within a religious community, an athlete from a team or sport one likes, or someone from your own city who has a positive effect on changing opinions. While I talked about ways that this could be done from a religious perspective, or from a general human rights-based approach (structured on arguments related to the rule of law), there is one other very interesting use of the in-messenger approach that seems to an effective way to appeal to those that were initially opposed to same-sex rights in Turkey. This approach is what LİSTAG has been doing with parents of children who are LGBTI. As Yakar explained, parents were able to move people based on their discussions centered on supporting their children, who were LGBTI. Sedef Çakmak felt that LİSTAG was able to serve as an organization that could break through barriers and speak to people from different backgrounds, saying that

one of the ice breakers we have in Turkey, which I also see it as another milestone, we have [a] families' organization. It is called LİSTAG and LİS-TAG is formed of mothers and fathers who ha[ve] ... LGBT children. Their formation ... really helped us to ... reach to several groups because when you're a young villain activist ... lesbian, and when you are talking about LGBT rights[,] some of the people generally do not take you seriously or some of the people just think that your mother and father didn't properly [bring] you up. But when a mother or father comes and says that ... I was either going to choose my child or choose the society[,] and of course I choose my child[,] and then when they start talking ... that conversation always ends in tears, which is good. I mean, both of the parties start crying ... The families' organization also help us reach to various groups because ... this is organized by various families; its religious families, its secular families, economically disadvantaged families, or economically advantaged families. So ... it's quite mixed in [that] respect.

Parents were relating to other parents, and this was being done through an "insider-based" model. Had the organization itself spoken to the public, but without the voices of parents, it most likely would not have been nearly as successful as what the activists saw happen during these film and conversational sessions.

6 | Political, Electoral, and Legislative Strategies for LGBTI Rights

I'm quite a fan of the [LGBTI] movement in Turkey because I'm quite fascinated by the fact that all these different people, with different ideologies, with different fears, with different hopes, can come together and can work on a common issue.

Sedef Çakmak

As important as traditional and "new" media is for LGBTI advocacy, activists for these rights have not limited their work to these realms. In fact, activities such as publically protesting injustices have been a critical avenue of activism for sexual minority rights in Turkey. As I noted earlier, human rights activists for LGBTI rights were very involved in the Gezi Park protests; it was here that these activists not only voiced their concern for how the government has treated sexual minorities, but also when they increased their political and rights advocacy networks with other activists. Goksel (2014) argues, "LGBT mobilisation was largely invisible to the general public until their organised presence in the Gezi Park resistance in May 2013, when the LGBT community virtually 'came out of the closet.' Arguably, this experience, along with the embracement of LGBT rights causes by parliamentarians of the main opposition party CHP and the Kurdish BDP [Peace and Democratic Party],[1] injected self-confidence, and motivated the LGBT community." However, following their activity during the Gezi Park protests, LGBTI organizations were able to hone in on their organizational capabilities and used the protests to further their political activity. Furthermore, the protests allowed the LGBTI to become more visible in Turkish society (Kafanov, 2015), something that they have continued to work for in recent years. It was the theme of "resistance" that the LGBTI activist organizers adopted during these protests (Pearce, 2014b).

Despite "reports of gay bashing by the police in the midst of other attacks on protesters[,]" the Gezi Park protests were not only seen as the event that brought together many different activists (Pearce, 2014b) but was also viewed as a turning point for how Turkish civil society viewed the LGBTI community. For example, before the protests, there were many that would not work with the LGBTI community, and/or they would not recognize them as members of Turkish civil society. However, during the Gezi Park protests, this seemed to change. For example, Asya Elmas, who is a human rights activist for LGBTI issues (and also a political candidate, as she ran for the Kadikoy city council with the HDP), spoke about her experience during the Gezi Park protests. She was quoted as saying:

When we went out to take care of our daily needs, police would bring us to the police station. While all that was going on, people applauded us when we entered Gezi Park for the first time. At first I didn't realise that they were clapping for us. I looked behind us, thinking they were applauding a famous person. After that, I met other LGBTI friends and we established a group called Hevi LGBTI. (*Turkish Weekly*, 2014)

Again, the protests also allowed them to work with other groups who have been facing their own struggles with Erdoğan and the AKP government. For example, "[d]uring the Gezi Park occupation, minority groups were able to raise their flags in safety, boosting awareness and support for their causes. Those with a well-established history of activism, such as Kurdish, feminist, and LGBT associations, were better organized and experienced with advocacy than their newly established counterparts and played central role in the movement as a result" (Beck, 2013). What the protests seemed to do is bring together those in Turkey who have been facing discrimination and repression by the Erdoğan regime. Many in the "majority" were now feeling what was historically an issue for minority groups. And because of this, a number of people in Turkish civil society were now at least more aware of some of the things that government has been doing to minority groups in the country. Writing after the Gezi Park protests, Beck (2013) explains that "[m]any of Istanbul's inhabitants are now experiencing a taste of the treatment faced by the minority groups for years. Banging pots and pans together – a common tool of protesters – is punished using the same laws once employed to harass transgender women, and censorship tactics employed to suppress discussion of homosexual issues and information on human-rights abuses in Kurdish areas were used to silence reporting on the protests."

Furthermore, the visibility of the LGBT associations during the Gezi Park protests has also led some in Turkey to reach out to these organizations, either to work with them or to even apologize for past behavior (Beck, 2013). The involvement of the LGBTI in the Gezi Park protests was also important for the pride of the community. Not only did it help bridge gaps between different communities and human rights groups, but to Yakar, the protests also allowed them to "[take] our pride back from society. It was important. [Pride] was already stolen from us . . . the pride with their homophobic words and discrimination[,] but they gave it back. We took it." He went on to say, "No one is going to give you back any pride of you. It was important."

Legislative Advocacy

As mentioned throughout this book, the LGBTI community has been very active in fighting for equal rights by pushing forward legislation that would recognize equality and rights for the LGBTI community. Many human rights organizations have been at the forefront of legislative advocacy. Groups like Kaos GL have been working on legislative advocacy since the early years of the organization's formation. For example, As Köylü explained to me, "KAOS GL brought [forward] the issue of this legislative influence and . . . legislative actions for the combat against homophobia . . . targeting the labor law, targeting the antidiscrimination law, targeting the civil law."

Another recent strategy has been for individuals to run in local and in parliamentary elections, with the hope of not only increasing awareness with regard to LGBTI issues but also with the goal of winning elections, and then in turn being able to introduce and pass legislation that would provide protections for sexual minorities in the country. In fact, in recent years, Turkey has witnessed a number of candidates from the LGBTI community, as well as current political leaders who have openly expressed their support of same-sex rights. LGBTI activists have placed a great amount of importance on activism through elections. For example, Barış Sulu, a former MP candidate, spoke about the need for advocacy through elections, and the presence of LGBTI individuals in government, saying, "This is one of the gains of the LGBTI movement, the fact that recently many representatives are proposing bills relating to LGBTI people. No matter how much they try to articulate some issues, the political representation of

LGBTI people, their presence in the parliament is more important. What I say [as an LGBTI individual] will be perceived differently" (Akpinar, 2015).

2014 Elections

The May 2014 elections in Turkey were local elections, with candidates vying for mayoral positions, as well as city council seats throughout the country. The LGBTI activist community used these elections to promote human rights, doing so in part by putting forward several LGBTI candidates. In fact, the 2014 elections had ten political candidates from the LGBTI community. These ten candidates were from one of two parties: the HDP (People's Democratic Congress) or the CHP (Republican People's Party) (Goksel, 2014). Having had so many political candidates from the LGBTI community has led some to call it "a new phase of the human rights movement" (*New Europe*, 2014). As Human Rights Campaign (2014) said in 2014, "The ten LGBT individuals that are running for city council represent several gay and lesbian candidates and one transgender woman and represent the Republican People's Party (CHP), the People's Democracy Party (HDP), and the Peace and Democracy Party (BDP) [which eventually became united with the HDP]. Seven LGBT Candidates are running for city council in Turkey's largest city, Istanbul, two in the Turkish capital, Ankara, and one in the city of Mersin." Obviously, NGOs such as Human Rights Campaign view the running of LGBT candidates as a great step for sexual minority rights.

Because of little legal support for sexual minority rights, negative statements by state leaders, and harassment LGBTI individuals face, being able to publicly run candidates, regardless of electoral success, has been seen as nothing but "positive strides" for LGBTI rights in Turkey (Human Rights Campaign, 2014). Other activists have echoed similar statements. For example, Murat Cekic, the former director of Turkey's Amnesty International branch, said, "It is a very important improvement to see LGBT candidates for local elections." Cekic went on to say that "[t]his is an improvement when compared with the past. The situation of LGBT people will change with their active involvement in the political sphere" (*New Europe*, 2014). Cekic also said that "[t]here has actually been an improvement in LGBT rights in Turkey," and added that "[p]olitical actors have put LGBT individuals and rights on the agenda through their statements, positive or not" (*New Europe*, 2014). Thus, it seems from Cekic's statement that the LGBTI movement can push forward by having candidates in local and national elections, along with an increase in overall political participation in Turkey.

Again, one must not judge this process a success only if one wins an election; there is a strong value in running as an LGBTI candidate, regardless of the electoral outcome. When one looks at the electoral results of the 2014 and 2015 elections, the vast majority of the LGBTI candidates did not win their elections; looking at the 2014 elections, the sole winner from the LGBTI community was Sedef Çakmak, who became the "municipal councilmember in Istanbul's Besiktas district" (Goksel, 2014). Yet, running in elections is a great accomplishment on its own terms. Political candidates from the LGBTI community have expressed their reasons for running in local and national elections, which seem to fall under one of two categories, with evident overlap. For some, they want their candidacy to aid in ending discrimination against the LGBTI community. Ebru Kiranci, who ran for a city council position in the city of Beyoglu said that "[t]he history of Beyoglu is full of expulsions, attacks, and tyranny against LGTBI people. A big portion of LBGTI individuals live in Beyoglu. That's why I became a candidate," Kiranci told SES Türkiye, "We want to have a say in the administration of our city. Our struggle is not new. Police would break down our doors and cut our hair. We had a hunger strike in Gezi Park in 1987 but the police dispersed us. Our struggle actually began then" (New Europe, 2014). Also, as reporter Irem Koker of *Hurriyet Daily News* wrote, years ago "it was a completely ignored issue." Koker added, "By definition everyone thought that everyone else was straight. Now we are talking about the existence of LGBT people in society" (Krajeski, 2014). This shift in the past ten years has been critically important, and must be examined to better understand how LGBTI activists were able to successfully bring the issue of same-sex rights to the forefront of Turkish society and Turkish politics.

So, for some, the visibility that running in elections offers is the reason why they ran. For others, it is about the potential that being in office can offer with regard to implementing legal changes for the benefit of the LGBTI community. Both strategies are useful with the context of same-sex rights. Whether one is brining about much-needed attention to the plight of the LGBTI community through running in elections, or whether they are in office hoping to make changes, both approaches allow Turkish society to see that LGBTI individuals are facing discrimination and can work to change current conditions. Metehan Ozkan and Giray Poyraz, two activists in Turkey, seem to feel the same way. For example, Ozkhan said, "It doesn't matter for us which party our friends stand for. The important thing is that the LGBTI movement is able to raise its issues and voices in the political arena with their assistance, and we support all friends who do this." Poyraz was quoted as saying that "I am a Kurdish LGBTI individual and unfortunately, in my country rights are denied to LGBTI individuals just like other excluded people. For this reason we support and care about all LGBTI candidates for the 2014 local elections, because the LGBTI struggle will help us to destroy LGBTI bias, exclusion, hate murders and systematic state violence" (New Europe, 2014). The Kurds have faced centuries of discrimination in Turkey from the Ottoman period through the rule of Mustapha Kemal (and his elevation of a common Turkish nationalism) to decades, with restrictions on the use of language in schools and the passing of a controversial law in 1991 that the government then used to go after Kurds, journalists, and political figures (with government accusations including support for terrorism, despite activists saying no such ties existed) (Ashdown, 2015), as well as incidents of violence from the state.

As mentioned, the two categories are clearly not mutually exclusive. Elmas, speaking about her candidacy, said: "I am just a city council candidate. If I am elected, I can't change everything," "I am not going to be the mayor, but I believe that to sit on city council as a trans woman will change people's views toward LGBTI people in a positive way. If I am elected I will try to extend municipal services like health-care to LGBTI people" (*New Europe,* 2014). This quote provides evidence that there is a value seen in just running; doing so allows people to see that the LGBT community exists. This helps in their strategy of visibility. However, it is evident that Elmas also wants to make changes, offering support to the LGBTI community if in office. So, the strategy is not necessarily just to show a presence in Turkey but also to make legal changes if voted into office. Nonetheless, the more that people hear about LGBT rights in the country, the more news attention that LGBT candidates receive (regardless of electoral outcome), the better that this can be for the rights movement. Again, as

Cekic argues, the mere mention of LGBT issues by politicians can be a positive effect for the movement, even if the statements are not always in support, because now the LGBT issue is one of the agenda issues with which political leaders must engage (*Turkish Weekly*, 2014).

2015 Elections

In June 2015, Turkey its held parliamentary elections. These elections were important for at least a couple of reasons. For one, many saw the elections as a vote on Erdoğan's power and influence in the country. While he himself was not up for reelection (having already been elected to the position of president in 2014), a strong showing by the AKP would have given Erdoğan arguably significantly more power in the country, something that troubled many given the rising authoritarianism of Erdoğan in Turkey in recent years. Instead of the AKP winning the outright supermajority that would have given them the power to pass legislation without trouble, they lost seats, leading them to have to form a coalition government with outside political parties. This is part of the reason that, at the time, this election was perceived to be an "electoral earthquake" in the country; what some expected to be an event that would give AKP a grip on governance unparalleled in Erdoğan's time office turned out to be one in which he now had no choice but to work further with non-AKP parliament members (Berman, 2015). However, the AKP gained back their majority in the November 2015 general elections.

Despite the AKP's ability to reestablish their hold on power through the November 2015 elections, and thus reversing the earlier trend in June, there is another reason as to why the June 2015 elections in Turkey were still important. These elections saw many LGBTI individuals running for political positions, and in some cases, for positions that no other LGBTI individual had openly run for. In addition, there was a push for NGOs to help elect LGBTI candidates and non-LGBTI candidates that are supportive of LGBTI rights initiatives. For this reason, many LGBTI rights activists have viewed the June 2015 elections as significant. For example, Hossein Alizadeh, who is a program coordinator at the International Gay and Lesbian Human Rights Commission, said of the elections: "The fact that Turkey's population has elected 22 acknowledged advocates for LGBTI rights is a tremendous victory." Hossein went on to say, "It is particularly important in a political landscape that recently has been quite conservative and where some high-level politicians have rejected even basic rights based on sexual orientation and gender identity" (IGLHRC, 2015). Despite the hostility toward LGBTI individuals in Turkey, twenty-two candidates who support LGBTI rights initiatives were elected; it is imperative that we examine who the various candidates were, why they ran, what they learned from running, and future ways in which activists can use this information and the lessons from the campaign trail for advancing LGBTI rights.

Barış Sulu

In 2015, Barış Sulu was the first openly gay Turkish parliamentary candidate. Barış Sulu was a parliamentary candidate under the People's Democratic Party (HDP), running in Eskişehir, in the northwestern district of Turkey. He ran on a platform promoting and advocating for LGBTI rights. However, it seems that his interest was more than the immediate importance of having an LGBTI candidate running for Parliament; his goal was to advance possibilities for the LGBTI community for years to come. Before the 2015 elections he spoke about what the future might look like for sexual minorities in the country, saying that "[t]he elections in four years will be utterly different. In the next elections, not just gay candidates will run but also lesbian or transgender candidates" (Brooks-Pollock, 2015). With regard to the reasons for his own candidacy, Sulu explained that "the accumulated wisdom of the LGBTI movement must be voiced in our own words" (Tar, 2015). He went on to say that "I support the self-representation of subjects. Therefore, I looked and saw that there was not much out there, and I acted fast. I thought there had to be someone. I have self-confidence, so I considered all the risks, spoke with my family, consulted many people and became a candidate for nomination" (Tar, 2015). In another interview, when asked about why he decided to run in the June 7 elections, Sulu stated that "[f]irst of all, I am somebody who thinks that the LGBTI people need to be interested/involved in politics. Boysan Yakar, Sedef Çakmak, and Tuna Şahin's assuming of municipal positions in the aftermath of local elections made me more hopeful. I thought another step was now needed. Therefore in order for different things to be talked about, subjects must articulate themselves" (Akpinar, 2015a).

Although Sulu decided to run for the Parliament in the 2015 elections, this is far from his first act of activism with regard to LGBTI rights. Sulu has been active in politics since 1998, saying: "I've been working on LGBTI issues for the last 17 years. I believe that I start doing politics automatically the moment I say 'I'm here.' I started my political life the moment I said 'I'm gay, I live in this country, and I'm not going anywhere. I start my struggle right here'" (Akan, 2015). Within his years of activism, prior to running in the elections, Sulu and his partner Aras Güngör tried, without success, to get married under Turkish law, being the first gay couple to apply for a marriage license (Kafanov, 2015). Sulu has made it clear that he ran in part because he wants the LGBT community to be able to speak out with regard to any challenges or problems that they may have, as they are also a part of Turkish society (NEOnline, 2015), saying, "'What we want is to be recognized as equal citizens of this country,' says Sulu, a candidate with the People's Democratic Party, a new leftist party" (Kafanov, 2015). Sulu went on to add, "Society is ready for a change and I believe the time is now for someone [whose] identity [is] to fight for LGBT issues in Parliament" (Kafanov, 2015).

In addition to his goal of being in Parliament so that he could bring about positive changes for LGBTI rights now, he also hoped that his candidacy will make it easier for LGBTI candidates in the future to compete and to win elections in Turkey, saying that "[i]n four years, elections will turn into something completely different. There may be more than just one gay man; there may be a lesbian candidate, a trans candidate. Things can be completely different in four years from now" (Akan, 2015). Related to this, Sulu was also quoted in another interview as saying that "I may not win, but the most important thing is we're now talking about LGBT rights" (Yackley, 2015). In an interview with Akpinar (2015a), when asked about what he would do to advance LGBTI rights if in office, Sulu stated that

[t]he new constitution process is quite stuck in the matter of LGBTI rights. LGBTI people have a demand[:] the recognition of sexual orientation and gender identity in the constitution. First, I think this has to continue. Next is hate crimes. Sexual orientation and gender identity were removed from the hate crime statute. LGBTI people are a group most affected by hate crimes and perhaps the group who introduced the concept to literature in Turkey. Bam! We were kicked out, in a very easy way! We need to focus on this.

This is obviously an important reason as to why one should run, particularly given the various levels of discrimination that exist against LGBTI candidates and the LGBTI community at large. In fact, Sulu himself faced discrimination and hate speech leading up to the election. For instance, it was reported that "[a]n anonymous pamphlet circulated ... [which] showed Sulu's image and read: "Do you want a homosexual from Eskisehir defending Kurds in parliament?" (Yackley, 2015).

Yet, despite such words, coming either from anonymous pamphlets, others in society, or even political leaders of Turkey, Sulu continued to stress the importance of his actions. For example, he spoke against actions by Erdoğan (as Erdoğan has spoken out against the LGBTI community, as well as others whom he often paints as not being religious or being against Islam), saying that "'regardless of what the president says, I am a citizen pursuing my rights' ... 'As a gay man, even saying "I exist," is a political statement'" (Yackley, 2015). Thus, every single candidacy by an LGBTI individual is great advancement for the rights of LGBTI individuals in Turkey. Sulu's bravery has given the LGBTI rights further attention as activists look to find ways to ensure that the community is protected from discrimination. And although he was not elected, Sulu still hopes that gains by opposition parties can help push for new LGBTI rights legislation and more overall rights for the LGBTI community, saying in an interview after the 2015 elections that "I trust the main opposition parties that will bring a change in the new legislative term. They should especially change the recently adopted Domestic Security Law that leads the way to arrest any transgender, even when going to the market to buy a bread, as a suspected or potential sex worker" (Tokyay, 2015).

Deva Ozenen

One of the other most-known Turkish political candidates in the 2015 MP elections was Deva Ozenen. Deva Ozenen is transgendered and ran for Parliament in the 2015 elections. Ozenen was running as a member of the Anatolia Party. Many have been outspoken about their support for a transgendered candidate, despite the fact that many did not think Ozenen would win. In interviews with different news outlets, Ozenen has spoken about the reasons for running for a political office. Within these discussions, Ozenen talked about the need to press forward on this issue, even if some in society may not be fully on board.

With regard to his candidacy, Ozenen spoke about the timing, saying that "[i]f we are waiting for Turkish society to get ready for us, we'll wait a long time." Ozenen went on to say that "[w]e are going against the tide. We are trying to get our rights and we don't care if society is ready for this or not." (Weise, 2015). Thus, Ozenen hoped to win the election and begin implementing an agenda that focused on LGBTI rights. However, campaigning was not easy. During the campaign, Ozenen would often face ridicule, as well as threats because of her attempt to win a seat as the first transgendered member of Parliament. Nonetheless, Ozenen continued with the campaign, and brought attention to LGBI issues. In fact, it seems that while she recognized the small probability of her chance to win the election, Ozenen also understood the importance that the act of running in an election as a transgendered individual has on the entire human rights movement. Ozenen is quoted as saying, "I am a pioneer. I opened the door. So, in the next elections, maybe there will be more LGBT candidates . . . It's a good opportunity for us to become more visible." She went on to say that "and I will try to get elected next time" (Weise, 2015).

It seems that this is exactly what activists are hoping for: visibility and increased awareness about the plight of the LGBTI in Turkey. Many of the candidates (and the candidate's supporters) understand the challenges that they faced and the slim chance that they had to win their seats. Yet, for many, that seemed to be entirely beside the point. Every time that LGBTI issues are in the news, whether it is speaking about a candidate or their platform, that is a victory for the entire human rights movement. The objective and strategy for LGBTI rights activists is to bring attention to the community, to continue to let Turkish society know that they are in the country, that they are an equal part of the country, that they are facing rights abuses, that they have a political voice, and that they are active in changing the political landscape in the country. Again, the candidates, while knowing that a victory may not have come this election, they also seemed to believe that their electoral activism as political candidates and members of the LGBTI community could help future LGBTI candidates get elected.

Niler Albayrak

Niler Albayrak is another well-known LGBTI activist in Turkey who also decided to run in the 2015 elections in Istanbul's third district under the CHP. Running under the CHP in and of itself is very significant, given that the CHP is one of the most noted and established political parties in Turkey (they came in second in the 2015 November elections). Albayrak spoke to Social Policies Gender Identity and Sexual Orientation Studies Association (SPoD) at their Politics School about why she decided to run for office. For Albayrak, it had a great deal to do with a physical attack on her life. Albayrak spoke about her experience, saying,

There was a craze of urban gentrification in Avcilar and we suffered attacks and lynching attempts that [were] related to this process. The attack[s] at Avcilar has [continued] with the homophobic and transphobic thinking by court judges. In the wake of these attacks in Avcilar, I decided to not quit the political competition and take it forward. We need to take this competition forward. In Poland, there can be a trans woman candidate for [the] Presidency. We still often remain as candidates for nomination, [unable to go beyond]. (Tar, 2015)

The 2015 election campaign was not the first for Albayrak. In fact, she ran in the 2014 local elections under the HDP political party; HDP did not meet the threshold necessary for political representation. Speaking about her decision to shift parties from HDP to CHP, Albayrak explained,

I believe that LGBTI individuals or especially trans women who are particularly visible must be in the parliament in order to represent themselves better and to defend their rights. This time I am proceeding with the CHP. I thought I would have a better [chance to win]. Surely, every party has homophobic and transphobic thinking in its ranks. Our society has not been able to accept certain things but I wanted to continue the race to transform both political parties and society. (Tar, 2015)

She also spoke about the discussion and process that took place between her and the CHP Secretary General Gursel Tekin before coming on board as a political candidate under the CHP banner, explaining that

[w]e established a great communication during our meeting with Gursel Tekin. Our talks progressed well. CHP parliamentarians such as Veli Agbaba, Gursel Tekin, Binnaz Toprak, Aylin Nazliaka, and others are now declaring that LGBTIs should be represented in the parliament. But, of course, this is a personal thing. The CHP's perspective in the 25th term seems to have improved in comparison to the previous terms. That is the impression I get. (Akpınar, 2015b)

For Albayrak, her strategy to advocate for LGBTI rights through an electoral campaign was because of her faith that human rights and change for LGBTI rights can happen through the national government (Tar, 2015). Thus, this is in line with others who are running for MP positions, believing that if elected, they can introduce and/or advocate for legislation that will guarantee rights for those who are LGBTI. For Albayrak, like many of the other political candidates discussed in this book, there is a history of political activism. Albayrak was active with the Istanbul branch of the Human Rights Association in 1987, where she wanted to improve human rights, with particular interest on LGBTI rights (Akpınar, 2015b). What made Albayrak run in 2015 were the abuses against trans sex workers in the country and her belief in the ability to make a change through the national government, saying that, for herself, "the best place to fight against this [discrimination against trans sex workers] was in the parliament" (Akpınar, 2015b). However, Albayrak has made it clear that critics who think she will only focus on LGBTI rights are mistaken. To her, as a human being, it is necessary to advocate for the rights of all. And just because someone has a particular sexual identity does not mean that they will only fight for the rights of that said group (Akpınar, 2015b). She also continued to criticize Erdoğan and the AKP for making promises to protect LGBTI rights (in 2002), explaining that they clearly failing to deliver, saying that the "AKP's slogan of 'what was once a dream is now a reality' became discrimination, hatred, violence, and suicides for LGBTIs" (Akpınar, 2015b).

Sedef Çakmak

Sedef Çakmak is also important to mention because, like the other individuals discussed above, Çakmak, as a member of the LGBTI community, also had a strong interest in activism and politics combined with the experience of running in elections. Çakmak ran in the 2014 local elections in Turkey, for the position of assembly member in Beşiktaş. At the time of writing, Çakmak was serving as the CHP city council representative and also working in the Department of Social Equality in the Beşiktaş Municipality in Istanbul. Çakmak was successful in winning the position of assembly member substitute. Now, she currently holds the position of assembly member (being given her mandate in March 2015). This is a key position, one with significant political responsibilities. What has brought additional attention to this case is that the victory made Çakmak the first openly LGBTI individual to win an elected position in the history of Turkey (LGBTI News Turkey, 2015b).

Çakmak has been very active on LGBTI issues in Turkey for the past decade. For example, she was the board president of SPoD from 2011 until 2013. Çakmak has also advised the mayor on LGBTI issues (LGBTI News Turkey, 2015b). Çakmak discussed the post with relation to conversations of identity, as well as the effect that holding the position could have with regards to activism and future advancements for LGBTI rights, saying that

[c]oming to such a position without having to hide your identity has, without doubt, an empowering effect in a country where people have to hide their identity from their closest for fear of oppression, violence, and exclusion and where LGBTIs face threats, blackmail, mobbing, and termination of employment once their identities are revealed. Policies and services in local administration for LGBTIs within the borders of the Beşiktaş Municipality will serve as an important starting point for developing democracy from the local for all social groups in Turkey. (LGBTI News Turkey, 2015b)

Çakmak has also accomplished many things for LGBTI rights during her time in public office. In a late 2015 interview with Research Turkey, when asked about the work that she had done, Çakmak responded by saying that: "together with mayor of Beşiktaş, as LGBTI activists, we have made awareness raising works on billboards on November 20th, the commemoration day of the transgender victims of hate crimes. To combat killings due to hate crimes[,] we came up with the slogan 'Spite hate, hooray for life' and made billboard advertisements. This was actually a first in Turkey. For the first time, a government agency has made such raising awareness work." Çakmak also spoke about other Beşiktaş Municipality-related activities that she has helped organized. For example, through the municipality, they have held a reception for Pride Week, something not done before in the Istanbul municipalities.

The Beşiktaş Municipality, along with the Şişli leadership, have also offered "established equality units in ... [the respective] municipalities in İstanbul. In these units, we have given trainings to citizens about the municipality services and LGBTI trainings to municipality employees. We have worked on the challenges faced by LGBTI individuals, how we are responsible on these issues as the municipality, how we can conduct studies in this regard." She goes on to say that "[t]he work was not limited to just these two municipalities. Requests are coming to associations from Sarıyer and Kadıköy municipalities for training regarding LGBTI individuals" (Research Turkey, 2015).

Boysan Yakar

Along with Çakmak, Boysan Yakar also ran for the city council, but in the district of Şişli. While Yakar did not win a seat, he was able to get on the reserve list. In addition, following the elections, the mayor of Şişli – Hayri İnönü – offered Yakar a position as a mayoral advisor. It is necessary to understand just how important Yakar's candidacy, and then subsequent advisory role for the mayor, were in the advocacy and advancement of LGBTI rights in Turkey. In discussing his political candidacy to the city council, Yakar was quoted as saying,

I believe that especially politicians were not ready for LGBTIs in Turkey to be so conspicuous until today. But we are part of the people and we live among the people. Contrary to popular opinion, we walk the city during the day as we need to. We live in this country but as a direct target to various discriminations and hateful actions. Our organized effort for equal rights have been continuing for more than 20 years and we expect our legal rights to be granted and our demands to be taken seriously. I think the politicians should just trust us. We are sure we will handle government duties and municipal duties at least as well as we do everything else we put our minds to! (Bianet, 2015)

Yakar (and Çakmak) spoke about how many in the government were not only open to working on LGBTI issues, but some of them were also upset with themselves that they were not the ones to reach out to the LGBTI community, instead of the other way around. There is a belief that visibility and presence will allow one to better advocate for their issues. Yakar made this point, saying that "This is how politics works in Turkey: if you're not here, your rights are not there either" (Durgun, 2015). By having LGBTI people in government, it allowed for conversations about LGBTI rights to happen. Again, for some, it was not a matter of an unwillingness to accept LGBTI rights. Rather, it was either a situation where they had not thought about LGBTI rights, or, if they did, they did not know the best way to go about fighting for these rights. As Çakmak explained,

I have seen that municipal employees are very open-minded about our situation. There was only one problem: since they didn't know what kinds of problems LGBTIs experience, they couldn't tell what they could do as a municipal government. What was mainly said was: "We are already a modern municipality, we welcome everyone." When I would ask[,] "Has a trans woman ever come here?" they would say no. This is the fundamental problem: why is a trans woman reluctant to go into a public building? We know that there are trans women who live in Beşiktas. In that sense, we have focused on awareness work, and we have organized training in cooperation with the SPoD Association. (Durgun, 2015)

Training Sessions with the Government

As government officials, both Çakmak and Yakar were instrumental in organizing and implementing training sessions for municipality workers. In these sessions, they discuss issues facing the LGBTI community, as well as think about ways that they, the government, can help this marginalized community. For example, for many in the training sessions, they share the fact that Çakmak and Yakar were the first LGBTI people that they have encountered, to which Çakmak responds that they most likely have met others but had not known that they were LGBTI.

Yakar and Çakmak were also active in offering training for health professionals. This is important because of previous cases where some doctors or others in the health field have been unwilling to treat transgendered patients. Yakar made it a point to push for health initiatives in the strategic plan of the municipality, saying,

When it comes to trans people, there have been situations that fly in the face of the Hippocratic oath, such as doctors refusing to touch them. To prevent these situations from happening, we have started a campaign for equal health service to stay in effect indefinitely. About 50 people who work in health departments have been trained on understanding LGBTIs. They have been informed about the homophobic situations that are often encountered. We can tell the positive feedback from the demand that we receive. (Durgun, 2015)

LGBTI Legislation in the Municipalities

For Yakar, working on LGBTI rights through municipality politics was very important. He was passionate about the role that his municipality played in helping LGBTI individuals living in the Şişli district. Yakar aided LGBTI groups in providing space for initiatives (namely, locations to hold meetings and events), given that the organizations are recognized and the issues are real issues. Yakar explained that if it were up to him, the municipality leaders "would like to give them money," which can be used for furthering LGBTI activism. But he understood that what the Şişli district was doing was just as important as money; they were giving these groups a "yes," permission to do things that other areas within Istanbul and in the country would not provide. He said, "[F]or twenty-three years they got too many "nos" from the state. But this time, the municipality is going to take the no."

While offering space for events is important, Yakar did much more to help the LGBTI community while he was working for Inönü. The office worked on improving social services. For example, Yakar explained that

we began to give equal health services by the healthcare directorate of the municipality. It is just happening here in Şişli [and] throughout the country, and what we are doing is ... [that] any citizen can come here, and that is important ... because some of them are using different names, and many trans women have male identity cards, and they don't want to show it or whatever, so if you skip that position ... now they can go to our healthcare, facilities in Şişli. There are like 6, 7 of them. And they can go freely. Whenever they would like to, and they can take healthcare services equally.

What was also important about these services offered in Şişli was that the staff was well trained. Yakar said that

[a]ll the personnel inside[,] all the labor inside ... these facilities, they're trained by SPoD, but not only the doctors or the servants, but also the guy who is responsible for the security of the building, even [the person] who's holding the gun on his belly, they were ... educated to make them aware of LGBTI instances. So these, they are ... some of the very first things we've done. And now it's more than a thousand people joined this service. They came, and they took the service. And it didn't stop just giving them equal service, we also let them come after ... After ... all [the] municipality and all the branches of the municipality works between 9 to 5[,] but just the healthcare initiatives of two centers were open from 5–8 for transwomen especially because they woke up really late, and they can go ... [at] six, seven in the night. Also ... [we] have ... services on health issues as well ... we are serving not only for LGBTIs, but for all Şişli citizens ... everyone is coming from around Istanbul for that, for that free test for sexual [diseases].

He went on to say that out of all of the municipalities in Istanbul, this is the only place where such a program exists.

In addition, the municipality was also active in "opening all of the cultural centers of Şişli municipality to LGBTI initiatives. Last year [2014], more than 1,500 people joined some screenings and some movies and some celebrations of the pride week." The municipality was also a strong advocate of the LGBTI events, promoting them on social media accounts. Related to this, the municipality showed their support for the Pride March in 2015. They provided marchers with placards. They also sponsor an event in the municipality called the "Rotten Tomato Awards," which is an "award" given to someone who has said something or done something outrageous against the LGBTI community (this serves as a shaming mechanism).

In our conversation, Yakar also spoke about his work to connect the Şişli district with other networks, whether this is with other cities in working to join the Rainbow Cities Network, or building linkages to the European Union, hoping to establish the municipality as a "gay-friendly municipality." Yakar believed that this label would make it easier to work on rights-based issues. This is why he was so excited about the Rainbow Cities Network, since he felt that by joining such a network, this would aid in providing support for the LGBTI community and ensure that whoever would be the mayor of the district would have to be committed to these issues.

"LGBTI Friendly" Political Officials

Along with running in elections directly, another strategy that LGBTI activists have taken with regard to furthering the rights of sexual minorities in Turkey has been to also form networks and relationships with "LGBT friendly" parties, political officials, and political candidates who themselves are not lesbian, gay, bisexual, or transgender. There has been a push by activists to form public alliances with political candidates or already-elected officials with regard to LGBTI issues. One of the clearest ways that this has been formulated is through what has been called the "LGBT Friendly Municipality Protocol." This protocol, established by SPoD (*Hurriyet Daily News*, 2014), states that candidates who sign are supportive of LGBTI rights and will work to end discrimination against the LGBTI community. In addition, these political candidates agree to work with LGBTI rights organizations and call (and advocate for) sexual identity, as well as gender equality (*Hurriyet Daily News*, 2014). The pledge, in English, states:

I, the undersigned, as a candidate for the Parliament, commit, if elected to the Parliament in the 7 June 2015 General Elections, to:

Display an approach that protects all human rights, including the rights pertaining to sexual orientation and gender identity,

Work in the Grand National Assembly of Turkey (Parliament) towards gaining recognition for lesbian, gay, bisexual, trans, and intersex rights, as protected by international human rights laws and regulations, and to ensure that Turkey fulfills its responsibilities as a party to any and all international human rights treaties,

Strive to ensure that the new Constitution drafting process, which is to begin after the elections, is transparent and inclusive,

Make efforts to amend laws that ignore discrimination on the basis of sexual orientation and/or gender identity in every aspect of life and to ensure that LGBTIs have access to the justice system,

Develop egalitarian social policies in order to make sure that LGBTIs are not excluded from or discriminated against in the spheres of education, health, employment, and housing, and that they have equal access to social services in these spheres,

Make LGBTI rights visible within my political party, in order to ensure equality in political representation and in political participation,

Take the necessary steps for the inclusion of openly-out LGBTI persons in every political position without them facing any discrimination,

And cooperate with other parties' parliamentarians who defend LGBTI rights and join them in leading the efforts towards the establishment of a permanent structure within the Assembly for this purpose. (SPoD, 2014)

In our discussion, Yakar praised Mayor İnönü for his willingness to support the Friendlies Campaign Protocol. He explained that İnönü was one of the leaders in signing the protocol; many others signed it, but they were waiting for the mayor to sign it because they understood the political nature of signing this document. Yakar explained that he knew that the mayor has many LGBTI individuals living in the district and that the groups needed and deserved equal rights. Thus, the municipality has not only been leading the way on LGBTI rights issues but it has continued to serve as a great model for other individuals and municipalities. In fact, when I asked Yakar what he would like other municipalities in Istanbul or around the world to learn from his work in Şişli, Yakar said that

[t]here is no anytime to wait for these things ... We suffered a lot. There's still suffering. Just a month ago, a woman committed suicide in her apartment in Şişli. I mean, she was [a] trans[gender individual]. It was just one thing about her. It was just one thing in her life. There are tons of other troubles we are facing ... There are no ... fields that we can work on with our identities as trans people or men. There [is] no educational equality with your identities.

Yakar went on to say that politicians have tried to say that "Turkey's like this" as if that argument is sufficient to not provide LGBTI rights. He said that this is not the time to wait to advocate for LGBTI rights. If one does not take the initiative to work on these issues, advocating for improving the lives of the LGBTI community, then it will not happen itself, and the horrible conditions facing LGBTI individuals will be forgotten. He mentioned that citizens by and large are supportive of rights and services for the LGBTI community, but that they are just now aware of what sorts of programs and services are being offered. It is therefore important to not only have these programs but there needs to continue to be work with additional political leaders who can create, promote, and implement programs and services for the LGBTI community.

Working with Political Parties Supportive of LGBTI Rights

Along with mayors and individual political candidates and officials, Turkish political parties such as the HDP and the CHP have also made much more public shows of support for LBGTI rights. For example, Çakmak explained that during the 2015 Pride Week in Istanbul, Turkey,

Cumhuriyet Halk Partisi (Republican People's Party) (CHP) municipalities began to publish support messages on ... social media. Obviously this was also a first in Turkey. They changed their official social media account logos to rainbows [and] issued messages condemning discrimination. While there were such developments in the CHP, the HDP also made an important attempt. During Demirtaş's presidential candidacy period, the *Halkların Demokratik Partisi* (People's Democratic Party) (HDP) issued an election slogan with the posters of our trans woman activist in Ağrı and this was on the billboards [as well]. (Research Turkey, 2015)

So, some of the political parties are beginning to better recognize the importance of advocating for LGBTI rights.

This work with political parties and leaders is not a new occurrence but a strategy that has been attempted by LGBTI advocacy groups for years. One group that has employed this approach of working with political leaders is SPoD. SPoD is a human rights organization that was founded in 2011 and that focuses on human rights of LGBTI members in Turkey. Their attention is primarily on social, as well as economic, issues facing LGBTI individuals, although their attention is toward ending any discrimination that exists (*Seattle Gay News*, 2014). For example, according to the organization, "SPoD works for the development of rights-based social policy that contributes to the full equality of LGBT individuals. SPoD's activities cover a wide range of social policy domains including labor market, social services, education, elderly care, healthcare, housing, and income poverty alleviation" (quoted in *Seattle Gay News*, 2014). This was an important milestone in terms of LGBT rights in Turkey. The reason for this is that "[o]ver the past 20 years of LGBT activism in Turkey, this was the first time the LGBT community engaged directly in mainstream politics" (Goksel, 2014).

Speaking on this issue of direct activism with regard to political elections, Erdal Partog, who is also a board member of SPoD, is quoted as saying that

[w]e have been working directly with politics since 2011. In this general election, we aim to run a campaign independent of political parties and to strengthen LGBTIs in both political representation and political participation. We want to support LGBTI representatives and representatives who defend LGBTI rights at every level of the Grand National Assembly of Turkey, to work together with them, and to tell everyone that this is a rights struggle beyond the issues of electing and getting elected. Pushing our struggle in the arena of politics like it is in many other fields will lead to gaining a legal and social rights framework for our demands. (LGBTI News Turkey, 2015b)

One way that they have been able to do this is through the pledge that SPoD created for political candidates to sign. During the 2014 local elections (which were held on March 30), there were forty political candidates that signed the protocol. As *Hurriyet Daily News* (2014) reported, "Three of the four elected LGBT friendly mayors are the Republican People's Party's (CHP) candidates of Istanbul's central districts: Aykurt Nuhoğlu in Kadıköy, Murat Hazinedar in Beşiktaş and Hayri İnönü in Şişli. The other is the Peace and Democracy Party's BDP co-candidate in the southern Mersin province's Akdeniz district Yüksel Mutlu, who won the race in his constituency, becoming the only LGBT friendly mayor outside Turkey's biggest metropolis."

Visibility of LGBTI Politicians and Municipality Workers

It is also important to note that having LGBTI candidates, politicians, and/or public municipality workers also helps with regard to visibility for the LGBTI community. The candidates and municipality workers themselves understand just how important it is for people to see an LGBTI individual in a public position. Yakar spoke about this to me, saying that

working on the local level is kind of important, you're meeting with every figure in this neighborhood. I mean ... [this] one year long period while I am working here, it's kind of working from the very basics. I am having each day [be] an experience of my life explaining it to the other [people who work] as an architect or somebody else. So ... when you're living and working at the same time, you're giving them that reality, a gay man with open identity with his personal life. He can live and work here. It's another experience, which is going on.

Political Education during Elections

Groups such as SPoD have not limited their work to political candidates; instead they have used the election season as one not only for supporting LGBTI rights through candidates who support the pledge (for example) but they have also mobilized during this time to advocate for other approaches in the name of LGBTI rights. In fact, Sedef Çakmak, who is a member of the board for SPoD (and former board president) was quoted as saying that "[i]n Turkey, individuals' political participation is confined to 'voting.' But political participation is all efforts to directly affect the decisions of decision-makers. SPoD LGBTI consciously uses all the tools of political participation such as election monitoring, face to face meetings with decision-makers, and political campaigns to emphasize LGBTI problems" (LGBTI News Turkey, 2015a).

While they were clearly targeting political candidates to sign a pledge related to protecting LGBTI rights if elected in office, SPoD has also been involved in launching other forms of activism campaigns prior to the June 2015 elections. For example, in 2012, SPoD began their Politics School for LGBTIs. This school brings together activists, academics, and political leaders (LGBTI News Turkey) to discuss LGBTI issues and strategies, and to increase visibility of the LGBTI community and LGBTI issues (LGBTI News Turkey, 2015c). The school serves a number of functions with regards to activism strategies. As LGBTI News Turkey (2015c) explains, the most recent

Politics School will inform LGBTIs of political participation mechanisms, conduct presentations and workshops to encourage active political partici-pation, and plan future political representation and participation activities. The school aims to involve participants in campaigns and monitoring for the general elections in their own cities. The subjects to be covered are: Democracy and freedoms, queer democracy, participation methods in decision-making mechanisms, civil society in law-making processes, [the] LGBTI movement's history and political participation, political parties and rights-based policies, gender[-]focused budgets, LGBTI[-] focused social policies, LGBTI rights in local politics, organizing election campaigns and election monitoring.

I asked Hüroğlu about the history of the SPoD Politics School. He said

That is also actually the work of the political representation working field activists from us. We did it [the workshops] three times, first of all during the constitutional process; it was not for the constitution, it was, in general, to create the potential for LGBTI people who can relate also other issues in LGBTI rights in daily politics. If they want to be an activist, mainstream politicians, they also need to have the ideas on environment, social . . . So to create that potential, we invited LGBTI rights activists to discuss all other issues in politics as well. It was a series of workshops . . . the first one was on the media.

While the first concentrated on media-related issues, he went on to say that:

[t]he second one was . . . before the elections to create a [list] of the potential candidates. At that time, the candidates were not certain, so we invited activists from all different cities, brought them altogether, and . . . the experts lectured on how municipalities work, what are LGBTI work on municipal-ities around the world, in Europe, what kind of networks do they have? . . . What do we want from the municipalities? What can municipalities do for LGBTI rights? And . . . at the end of the school of politics, they, with all the

representatives of all the different LGBTI groups, came together to create a list of demands for the municipalities and we created that protocol, and ... signed [it] too. We asked the candidates to sign that protocol. And when they are elected, they are going to do certain things to protect LGBTI rights. And we [published it], we had the names of the people who signed that published [protocol], and ... ensure[d] that if you are campaigning, the LGBTI people are going to support you if you sign that protocol.

Hüroğlu explained that there were many who decided to sign the protocol, but that "it was also a lot of work to find the people" that were willing to do so.

Along with this work, one of their more recent campaigns before the 2015 general elections was called "In School, in Work, in the Parliament: LGBTI's Are Everywhere!" The idea behind this campaign is for the LGBTI community to increase their visibility in Turkish society, showing members of the public that they are as much of society as non-LGBTI individuals are. SPoD feels that this approach is effective since it shows a presence of LGBTIs in Turkey, which in turn can then lead to effective demands for their human rights. Çakmak did actually say that while they use various methods of political participation, in her mind, "there is one method that is the most effective and that is the thought that 'you don't have rights if you are not present'" (LGBTI News Turkey, 2015a). The idea is that to offer visibility and show that presence. It demonstrates to Turkey that being lesbian, gay, bisexual, or transgendered is not some sort of sickness or problem and that the community should not have to hide or feel alienated, with Çakmak noting that the community "must actively participate in politics with our LGBTI identities in order to show decision-makers that being LGBTI is not something that needs to be hidden, shunned, treated or eliminated, to pass laws for LGBTIs, and to repair the negative associations in society. Only in this way can we ensure a truly participatory democracy in society, in the parliament, and in political parties" (LGBTI News Turkey, 2015a). Related to this initiative, SPoD has been meeting with the leaders of different political parties in Turkey. For example, before the 2015 general elections, SPoD met with the HDP, along with the co-president of Istanbul's HDP, Ayşe Erdem, where the two discussed how the organization can work with HDP political candidates for the June 2015 elections, as well as the party's overall strategy and approach towards further advocating LGBTI rights issues (LGBTI News Turkey, 2015b). When asked in an interview (Akpinar, 2015a), Sulu, who spoke at the school, talked about some of the things that the Politics School has focused on, saying that

[i]t is going very well, very intense. We discussed perception of democracy, the political representation of LGBTI people and how to articulate their rights demands. We are learning very technical things actually, like a camp; quite good. After we say we are victimized, we are lacking in our efforts at the point of demanding our rights. We repeat these continuously, but we need to rid ourselves [of] the victim psychology and remind [people] that we are citizens, paying taxes, needing access to health services. At the Politics School, we discuss a range of topics from politics, how to do politics to being a citizen.

Hüroğlu explained that what was great from these Politics School education sessions was that some of the candidates who won local elections did in fact implement parts of the protocol by hiring individuals from the LGBTI community onto their staff. Thus, this specific advocacy not only centered on educating the media and political candidates (at the local and national level), and also teaching individuals on how to lobby political leaders, but the sessions were also successful in having more LGBTI diversity present in public office positions. Thus, people like Sedef Çakmak and Boysan Yakar could then advocate for rights within the system. The Politics School is a very important workshop for LGBTI rights. They are able to educate people about working through the political process to advocate change. However, it is important to note that SPoD is not the only LGBTI human rights organization running activist workshops with regard to strategies for LGBT rights advocacy. The idea of NGO training and workshops seems to be common across many human rights organizations.

However, SPoD is not limited to community activism alone. In fact, one of their other branches of concentration is related to working to support LGBTI candidates in Turkey. In fact, Hüroğlu argues, "[T]he most visible work of my organization isn't really that [namely, the roundtables with doctors and others to improve social issues]. In the last three years, it became the elections and our cultural campaigns." On this point, Hüroğlu says,

First of all ... the strongest one was our local elections campaign where we supported the ... different LGBTI candidates. They were not campaigning for the mayorship ... [but] for the city councils. And at first, none of them became successful, but then Sedef [Çakmak] ... was able to get into the city council. And at that time actually we had a lot of contacts with MPs because somehow ... they ... had to put pressure on the mayors, on the party representatives – who have to create the list of city council members – to put the LGBTs at a little bit higher rank. So there you had to really contact a lot of people to make it possible to make yourself more visible, to make them understand the importance of the issue.

Hüroğlu went on to say that

[m]eanwhile, they also accepted the fact of LGBTI rights and problems in a powerful way, those MPs also put some other efforts in parliament, Such as one MP from CHP ... has given a proposal to parliament to create a kind of research group of parliamentarians researching the LGBTI rights abuses. Of course it was refused, but it was a good attempt with, I think, 59 signatures of social democrat MPs. And we don't have that much contact with MPs ... We didn't know until then that we had that many allies in the parliament. Well, they of course are not visible, they didn't give us the list, but we know who signed the agreement.

Given the attention and resources that SPoD has committed to focusing on LGBTI issues in the context of legislation and elections, it is interesting to understand how the organization moved to that position. Asking Hüroğlu if there was a discussion or decision to focus on elections as an advocacy strategy, he replied,

It was not a decision at all ... At the beginning we thought, okay we will have four directions. We want to have expert trainings on economic and social rights ... to strengthen the representation of LGBTI people in politics. We want to work closer with academic missions, support them and create maybe our own academic work. And ... we want to support LGBTI people in their legal processes, create some campaign, law cases ... Everybody is working, I am working for expert trainings and other ones, writing projects on legal campaigning. But the ... elections became a bigger area and more sexy because ... for new volunteers it was more visible and our work bec [a]me more visible. And for politicians it can catch [their] ... attention [more] than the training ... So it became somewhat more important, but not for everybody. Of course, everybody was working in it some, but ... there was no decision.

Hüroğlu spoke about his activities and how he works to still maintain other aspects of activism not directly related to political campaigns, saying:

I am still trying to keep myself out of all [this] political presentation work because I think there is enough people working on that and ... very successfully. ... I myself am still trying to create more ideas for more interesting people, experts, academics, local municipality workers, prisons, like prison guards, and all [the] people we had trainings with ... It is going good ... [as they are] interesting people.

He went on to stress his role in setting up an activist network, which includes helping other organizations like Lambda Istanbul with their "shelter for older trans[gender] people ... [as] that is a very important ... [initiative]." They have even thought about "creating another shelter within the Beşiktaş municipality for all LGBTI people as well," although he views that shelter as "a long-term project," and one that the community in Beşiktaş may or may not want.

Moreover, SPoD has also been very active in organizing mental health professionals. In fact, he explains that there has not been as much support for mental health, which has led the organization to focus more on this matter. Hüroğlu said that they "are trying to create a methodology for mental health experts. We have an expert now," and individuals are able to apply as volunteers through the site. The organization offers specific training in mental health. This training is not "one day training," but rather about "40 hours [of] training." He feels that this allows those attending to have some at least basic idea of being able to help the person(s) in need. The organization is not limited to mental health; "we are already trying to build [that kind of system] ... That's what we thought was lacking. But this is kind of ... more invisible work because you do not come up with ... the media attention." So, as we can see, there are many strategies taken by LGBTI activists and organizations in Turkey as it relates to media, legislative work, and elections.

7 | *Other Forms of LGBTI Rights-Based Advocacy*

Our strategy ... [is] to be more and more visible and to tell people about us because maybe we can change something.

Murat Renay

While the previous chapters concentrated on activism pertaining to digital and social media, as well as political, electoral, and legislative activities carried out by LGBTI activists, this chapter will look at additional strategies, which include the role of social services for sexual minorities in Turkey. We will also discuss other activities like educational workshops, human rights research, and cross-issue advocacy. In addition, we will also examine the question of whether activists are pushing for same-sex marriage in Turkey and how this compares to advocacy on the issue in Western Europe and the United States.

Providing Social Services to the LGBTI Community

Social services continue to be one of the central components of LGBTI human rights-based advocacy for quite some time. For example, organizations like SPoD actually began primarily with a focus on socioeconomic rights. Cihan Hüroğlu works on social and economic issues for SPoD and leads training sessions with regard to LGBTI activism. Prior to SPoD, Hüroğlu worked for Lamba Istanbul for ten years. I was interested to understand how SPoD came to exist as a domestic LGBTI rights organization, as well as the direction that SPoD has taken with regards to LGBTI rights advocacy. Hüroğlu explains how SPoD came to exist in light of other LGBTI organizations in Turkey, and more specifically, how they provided socioeconomic support for the LGBTI community, saying that

we are established to fill the gap we thought that exists in the LGBTI rights movement, to focus more on economic and social rights [for] the LGBTI people. That includes [things] like education, health, housing ... but also, in

159

Istanbul, there was a great potential for LGBTI people, international connections, media, financial resources and everything. And we thought organizations in Istanbul were not capable of ... absorbing all that potential
because the organization of Lambda Istanbul and some other initiatives[,]
they were more about community organizations and supporting the community or more focused on that.

He went on to speak more about the issue of community support, and
its relation to the formation of SPoD, saying, "[I]f you are focused on
community, you have a lot [of] circulation of volunteers." However,
this could also result in

more experienced people ... [leaving] because they don't ... feel
strengthened, and... their friendship circles may not need that community
support. So they leave the organization, but nobody really stays to ... keep
the contacts to ... make an archive ... [Those] sort of relations are lacking in
the moment in Istanbul. In Ankara it was going more institutionalized, but in
Istanbul it was not. But we actually wanted to keep that as well, so we found
[ed] SPoD, and well it was maybe luck, or maybe I don't know, unlucky, but
afterwards in the last two years we had three elections and we actually
wanted to focus on socioeconomic rights.

This specific socioeconomic work is necessary for the LGBTI community in Turkey, and even more so for the transgender community,
because the government programs supporting women's rights, for
example, are not available to transgender persons. Janset Kalan of
Pembe Hayat explains that the

legal gender recognition itself doesn't exist in Turkey so we know in order
for you to change your legal gender marking, in your official documents, you
need to go through gender reassignment surgery, and you need to go through
a long legal procedure, and unless your document is not changed ... you
cannot have access to those mechanisms. Because they say that "okay you
look like a woman but your ID says you're a man, and you're registered as a
man in the system, in the national system ... we cannot provide you with
these services."

However, organizations like SPoD have also been quite active in
economic and social issues in other ways. Hüroğlu explained that the
organization, through President Volkan Yılmaz (along with Boğaziçi
University), carried out a survey regarding LGBTI access to socioeconomic rights, such as issues with health services. He felt that to truly be

effective in LGBTI rights, one needs figures. He said that there were "about 200 interviews" which were done "face-to-face[,] but in focus groups." They were also able to utilize the Internet and had some websites publish the survey on their own sites, including a particular dating site. This helped them get to "around a few thousand" respondents. They were not only able to gain valuable information on how the LGBTI community members felt about social services, but their survey had questions that were like those asked in European surveys, which allowed them to put their results next to those found in the other works.

Continuing on the issue of socioeconomic rights, I asked Hüroğlu whether SPoD's social and economic services were being utilized in Istanbul. Since SPoD was offering such a commitment to this realm of activist engagement, it is interesting to examine the level of reach that these sorts of programs are having in the city. In response to this, Hüroğlu said that this is happening, although there are some difficulties due to the fact that Istanbul has such a large population, and so there are many more LGBTI individuals who require these services than what the organization is able to offer. Specifically, he said that while people are taking advantage of SPoD's services,

[w]e do not have the voluntary power or professional power ... to increase that. If you do that, you have demand always. Until now maybe we could help around like 100 people for ... our mental health services. And we have now four or five legal campaigns like on one health, one on right to education, one employment, one murder case. We are picking the most dramatic cases ... But it's not enough.

Hüroğlu also noted that they do not publicize their entire range of services because of a concern that they would not "be able to satisfy the needs if everyone knows" about what they offer. They want to provide additional services, or a presence in areas where poorer people would have an easier time accessing what they offer. Some organizations like Lambda Istanbul have moved to Kadikoy, where "lower class people can reach Kadikoy as well. But the European side is kind of bigger and we do not have a cultural center on the European side. All of our offices of LGBTI organizations are very small. We have a meeting room of 30–40 people, it's sad really, it's pathetic even." But he recognizes that they have other more important priorities than the meeting room size.

Even organizations such as Pembe Hayat, who, while they themselves don't consider it a strategy to specifically put forward transgender individuals for political office (since some organizations see the choices people make with regard to politics as an individual choice), do find other ways to be helpful. For example, as Kalan explained, "if there is a trans candidate, and there were for the last two elections now, we are trying to make them more visible. We are helping them by providing technical and capacity assistance in their campaign management, and with ... raising their own campaign funds." Kalan went on to say

that just because you are transgender, we are not giving our support, direct support to you, but what we can do is to make your presentation through media to different media channels in a proper way [i.e., spread the message of a trans candidate to other media channels]. And ... we are behind you, and we are here, always ready when you need some assistance ... we are also trying to ... monitor any hate speech or any targeting against them by mainstream media or by other politicians and make it also public so people can react to that.

NGO Workshops

As mentioned, while some of SPoD's activities include workshops focused on working within the political system, other workshops are organized around other issues. Hüroğlu explained that SPoD is focused on a number of activities, but his role more directly involves working on a variety of social issues facing the LGBTI community. He says,

I personally am dealing more with the trainings, mental health experts especially. This is a really, really key issue for LGBTI rights, and we are doing that with ... universities since three years now. But we also did a lot of meetings with trade unions and we are organizing roundtable discussions with social workers, with health professionals, health doctors and trying to find some strategies to solve the problems for LGBTs in relative fields.

Other groups also emphasize training workshops. Take Pembe Hayat, for example. In one of the interviews, Kalan explained that

our trainings are going on in multi-levels, so in the first level and the most [important] thing we are focusing on is the trainings toward teachers and lawyers. So we can create a network of teachers who can create some safe spaces for ... trans school children. And the other training is for the lawyers.

So we can create a network of lawyers who can take up issues of human rights violations as well as discrimination issues and specifically on transgender, trans legal processes. So they can help actually give consultancy to any trans applicant who can approach them. And [the] other level of training is toward academia. So we are trying to encourage academic admissions and new academic admissions, newcomers in academia to work on queer studies.

They also are working to

train activists to ... actually report human rights violations in the cities where they are living. ... if they face discrimination ... we encourage them to report it and send it to us, or keep it in their own archives if there is an organization there, an LGBTI organization or human rights organization there and to create a segregated information [listing], [a] segregated database which we can use [at] both national and international level[s] during our advocacy activities.

They also have training for NGOs, and Kalan explains that these sessions are "actually about enhancing their own capacities to encourage them to build their own networks and ... to get them to engage with their local authorities ... local administration and local policy makers. And the other level of this training toward the LGBTI organization is to help them build their own skill analysis and create their own sustainability in their own local level," which can then be used "[at] a national level or to an international level so they can get engaged with the international process." Related to working with NGOs, Pembe Hayat also has training sessions for individual activists working on transgender issues. Pembe Hayat has a summer camp that brings together different activists (summer camp topics have included one that focuses on transgender women and another one for transgender men. They hope to have the following summer session focus on gender nonconforming persons, as well as queer persons.

One of the other most well-known LGBT rights organizations, Kaos GL, has been hosting an event entitled "New Media School." 2015 was the first year for the event. It is here that Kaos GL brought together over twenty reporters from throughout Turkey. The primary objective of the New Media School is to train journalists with regard to social media as it pertains to LGBT rights. In addition, there is also a push to expand the influence of volunteer reporters in Turkey. The New Media School featured different workshops that journalists attended. While the topics varied, there were workshops on "Digital

Security," "Digital Storytelling," and a workshop on social media, with emphasis on Tweetdeck, as well as Twitter (Kaos GL, 2015b). One of "[t]he first workshop[s] of the school started with the speeches of Secin Tuncel and Yildiz Tar from Kaos GL[,] and Journalist Bugra Tokmakoglu conveyed the historical background of the 'news' and 'journal/newspaper' concepts. Tokmakoglu also mentioned the significance of LGTI journalism while conducting a practical workshop concerning news elements, components, subjects and methods" (Kaos GL, 2015b). In addition, Tokmakoglu went on to say, "We need to strengthen the news channels in order to make the ones who are not heard visible and to improve social awareness. In this respect, Kaos GL's publishing and what they have done up until today set an example. In fact, [LGBTIs] become visible as a whole with a correct representation via Kaos GL[,] who makes the LGBTI agenda visible through a rights-based point of view."

The objective behind this workshop seems to have concentrated on providing advice on how journalists' voices can be better heard with regard to LGBTI stories. A common theme that we are seeing with the activists interviewed in various outlets is their emphasis on the importance of visibility within the context of activism. Being heard and being in front of the public is a necessary (and important) form of activism for advancing LGBT rights. Tokmakoglu seems to share this position, being quoted as saying: "Gays and lesbians are changing the world by making news. They tell about themselves and ensure their fights to meet the society through different channels" (Kaos GL, 2015b). Thus, telling the story about gays, lesbians, bisexuals, and transgendered individuals allows civil society to see that these persons are also members of society, that they are as much a part of Turkey as is anyone else. And with continued visibility, the hope is that perception towards the LGBTI community will continue to change for the better. It seems that this sort of workshop provides journalists with the tools necessary to navigate media and social media fronts. Others, such as Pembe Hayat, host "expert workshops on psychosocial support mechanisms towards transgender people."

Research and Reporting

As discussed in Chapter 4, NGOs also focus on research and reporting. This has also been a strategy used by Turkish NGOs, as well as international NGOs, in collaboration with local organizations, as they attempt to bring attention to the plight of the LGBTI community in Turkey. For example, LGBTI rights-based organizations Kaos GL, LGBTI News Turkey, and the International Gay and Lesbian Human Rights Commission (IGLHRC) (2014) gather information, research, and write reports to the United Nations Human Rights Council with regard to Turkey's Universal Periodic Review as it relates to LGBTI rights. These United Nations reports are critical, as they often document – in fine detail – the types of rights abuses (often perpetrated by the state) or the state's indifference towards abuses, thus presenting a very different situation than the one the country presents to these different human rights councils. Because one is often skeptical of the motivations and interests behind a state's report during their periodic review, NGO research and reporting becomes a vital element in terms of seeking truth with regard to the human rights conditions within a state. With these reports, NGOs not only document state abuses, but they also make recommendations on how the state should alter their behavior to protect the human rights of the LGBTI community. For example, in the 2014 Universal Periodic Review report by Kaos GL, LGBTI News Turkey, and the IGLHRC), following their report on human rights abuses against the LGBTI community in Turkey, they ended the report with a list of recommendations that they would like the Human Rights Council to bring forward to Turkey. They are as follows:

1. Include the terms "sexual orientation" and "gender identity" in constitutional clauses on equality and nondiscrimination, as well as in hate crimes legislation.
2. Take all administrative measures, both on the national and local levels, to prohibit and prevent discrimination on the basis of sexual orientation and gender identity, in order to provide effective protection of LGBT people in Turkey.
3. Conduct full and independent investigations into all allegations of harassment, violence, or abuse of LGBT individuals, and prosecute perpetrators.
4. Monitor, aggregate, and publish data on the number of complaints of violence against members of the LGBT community.
5. Provide mandatory trainings on the international standards of nondiscrimination to government officials, police, military,

prison/detention staff, and to the judiciary with specific emphasis on sexual orientation and gender identity.

6. Provide a comprehensive framework for public school education on sexuality that includes sexual orientation and gender identity.
7. Cease to categorize homosexuality and transsexuality as illnesses of any sort.
8. Ensure that an individual's mere existence as an LGBT individual is never considered "unjust provocation" of a criminal act, nor "contrary to law and ethics."
9. Provide legal protection and equal treatment for LGBT people who have faced discrimination and abuse due to their actual or perceived sexual orientation and/or gender identity.
10. Guarantee the freedom of speech and assembly for LGBT community members and their allies (11).

Cross-Issue Advocacy

I have spent much of this book discussing the different ways NGOs and individual activists are working to advance LGBTI rights. However, I want to also note that many of the LGBTI activists do not see these rights in a vacuum. In fact, they understand and stress that what they are fighting for is not only the rights of the LGBTI, but rather, their work consists of an intersectionality with many other groups' issues, whether it is the advocacy of rights based on ethnic, gender, or any other forms of discrimination. In fact, there exists a strong belief that one cannot advocate for human rights for the LGBTI community without also – and at the same time – speaking equally about the rights of everyone.

As I have discussed throughout book, it is impossible to isolate LGBTI rights as one category of rights as if they are somehow separate from all of the other forms of discrimination (economic discrimination, gender discrimination, ethnic and religious minority discrimination, refugee rights, etc.). As Rahman (2010) notes, "Understanding the epistemological and political provenance of gay identity and LGBT rights suggests that the equation between secularism, democracy and social justice for LGBT is not inevitable, but rather that it has been and remains contingent on dealing with a variety of intersecting oppressions; on social change in gender divisions; on the ability to organize political action; and on moral cultural codes becoming detraditionalized" (955).

LGBTI activists, while focusing on issues that may only seem directly related to the lesbian, gay, bisexual, and transgender community, have also been employing a variety of cross-issue advocacy tactics, aiming to work with other human rights activists and organizations. The LGBTI communities and affiliated activists recognize that the issues impacting LGBTI community often overlap with other human rights categories. For example, there is a close linkage between LGBTI and women's rights activists. As discussed earlier in the book, for example, many within the HDP find it necessary to fight for both LGBTI as well as women's rights; both groups are discriminated against by what are often pegged "traditional values" arguments (often based in some interpretation of Islam, although not necessarily). From early onward in the history of the LGBTI rights movement in Turkey, activists pushing for more LGBTI rights were also just as vocal and active for women's rights, ethnic and religious minority rights, etc.; they understood that increased women's rights might help with regard to more LGBTI rights, and if religious and/or ethnic minorities received more state attention as far as rights protections, then this could also help LGBTI rights. Plus, many individuals fall within multiple so-called categories. There are many women who are also members of the LGBTI community, there are ethnic and religious groups that cut across different gender and sexual identities, as well as political ideologies. Thus, LGBTI activists often make little distinction between rights for the LGBTI community and human rights for women, Kurds, Jews, Alevi, etc.

In fact, this can be seen in the various advocacy networks that have arisen in Turkey, whether at the individual level, the organizational level, or within and between political parties. Again, for example, the HDP calls for the rights of all humans in Turkey. Their manifesto explicitly states support for women, LGBTI, ethnic groups, religious groups, etc., and their candidate nominations have group thresholds. But it is not only the HDP that is focused on cross-issue advocacy. As Nurtsch (2015), explains, "The LGBT movement does not limit itself to calling for the recognition of sexual identities. But [it] also lobbies for social justice, women's rights and against racism. For example, for what was billed as the "Dignity March" of 2013, 50,000 people took to the streets under the slogan 'For bread, justice, and freedom.'" The activists understand how important human rights for all individuals are and recognize that these issues are not isolated from one another.

For example, women who are also within the LGBTI community are often discriminated against because they are women as well as because they are being lesbian, transgendered, etc. This is often an issue with family members who may not be understanding, in education systems, in the workplace, or in politics for political candidates. In a 2011 report on conditions facing the LGBTI community in Turkey, Amnesty International stated that when discrimination against the LGBTI community exists, it leads many to hide their identities. They explain that while this occurs for many within the LGBTI community,

[t]his is particularly the case for lesbians and bisexual women who, due to their often-lower levels of economic autonomy and independence within the family than men, suffer different problems and have less access to protection mechanisms. While women have equal rights in law to men, they experience grossly unequal treatment in practice. This multiple discrimination contributes to the frequent invisibility of lesbians and bisexual women in Turkey. Gay and bisexual men risk violence and discrimination when they are open about their sexual orientation and are often perceived to violate narrow concepts of masculinity. Many transgender women and men, unable or unwilling to hide their gender identity from prejudicial audiences, suffer some of the most serious acts of violence and intolerance due to their gender identity and perceived sexual orientation. Transgender women in particular face the greatest barriers to entering employment and are in a great many cases forced to engage in illegal sex work, adding another layer of prejudice against them and providing an additional subtext for their harassment by law enforcement officials. Of great concern – yet largely ignored by the authorities – is the continuing prevalence of hate crimes – including violent attacks and murders. Transgender women in particular are targeted. (Amnesty International, 2011: 6)

As we see, these issues are not separate from one another; discrimination because one is in the LGBTI community could also be compounded by discrimination that a woman may face in Turkey, for example, because they face additional discrimination and various sorts of inequalities in their day-to-day lives.

Beşiktaş City Council member Sedef Çakmak explained the importance of advocacy for all rights when she spoke about the many rights abuses that different groups are facing in Turkey, saying,

[T]here is no hierarchy among human rights. There cannot be a situation in which we would say we will solve this first. For example, there is a certain phrase that we the LGBTI activists hear a lot: *"even men and women are not equal in this country."* Sexual equality is not fully secured even in many countries where LGBTI rights are respected and recognised. This is why we cannot set up such a hierarchy. Instead, what I understand also from democracy is that we need to think all of it as a whole since none of the concepts is inferior to the others. After all what we care about is a healthy, happy and peaceful human since those humans create a healthy, happy and peaceful society. (Research Turkey, 2015)

In another interview, Çakmak continued to speak about the intersectionality of LGBTI rights with many other human rights abuses facing people in Turkey:

Being LGBTI is not our only identity. You can be LGBTI and Kurdish, Alevi, disabled, poor ... If you look at our struggle of 22 years, we have been discussing the income gap, the effects of gentrification, and the effects of violence. As far as these three issues go, LGBTIs are among the first groups to suffer. When you talk about LGBTI rights, you have to expand the discussion to other subjects: employment with no benefits, discrimination in health care, deprivation from the right to education. (Durgun, 2015)

Çakmak was also quoted as stating,

At this point, during the ban on the Pride parade and the following two months, there have been systematic attacks on the LGBTI community because if the government acts this way, the people on the street draw power from this and continue their attacks[;] the political agenda is always busy, these kind of attacks are not mentioned. This is one of the problems of the disadvantaged groups. The violence that they go through is never visible. Especially when the agenda is full like in our country and there are harsh events happening one after the other every day. (Research Turkey, 2015)

A high level of fear and violence, whether state-related or not, has led to security concerns and with it a willingness by citizens to overlook certain rights and for the state to go on repressing citizen rights, knowing that much of the public will not stand in their way and will almost accept, if not tolerate, their actions, all in the name of domestic security. If we recall, the AKP government won the majority of seats in the late 2015 elections and has continued to be involved in many repressive domestic and foreign policy activities. The violence in southern Turkey against the PKK and Kurdish citizens, Turkish government responses to multiple terror attacks (whether in Suruc, Ankara, or Istanbul), their international activity in northern Syria against the

Popular People's Movement, their crackdown on Fethullah Gulen and Hizmet, and on journalists and other free speech in the country has left little room for a public international conversation focused on LGBTI rights.

Cooperation between Activists and NGOs within Turkey

While I have addressed the different ways that activists and NGOs are working in Turkey to promote same-sex rights issues, it is also important to discuss the levels of cooperation between NGOs within Turkey and the network linkages between local NGOs and activists and international actors (both states and nonstate actors). One advocacy strategy is the ability and willingness of NGOs to work together. Different human rights organizations in Turkey have in fact worked together on many events and points of advocacy. Many are members of coalitions, and they often share ideas, tactics, and other strategies with one another. There are many examples of cooperative behavior amongst LGBTI and other human rights organizations. For example, "Lambdaistanbul and other LGBT organizations in Turkey have formed an LGBT human rights watch platform in late 2006 and have reported and published annual LGBT human rights violations and have sent it to all 550 members of the Turkish parliament" (Lambda Istanbul, 2015). Other examples include collaboration on research (such as shadow reports to international bodies such as the Human Rights Commission) or logistical cooperation for organizing Pride Marches in Turkey. Furthermore, Lambda Istanbul explain on their website that, "[t]ogether with Kaos GL (Ankara), the other main LGBTI group in Turkey, we have worked out our demands on twelve articles of the new Penal Code and presented our suggestions to a member of the Commission of Justice of the Parliament in Ankara, which we also declared through a press conference, broadcast in various Turkish television channels" (Lambda Istanbul, 2015). They have also been active in trying to have "sexual orientation" and "gender identity" language included in national law, something that the AKP-dominated government has thus far refused to do. Again, there are numerous ways that the organizations either directly cooperate or indirectly do so by sharing information and asking each other for advice or other types of support as they work on their respective projects as separate organizations.

However, this is not to suggest that challenges don't exist. One challenge for cooperation within the LGBTI activist movement in Turkey is related to questions of visibility strategy. As Sedef Çakmak explained, there is a division between some who want to be more "mainstream" in Turkish society, and those within the movement who do not want this. Çakmak said, "This is one of the heated debates in the LGBT movement because some people see ... becoming the mainstream as a threat. For me, of course there are threats to becoming mainstream but the benefits [are] much higher than the threats, in my opinion. I mean, that's my opinion, if it's going to prevent hate crime, if it's going to prevent people committing suicide[,] then we must be mainstream. That's how I perceive the whole situation." There is a concern about whether the LGBTI community should be open and willing to work within the political system, with political parties. Çakmak is open to this, as she herself is a public official. However, others are concerned that if they begin tying themselves to political parties that the agenda will not continue to be a diverse one: "[P]eople are just afraid that it will be just like in the [United S]tates, that you will be talking about the gay marriage but you will not be talking about the refugees, you will not be talking about the inmates, you're not even talking about the transgender so people are afraid of that."

In my interviews, I asked several of the activists what sort of cooperation exists between them and other local and/or international human rights activists. The response that I received largely suggests that these different actors are actively working with other LGBTI rights organizations to promote these issues in Turkey. But of course this depends on the type of work on which the different organizations are focused. When the NGOs are concentrating on different tasks, there may be less cooperation and overlap in the work. However, when they are working on similar (or the same) issues, then coordination is not only possible but in many cases actually does happen between these groups. One example of cooperation between NGOs in Turkey is that of SPoD and Lamba Istanbul. Now, since they have different concentrations with regard to the exact type of LGBTI rights activities that they are engaged in, the amount of cooperation will not overlap completely. However, as Hüroğlu of SPoD explains,

[F]or the Pride Week we can collaborate with them. And it was okay, but Pride Week is not just Lambda and it's an independent group, but mostly people from Lambda. For example, for mental health issues we are also in touch with them, they are also working on mental health nowadays. They have their own people training, but ... more students. With KAOS and Pembe Hayat we are collaborating on certain issues.

Kaos GL has also been active in building linkages between them and international actors, whether it is states or other LGBTI and human rights organizations. They have worked with organizations such as Amnesty International, Human Rights Campaign, Human Rights Watch, Freedom House, and Outright Action. One other way that Kaos GL has been working with international actors is with regard to the issue of funding the activities of the organization. Köylü explained that while he would like to get financial support domestically (from the government and nongovernmental actors) for doing important human rights work in Turkey, there is a fear by many private entities to support LGBTI groups. Köylü believes that these individuals worry that if they fund LGBTI groups, there is a worry that "tomorrow one of the AKP people would attack you in a very, very unethical way." Thus, the political costs of being funded are high. Because of this, "unfortunately, more than 90% of our financial national resources are coming from international solidarity."

So, there is a clear linkage between domestic NGOs and international actors. However, Hüroğlu pointed out an interesting fact with regard to the history of cooperation between these different NGOs in Turkey. In years past (Hüroğlu says ten or 15 years ago)

we had a yearly meeting with all the LGBTI organizations in Turkey and back then there was three, four organizations. Nowadays it's like more, and it stopped somehow, and I didn't want it to stop but anyway, I mean the discussions among the organizations sometimes are more personal. But it stopped and we [–] this year we are going to try to start it again. So, LGBTI network [in] Turkey meetings at least once a year at least to discuss the whole movement's priorities. I mean, we are certainly going to do that, but of course there will be a lot to the discussions. We actually wanted to call it a parliament at first. But it can be ambitious to call it like that and not everybody is comfortable with that idea, because ... "parliament"... who is going to talk in the name of the parliament? Will there be such a person, and who, and why? Probably it will stay the network. But if they want, in that meeting it can turn to a parliament. I mean that will be probably, I hope, the basic ritual where the LGBTI organizations can come together and interact, but there are already some other organizations like Pride Week, the Week against Transphobia, KAOS, sex workers, they have their symposium.

He goes on to say that "people come together in certain meetings as well but one has to be more essential." Thus, Hüroğlu believes that reestablishing a yearly meeting between NGOs – alongside any other sorts of meetings that exist throughout the year – would be helpful for the LGBTI rights advocacy taking place in Turkey.

Janset Kalan of Pembe Hayat said that, along with their training sessions, they are also in working on a conference bringing together human rights activists from around the world in Turkey to discuss human rights in general. As Kalan explained, these activists

come together to build up [a] strategic way, a strategic world map and encompass a larger manifestation. We are giving them basic human rights trainings, at first, and then if the activists would like to focus on specific teams of law, we are trying to facilitate it for them, as well. We are also training them in regard to fundraising, and resource management ... project cycles, and how to administer specific project, too, in case they would like to get engaged with the ... largest civil society organizations. They would have to get prestige, or apply for an adjunct position. It doesn't have to be an LGBTI organization, but it could be any subject because most of the activists are also engaging with different levels of activism and with ecologists also and with anti-militarist groups[,] as well as with children rights and refugee rights, so at least ... we can provide them with basic knowledge that they cannot get ... from the education system in Turkey, actually.

Another very interesting issue that Hüroğlu mentioned that was of serious concern to him was what he called the "the potential split between the transgender community and LGB community." He argued that this has happened in Europe, where lesbian, gay, and bisexual rights groups are advocating for LGB issues, and transgender advocacy groups are working for transgender rights, and there is little overlap or multiple rights advocacy structures. For Hüroğlu, it is essential to try to ensure cohesion among all of the rights groups. Some of the issues are agenda-based (LGB groups not working on transgender rights), or, in other cases, it might also be how a group presents itself. For example, Hüroğlu noted that Kaos GL, a very important rights-based group in Ankara, has still not changed the name of their organization to reflect "T" transgender individuals.

He expressed his concern about separation between LGB and transgender rights groups, saying:

I'm afraid that it will be also similar because I don't really want that. But we are not really working on … hindering that. What I see is that transgender people mostly … it's not their priority to have concerns to be together with the LGBs, not politically, not individually. We don't see that because they think they are the victims and they are blaming LGBTI organizations for … selling out their agenda, for getting funds through that, that their problems have become [a] commodity to be sold to funding organizations and that all. And they do not trust LGBTI organizations.

I asked Hüroğlu if the reason that the transgender groups did not trust the lesbian, gay, and bisexual rights groups was because these groups are not adequately representing transgender rights issues. He answered by speaking about the activities that the groups took during the 2015 Pride Parade, saying that the transgender community felt that the rest of the LGBI community was misrepresenting them during the Pride Marches, saying that

the more conservative ones for example, they said … [that for] one day, the gay people … are acting as gender queers, drag queens, whatever, and that appearance does not come close to us and does not represent us. But people think that that's what we are, and the rest of the 364 days, we are on the street, and we are then perceived in a wrong way as acting crazy on the street and looking for sex all the time, which we are not like that. So you are representing us wrong, and you don't care about that, and after that day, you became … you're all normal gender performance, whatever you do and you do not have that problem on the street. That is one of the other factors [that] may go towards the split. I have concerns on that. That's one concern for the moment for me.

A second concern that Hüroğlu has with regard to ensuring that LGBTI advocacy groups and networks are working together, and that the movement as a whole continues to become stronger, has to do with the age of the activists within the LGBTI networks. As Hüroğlu explains,

[M]ost of the people you will meet [are] young. The movement is very young, I mean even younger than it should be. I mean, we start[ed] 12 years ago, but … 90% of the people [are] below 30. And … I am one of the older ones … and that also hinders the movement from becoming more professionalized, more institutionalized and… [to] make [it] stable and consistent work, because young people go back and forth, they study, they write [a] PhD, they go abroad, they find a job, they leave, they quit.

Because of this, he feels that it is essential to find ways to help these young activists not only stay in Istanbul but also to continue working within the advocacy networks and movement.

Interestingly, a related concern is that while the young people he noted want to be a part of the movement, for some, they actually don't want to do it on a full-time basis. But what happens is that if the organizations are unable to bring them in, then the organizations are losing people who are willing to help on some level. It seems that many organizations [whether they are LGBTI, other human rights groups, religious organizations, other political groups, etc.), many of them seem to have these sorts of challenges. On the one hand, groups want people who are committed to the cause. However, if there is little outreach and recruitment, or if other groups have stringent conditions for accepting volunteers, then this can potentially affect overall numbers of activists within organizations.

International Cooperation

While much of the discussion thus far with regard to issues of NGO cooperation has centered on local advocacy networks and their successes, as well as their challenges for interconnected advocacy, there is also a number of academic and policy literatures that concentrate on the role of international transnational human rights advocacy networks (Keck and Sikkink, 1998). In fact, in the case of Turkey, one should not think that the NGOs in Istanbul and Ankara are merely focused on local relationships with other rights NGOs and individual activists. For example, SPoD has within its network various NGOs and state agencies that it cooperates with when working on LGBTI rights. When asking Hüroğlu about whether SPoD works with international NGOs, he replied:

Sure. I mean we are a member of Transgender Europe, IGLYO [The International Lesbian, Gay, Bisexual, Transgender, Queer and Intersex Youth and Student Organization], ILGA-Europe ... We work together with Human Rights Campaign ... Most of the funds we get from the consulates; Dutch Consulate, English Consulate, American Consulate, and [other] consulates because we are in Istanbul, otherwise, embassies, but we have contacts with embassies as well. German ... foundations ... [the] Swedish Consulate of course ... We participate in international meetings as much as we can.

Sedef, Boysan Yakar, Pembe Hayat, and Kaos GL also mentioned that they too worked with state leaders.

Boomerang Pattern

In their seminal work entitled "Activists Beyond Borders," Margaret Keck and Kathryn Sikkink discuss an activist strategy called the "boomerang pattern." Activists within a country are often unable to put pressure on the state to address rights abuses. The leaders and authorities of the state may themselves be the ones committing the human rights abuses. Or, they might show an unwillingness to respond to the rights abuses by others. In these instances, activists may have little success in pressuring their own government. However, what they can do is share the information about the rights abuses with other NGOs and governments elsewhere in the hopes that they can these bodies pressure their own state leaders, as well as other governments and international organizations (such as the United Nations), to put pressure on the first state to address said rights abuses.

Activists in Turkey have used the boomerang pattern, where domestic activists establish and maintain contact with international cooperation with transnational actors. The reason for this has been the reduction of the cost of traveling to and communicating with others internationally (Kollman and Waites, 2009). In the case of Turkey, this was evident as early as 2006. For example, when the government attempted to close Lambda Istanbul, the members of the organization not only attempted to lobby internally in Turkey, but they also shifted their attention to sharing what was happening with international activists, who in turn used their time and resources to help Lambda Istanbul in Turkey. The attention to lobbying really picked up during this time in 2006. As Çakmak (who at the time of this closure case was working on international relations issues) explained, during this period, "when the court case opened up against us[,] it really shocked us and we ... actually started shouting" as they were trying to be heard. Unfortunately, there some who felt that their organization was actually "promoting prostitution because we would be having lots of transgender women meetings in our office, [and] generally most of them are sex workers." So, while the LGBTI human rights movement viewed and continue to "see sex working ... as an employment like any other employment," others did not view it this way. So, while they attempted to set up "a huge campaign," which included "reach[ing] out to [the] national assembly and back," Çakmak admits that while they "were good activists" and "good at explaining ourselves," they were not as effective in "getting into contact with the authorities."

Thus, Çakmak explained that this was a an important moment for their activism, saying:

I always see this experience [as one in which] ... we learned the power of lobbying during that time ... We learned that ... [when] we always have problems with the authorities, within our lives, always have problems with your family or always have problem[s] with your school, you have a problem with the state ... we generally try to stay away from those authority figures. But ... when things get too serious you just have no choice but to ... talk to them [the authorities] ... And this was also what has happened too ... I remember that I was going to Brussels or Stroudsburg ... to meet several parliamentarians, and I was just cursing at myself saying that I cannot reach my own members of the parliament whom I voted for, and now I'm calling the big sisters and brothers outside. So I'm seeing [this] also as ... an ethical problem, to be honest. But then, I realized that is politics ... and I really see that ... we are doing this ... for a good cause, so that's how I justified my actions.

This sort of strategic engagement with the international community – in the form of the boomerang pattern – has not let up. For example, in early 2016, following the continued human rights abuses by the Turkish government against its citizens, many academics, journalists, and other activists have been appealing to the German leadership with the hopes that they will pressure Turkey to stop its abuses (Williamson, 2016).

Kalan of Pembe Hayat also stressed that they would like expand engagement with the international community. Kalan spoke about this relationship, saying:

for about a year now [this interview was conducted in early April 2016], we started this new strategy regarding ... the international level of advocacy, that we are trying to include more local activists from Turkey to directly get engaged with the process because it has been ... such that only ... activists who can speak and communicate in the English language would go to the meetings, the trainings, and also do the advocacy at the international level, and never [bring] back the information to the local activists. There was a disconnection ... So we try to get local activists to be engaged directly in this level, and we also encourage them ... to approach us if they do not have ...

the capacity of English language so we can translate whatever they are, their proposal, their criticism[s] and ... actually facilitate it for them, and they can reach out to the international level. ... we also bring the international arguments in terms to be discussed. We try to make other trans organizations ... and trans activists ... know what kind of arguments and discussions are going on at [the] international and global level, in regards to transgender human rights.

For Pembe Hayat, it is not solely about building international cooperation and linkages with international activists. Rather, they are concentrating on processes that would allow for the exchange of strategies. This information, what actors abroad are doing, is now being received by Turkish rights activists and shared within the organization. New ideas are introduced, discussed, and debated, and then either passed on, altered, or adopted. This is an effective way to grow a movement, as it allows for continued creativity and the fostering (and potential) implementation of new ideas and actions.

Yet, despite the international linkages, and the important function that such a network can do for LGBTI rights advocacy in Turkey, for Köylü, the most important point to keep in mind when networking and working with other human rights organizations is to ensure that the attention continues to be on those who need help and that their voices are included in strategies and activism. It can be a problem when NGOs are not incorporating non-NGO voices into strategy, as Köylü believes it actually "creates an NGO world ... an NGO paradise" where,

because NGOs [are] working with NGOs ... after ... [a while] you know everybody, everybody knows you, and you always hear your [own voices]. You ... [are] always in a kind of comfort zone and its important when you touch an NGO that you haven't touched before, that [it is] an NGO coming from a constituency that you haven't seen before ... But if you are always together in that world, like we did it for the last thirteen years ... [along with project based work], we should communicate with the people from every aspect of the society.

Köylü believed that it was even more important that they should speak with supporters of the AKP, since he believed that "if we don't communicate with them as NGOs, [the] AKP [is] communicating with them" and the people are hearing messages after the AKP translates them."

Thus, Köylü felt strongly that there needs to be an assurance that NGOs are speaking to the public, not soley to each other, and not only in an academic fashion. This includes language in documents that is understandable to nonacademics. Köylü explained that "we should speak with the people and not with human rights terminology[,] only with certain human rights terminology or with society terminology." Asked how organizations can better connect with the people, Köylü responded, "Well, local scale, face to face communication, I would say. Of course, in addition to all other [work]". He also said that even the language should be altered, arguing that

we should start changing our language, we should ... be less academic ... I'm talking about the NGO people, I['m] not talking about the academics, I'm talking about the NGO people ... We should be more practical, we should go and ask people what is their demand or ... how they are, pronouncing their demands. Of course their demands are rights[-]based demands but how we will create that interface between the right holder and the rights[-] based NGO[?] And how we will expand our network among the right holders[?]

So, Köylü's emphasis is to really shift attention more toward those affected in society, speaking in a way that they can related to, and not only dealing with other NGOs that they have known for a long period of time. However, this is not to say that there are no drawbacks to working with international organizations. I discuss this issue, and activist concerns with regard to international partnerships, in the next chapter.

Same-Sex Marriage in Turkey

I previously examined the strategies activists are using in Turkey to advocate for and advance LGBTI rights. However, I wanted to set aside a separate section in this chapter to discuss the issue of same-sex marriage advocacy in the world and as it pertains to Turkey. The issue of same-sex marriage continues to be one of the most discussed LGBTI issues in many "Western" countries. In terms of recent activity on the issue, in 2015, the US Supreme Court offered a ruling that legalized same-sex unions. Then, in Ireland, the issue of same-sex marriage was brought to a national referendum, where the public voted to support the measure. On June 30, 2017, the parliament in Germany also approved same-sex marriage. And as mentioned earlier, a referendum is going to be held in Australia on the issue. In fact, since Denmark's law on same-sex unions in 1989, many additional Western states have implemented a similar policy (Kollman, 2007). The advancements on the issue of same-sex marriage rights in these countries, and the role of transnational advocacy, as well as perceptions of international norms (Kollman, 2007), has not only led to this push for same-sex marriage laws but it has also led some to wonder whether advocating for same-sex marriage in Turkey would also an effective strategy and if it something that could be realized in the country. Given that it has prevailed elsewhere, could it also work in Turkey? To help answer that question, it is important to understand marriage, and also same-sex marriage in the Turkish context.

In September of 2014, two individuals, Ekin Keser and Emrullah Tuzun, wanted to get married in Istanbul. Keser and Tuzun knew that Turkey did not (and still does not) recognize same-sex marriages. As we discussed earlier, the Turkish Constitution does not recognize LGBTI status as a category for protection. Nor does the Turkish Civil Code recognize same-sex marriages (Alkaç, 2014). However, they wanted to get married publicly. Once they made their announcement that they wanted a public wedding to express their love for one another, they were met with harsh criticism from some family members who were uncomfortable with the idea of the two getting married. Nevertheless, they were married in an open ceremony on a ferry in Istanbul in early September 2014 (Alkaç, 2014). But even after the marriage ceremony, the threats continued. These came from family members, as well as from people online. As reports note,

Keser said he was also receiving threats over social media and could not go to the university to attend classes. "I am originally from Antakya. I am accused of giving Antakya a bad name and am getting death threats because of this. My family knew I was gay, but they reacted very angrily to my getting married," said Keser. He said they had gotten married to break down taboos and that now all they wanted was for their families and others to leave them alone. (Idiz, 2014a)

To add to their struggles, the couple was also kicked out of their residence after their landlord got word of their marriage (Alkaç, 2014). Moreover, Emrullah was also fired because of the wedding. He explained that "I used to work as a waiter in Istanbul's Kadıköy district. When the threats increased, my boss learned about the situation and

I was laid off. Ekin is not working, as he is an undergraduate student. I was the only breadwinner, but I lost my job" (Alkaç, 2014).

Because of this, many have felt that it may take years for a government in Turkey to recognize same-sex marriage. For example, human rights lawyer Rozerin Seda Kip has stated that with so much negative conditions facing the LGBTI community, "[t]opics such as gay marriage and child adoption for gays are for the future" (quoted in Idiz, 2014a). Given this position by some in Turkey, and the attention that this issue was receiving elsewhere at the time of the interviews, it was important to see whether the numerous LGBTI activists and organizations in Turkey were advocating for same-sex marriage. As we shall see, many of the responses were quite similar in nature to one another: advocating for same-sex marriage was not their primary agenda issue. Regarding this topic, Sedef Çakmak said that:

the LGBT associations never, ever, ever made the demand on gay marriage-... we are actually quite questioning the whole importance on gay marriage ... because we know that, even in the [United] States ... you're focusing too much on the gay marriage and you're totally forgetting the other parts of the problem and it's not just marriage. And there ... [are] also lots of people who are ... questioning ... marriage as an institution. So ... it ... [has] never ever been a demand of the LGBT movement in Turkey. But, unfortunately, both the government and the people who are not familiar with this issue ... always understand the issue as a demand of gay marriage and I always see this as something tricky because ... as an activist, of course, you cannot say that "no[,] we don't want gay marriage." You cannot say that because there [are] tons of people who wanted to get married and it's also a part of becoming an equal citizen. ... But ... you just try to show them the other way around where you just talk more about the hate crimes; we just talk more about the discrimination.

Çakmak went on to add:

So ... that's the understanding of the people working at the municipality too. They just think, "What does [the] LGBT [community] want? They just want to get married." But it's not something in our hands ... Then you started to talk more about [other issues. For example] ... there are lots of homeless LGBTs. There's lots of LGBTs who are facing violence, so we can give them ... some counseling services or we do have some services for ... the older folks. We could involve the LGBT people for this ... So ... these are the concrete solutions which we came up with, but I realize that it just takes time for people to totally understand the idea.

In another interview in *Research Turkey*, Çakmak, when asked about same-sex marriage in November 2015, responded by saying:

[T]he first question I encounter is the question of gay marriage ... you have to explain patiently, one by one[,] that this issue is not only about marriage. People are repressed by their families, imprisoned at their homes, beaten up on the streets, get murdered, experience mobbing at their workplaces, miss out on their education from the constant humiliation at their schools. What we are talking about is in fact about a group deprived of their social and economic rights. For this to be understood it has to be constantly expressed. (Research Turkey, 2015)

Again, the strategy of same-sex marriage is not one on which activists in Turkey are focusing.

Boysan Yakar made similar arguments, pointing out "We're not asking for marriage ... it's not a preliminary thing. We're asking for equal rights for sure ... I'm not dying to marry with a man like American gays, and I don't want to put all the money on that issue." Yakar spoke about how opponents are framing the issue of LGBTI rights as one of gay marriage, where he felt that "they are putting us in a position against the society, [that] we're just asking for marriage rights. So it's kind of like [a] battlefield right now. When we're asking for social rights, equal rights for example, they are saying ... 'No, they are asking for equal marriage rights.' So we are not asking for that privilege to marry." Again, he indeed did believe that the government was framing LGBTI rights as marriage rights.

This position seems to be in line with what other activists and NGOs felt. Regarding the amount of attention the issue of same-sex marriage gets as a strategy within LGBTI human rights organizations, Cihan Hüroğlu of SPoD pointed out that they themselves do little with regards to same-sex marriage issues in the country. There are different reasons for this. For one, there are many within Turkish society that equate the LGBTI rights movement with the right to get married, which takes attention away from the other problems facing the community. As Hüroğlu said,

[I]f you talk about gay rights in Turkey, that will be one of the first speculations people will think, or first they ask ... "[D]o you really want to have marriage" ... What we are trying to say is that that is not really our primary goal, but yes indeed, we are for marriage rights. Not only because we want to marry, well not necessarily [because] we want to have [a] ceremony ... it's because of the social rights and benefits.

So, same-sex marriage is just one right within a series of human rights for which the human rights organizations are fighting.

Yet, time and time again, political opponents of LGBTI rights have continued to try to frame the LGBTI activism as one that is solely centered on same-sex marriage. This was happening when activists were trying to push for sexual minority rights to be recognized in the Constitution (in 2012); some of the political leaders kept referring the movement back to one of marriage in attempts to scare people. As Hüroğlu explains, when they were advocating for the inclusion of language viewing sexual orientation as a specific group that deserves equal rights, "all the politicians who actually are conservative were saying, 'we shouldn't allow gay marriages and that will happen, and we are defending our species, and we don't want to get it extinct because of gay marriage.'" He went on to say that other than a short press release on how marriage can be helpful to LGBTI individuals during the 2012 constitutional amendment process, there was little talk about the topic from SPoD. And since that release, Horuglu added, "[W]e didn't talk about marriage at all, we had three additional elections after that, local elections, presidential elections, and then, general elections. ... Elections ... [during] all of [those periods], we were talking about discrimination," and not the issue of same-sex rights.

For example, rather than focus on same sex marriage, SPoD's attention was on training sessions for social workers and other professionals, along with advocacy of positive rights for the LGBTI community. It is also for this reason that groups like SPoD and Pembe Hayat are not spending time on same-sex marriage, but are instead focusing on other advocacy issues. Hüroğlu explains that same-sex marriage is not at the forefront of rights advocacy, and it has to do with what was mentioned earlier: in Turkey, the LGBTI community face death, other violence, economic discrimination, etc. As Hüroğlu notes, "[T]he social benefits is not the most important agenda right now. There are hate crimes, murders, discrimination at work, discrimination in health services, and all kinds of problems in the trans process, and health issues." He went on to say that initially, activists in Turkey believed that they could focus on all of these issues, along with same-sex marriage. However, Hüroğlu believes that before working on same-sex marriage, "discrimination has to be abolished. You have to have some sort of safeguards in the law. That first, and then, you can talk about some additional ... benefits, social benefits. And then, to conceptualize all the benefits, you can [maybe] talk ... [about] marriage rights; there's obviously some time for that."

Janset Kalan of Pembe Hayat made similar comments. When asked if Pembe Hayat advocates same-sex marriage as a strategy, Kalan responded by saying "no," because

it is not in our agenda because there are much more important problems, issues, and human rights violations that we need to take care of, so, the same sex-marriage thing ... is in an argument that we discuss inside our LGBT community and also within our own lives, but turning it into a campaign or discussing it with public authorities or political figures, it doesn't happen, because it is only counter-productive for us.

In a follow-up regarding why this strategy might be viewed as counter-productive, Kalan's responded by saying that

the first reason is that people are not well informed about LGBTI identities ... So let's say there are like 80 million people living in Turkey and like 10–15% of them actually know what LGBTI stands for. What we try to do is actually get our own identities recognized, that we exist, and maybe in the future, if we [succeed] ... then the same-sex marriage argument could turn into a campaign, I don't know. I am not sure if I will see those days or not.

Murat Köylü stated that Kaos GL's position was also quite similar to the comments made by the other activists, saying that for his organization, same-sex marriage not a strategy being pushed. It is not that Köylü didn't want same-sex marriage in Turkey, but right now, "sexual orientation and gender identity is not even included in the hate crimes legislation among discrimination legislation." So, being unable to include "sexual orientation and gender identity in the ... very fundamental human rights legislation or policies" in Turkey means same-sex marriage is not something at the forefront of activism. Like other activists, he also believed that "conservative and especially AKP leaders started to use it as a anti-propaganda for any kind of LGBTI rights ... They say that all the time in discrimination law, all the time in the constitution, and all the time in the hate crime legislation ... sexual orientation [will be] a recognized category if people end up in the marriage, they ... use it to scare their constituency."

There are a few things taking place here. For one, needs such as physical safety, employment, and health services are taking priority for activists. But along with this, there is not only an authoritarian slide in Turkey (which is clearly in opposition to international norms of just governance) but the current government is also unwilling to recognize LGBTI rights as an accepted international norm, an important variable in the literature as to whether same-sex unions are protected in a state (Kollman, 2007). With the continued oppression of LGBTI rights by the state, their focus on fighting the Islamic State and Kurdish forces, and a situation where socioeconomic LGBTI rights are not protected, the likelihood of same-sex unions in Turkey may remain out of reach for the time being. So, while it is certainly a possibility that this issue could be one that will be advocated for in Turkey, there seems to be a general consensus that there are other issues that are deserving of more time, attention, and resources.

Conclusion

LGBTI activists have taken a number of approaches in their fight for same-sex rights in Turkey. For many, they have worked to increase the visibility of the LGBTI community, believing that with greater visibility will come more acceptance of the community in Turkey. It is for this reason, in part, why events like the LGBTI Pride March are so important. As Gorkem Ulumeric, one of the representatives of the Istanbul Pride Week group, said, "LGBT people go through different unfair treatments in various areas of their daily lives, such as work, health, education and even life itself. Therefore, it is important for us to express ourselves on one day in a year at the centre of the city" (Uras, 2016). They also put out a petition calling for a safe Pride March, one that is protected by Turkish authorities. Pearce (2014b), citing Enguix (2009) and Johnston (2005), notes the importance of why people are involved in Pride Marches, arguing "that Pride events help the LGBT community as it carves out "a space for vindication, [visibility], and commemoration": victims of homophobic violence were recalled and honored in Istanbul, for example. And, as Johnston (2005) has suggested, such events also help the community of sexual minorities to claim access to heteronormative public space physically, at least momentarily."

Overall, for those who have adopted this strategy of visibility politics, they have focused on letting Turkey know about the LGBTI community, whether it is through the creation of a magazine, reporting on the community through traditional media or "new" media that includes social media, or through related projects. However, others have preferred to focus on elections as an effective strategy for improving the conditions of the LGBTI community. For those who work through elections, they have focused on political candidacies – namely LGBTI members running for office or finding support amongst non-LGBTI political candidates or current political officials.

The literature seems to support this position. Visibility of LGBTI individuals will help move the country towards increased acceptance. As Reynolds (2013) writes: "Public acceptance of LGBT people is a predictor of progressive law. At first blush this finding is unsurprising. But it does indicate that politicians and governments have been responding to public opinion, and it suggests that, if the general public becomes more supportive of sexual orientation equality, then governments may respond with broader laws accepting same-sex marriage, adoption and legal protections" (26). Again, given the findings related to my fieldwork, activists in Turkey are not centering their efforts on same-sex marriage or on adoption. They believe that other rights advocacy (such as the protection from being injured or murdered, fair housing, etc.) is more pressing. But, increased visibility, whether in the media or through electoral candidates and campaigns, can have a variety of positive effects on Turkish society. Right now the AKP has done little to protect the rights of the LGBTI community. But with increased civil society pressure (which could come from a continued shift in attitudes toward the LGBTI community because of the visibility approaches), this could eventually lead to government shifts in positions toward LGBTI rights.

Some groups still have had a more evolutionary position with regard to the sorts of activist strategies that they have adopted. For example, for a group such as SPoD, they began with an emphasis on visibility, as well as dissemination of knowledge (such as publicizing rights abuses against the LGBTI community), but then shifted their strategies to also include elections. As Erdal Partog stated,

Why shouldn't we use the right to political representation and participation, which are the most important aspects of democracy? Why not have our voices be heard more strongly through the parliament's podium and through political parties? Through this campaign, we want to make LGBTIs existence more visible in the general elections. To deepen democracy, we aim to ensure and strengthen access to justice for LGBTIs in representation and participation. (LGBTI News Turkey, 2015b)

So, sometimes the notion of visibility can be the driving factor, it but can manifest itself through either media, or through the backing of LGBT candidates. For all that the recent elections have been about (namely, the increased power of Erdoğan and the AKP), people have been talking about the elections with regard to the LGBTI candidates that were running, which is a success as far as activists are concerned. In addition, the fact that twenty-two officials who support LGBTI rights were elected is seen as another victory, particularly given all that those who oppose LGBTI rights did in attempts to reduce the support of LGBTI groups and LGBTI-friendly candidates. As Volkan Yilmaz of SpoD explains, "Despite former Prime Minister Davutoglu and current President Erdoğan's public statements against the involvement of LGBTI organizations in the election campaign, including the candidacy of Baris Sulu, a LGBTI rights activist from the Peoples' Democratic Party (HDP), the election results proved that homophobic and transphobic statements do not have any negative impacts on the voting behavior of the constituents" (IGLHRC, 2015). Yilmaz went on to add that "Thanks to the 'LGBTI in the Parliament' campaign as well as the efforts of LGBTI rights activists in different political parties, we have now at least 22 MPs in the new Parliament who have declared their commitment to LGBTI rights" (IGLHRC, 2015).

Overall, there seems to be an underlying theme that Turkish society should not only know that LGBTI individuals are also members of society, and that they have a voice, but also that there is no need for fear or hate with regard to the LGBTI community. Sulu spoke on this issue, when asked about the Kurdish peace process, relating it to the LGBTI situation:

There are groups that society needs to make peace with. Society needs to make peace with the LGBTI people as well. We need to be rid of discourses we have been hearing so far that say "This is a 99% Muslim country, society has general rules, general morality," and so on. LGBTI people are oppressed within the heterosexist system, a system where heterosexuality is imposed and we need to make peace with these individuals. We should be reading the peace resolution process in this light. Just as Turkey as a society needs to make peace with Kurdish people, they need to make peace with LGBTI people. We can read "peace" in these terms in the context of the peace resolution process.

Ali Erol from Kaos GL Association has a saying ... "End the undeclared war on the LGBT!" Society must make peace with us, too. Because we, too, live in this society. We walk past you when you were walking, our shoulders brush, we are that close. When you take public transportation, perhaps that person sitting next to you is gay. You are never aware of this. Because you never see us, hear us, and you act as though we do not exist, we have problems. Stop this undeclared war. (Akpinar, 2015a)

Thus, issues of intersectionality are right there within the LGBTI struggle. NGOs and other activists continue to understand and fight for the human rights of everyone, not just LGBTI people.

8 | *Challenges Facing the LGBTI Movement in Turkey*

What we do now is to create excess opportunities to [access] already existing state social services and psychosocial support mechanisms where we can . . . [have] authorities to include or to provide an alternative way to help, support and access . . . the transgender applicants.

Janset Kalan

Despite all of the progress that these LGBTI rights activists and organizations have made in Turkey, there are still a number of challenges that they continue to face. The difficulties range from issues of funding to government oppression, threats of terrorism, and other forms of physical violence. In this chapter, I shall lay out the various challenges that activists raised that make it difficult to fully realize human rights for all people in Turkey. As important as it is to speak about the numerous successes of LGBTI activism in Turkey, it is also necessary to understand any difficulties that exist within the movement. This can help to not only learn from mistakes but also in raising additional awareness to challenges to be remedied. Below are some of the main issues with which activists are dealing.

Funding

A lack of funding is one of the most noted roadblocks for human rights activism in Turkey, it and continues to limit NGO programming and services. Looking at the various challenges the different activists brought up, NGO leaders were all in rather strong agreement about financial limitations and the implications of this on their work. For example, Hüroğlu of SPoD iterated that funding was indeed the greatest challenge for the organization. Because of this, I asked him if the organization tries to fundraise, to which he replied:

[W]e are applying for various grants. We are trying to find new strategies for our members and we are trying to keep in touch with our members . . . And

189

we have, from time to time ... our social events. We are not that professional, and ... I'm not sure how professional we want to be ... on fundraising because it can get ugly ... We are thinking of new methodology. For
example, this network of mental health experts can actually turn [on] itself.
The trainings are not free, so people really want to pay to get that. So we can
pay all the experts taking part in it as well. And all the experts are doing these
voluntary counseling sessions[,] [and] they ... [also get paid], [the money]
which can derive from organizational ... and financial resources ... So first
of all I'm trying to create sustainability in of these things so whatever you do
[is to] try to make it sustainable.

Hüroğlu added that

[i]f you want to start with something new, if you want to have a place with
around 400 Turkish lira [rent] per month, it is hard to sustain that. And we
have trained professionals. To pay professionals, it is not cheap. Lambda
[Istanbul] for example, does not have any [professionals] so they have more
money to pay for the rent so they can sustain a bigger place, but we think
also that professionals are most important.

He said that SPoD would like to be more active in fundraising, but the
problem that they face is that a small number of people work within
the organization, and because of this, "there is not enough professional
staff [that] would prepare the [grant] applications."

For SPoD, the lack of funding has not only hurt their ability to do
more work on existing strands of advocacy, but it also made it difficult
to expand to other LGBTI rights-based issues. Hüroğlu explained that
additional funding would allow them to do much more work for the
transgender community in Turkey. However, the limited staff hinders
their ability to improve their capacity for expanding work on transgender rights. As he noted:

We have two people as staff, transgender people, in our association. And one
of them has also in this campaign [these] legal cases and they are working
very [well] to create ... contacts with the community. But, for example, they
cannot prepare an application in English. So ... you need to keep the
balance ... you don't have enough resources, to have many people ... At
the end, you have one or two people that can create such an application.

Thus, without having people on the staff who can write grant applications in English, the chances of SPoD getting funding in order to
expand their work on transgender rights will continue to be unlikely.
For SPoD, they are so underfunded that the majority of their staff are

volunteers, and because of this, Hüroğlu says that they may not have the experience that a full-time employee may have.

This issue of funding also came up in my conversation with Sedef Çakmak, who also has ties to SPoD. Çakmak said,

[W]e don't have money and there are generally ... more volunteers at the associations than professionals workers ... In SPoD we are like, let's say 35 people, but only 3 of th[ese] 35 people [are] ... professional[s]. [T]he others are ... volunteers and you cannot see the difference between [the] voluntary person and the professional person. So, in that respect we also have too much [of a] problem funding our own organizations or funding our own activities because, in some ways, we are also ... doing some services which should be done by the states ... We are arranging lawyers to attend to cases or to coun[se]l when someone is taken under custody and cannot do this on a voluntary basis ... we are offering psychiatric consultation but you cannot do this for the extremely poor person. Yes, we try to do it for free but then it is very hard to sustain all of these services too.

It should also be noted that the funding limitations are not limited to NGOs but also individuals who are looking to run as political candidates. Çakmak was one such candidate, and she talked about the difficulty of running without large amounts of money, explaining that individuals such as herself and Boysan Yakar were trying to run a campaign in such a situation.

The same funding issues have also been an issue for Pembe Hayat. The organization knows that that the Turkish government is not living up to its responsibilities, but, as Kalan explained,

[W]e are considered as a small organization and with our limited capacity and our resources, it becomes very difficult for us to provide direct social services to the applicants. What we do now is to create excess opportunities to [access] already existing state social services and to psychosocial support mechanisms where we can ... [have] authorities to include or to provide an alternative way to help support and access ... the transgender applicants.

Even when the state is providing some resources, there are always additional roadblocks for the transgender community. As Kalan noted, there are cases when the organization will apply for someone to get help (at shelters or violence prevention centers), and there will be promises made by the state, but these are just that: promises.[1] Thus, it becomes clear that for organizations such as Pembe Hayat, the necessary funding would go a long way to provide much-needed resources for transgendered individuals in Turkey.

The issue of funding is also a primary problem for Renay's *GZone Magazine*. Despite the importance of the magazine with regard to raising awareness on LGBTI issues, Renay and his team have had some trouble funding the magazine due to low advertising because of what many believe was a reluctance by a number of businesses to promote their company in the gay lifestyle magazine, even if the company itself catered to the LGBTI community. However, after the difficulty in finding initial financial support for the magazine, Sean Howell, the founder of the US-based-company Hornet stepped up and offered to help with printing and distribution costs (Feldman, 2014). Renay saw this as very beneficial for the magazine, saying that "now we are reaching out [to] like 300,000 people or more with Hornet app," and that the app is very useful in promoting the magazine. Renay realizes the importance of a platform on which Turkish citizens can not only read and learn about the LGBTI community but also a place where connections can take place (Feldman, 2014).

However, despite the early funding by Howell, the issue of funding continues to be an ongoing challenge. Again, Renay explained that their biggest challenge is finding companies who are willing advertise on the magazine's website. In my first interview with him, he said as much. In my follow up in late July 2015, he said that they are unable to physically print issues of the magazine on account of a lack of funds. However, he went on to say,

To be printed is not a big goal for us because we are reaching many people from here. Even if we are only printed we won't be reaching this crowd[;] you know about this. But it's maybe [a] matter of honor with us to be printed. For example in the Sezen Aksu issue, people said that you must print it and then ... we said we are a digital magazine and we don't do it[,] then they did it.

Because of the difficulties of paying for parts of the magazine (especially if they wanted to make a print version), Renay went on to say that their

goal is also getting much more ads. We don't have any ads or we don't have any financial support ... By all these eleven issues we did it ourselves. Only we have [some] supporting us through app sites[,] then we have partners that are publishing the app, publishing the magazine every month, for free. And also Hornet is supporting us, for free. They are sending a message for us. But, other than that, we don't have any financial support [besides one gym/fitness company].

Renay spoke about how he and his team have tried to increase the magazine's exposure to companies who he would hope would be willing to advertise in the magazine. He said that the magazine attempts "to be more active on gay marketing with the brands," and that they tell clothing companies, for example, that they would be able to market to those who are LGBTI in the country. They try to convince companies to "rethink ... [their] brand strategy" and work to advertise to the LGBTI community. Renay went on to say in a later interview that there are some brands in Turkey backing LGBTI rights but that the magazine volunteers don't have the time to reach out to speak with these companies due to the time and commitment it takes to run the web portal and because it is so important to publish the stories on time. Furthermore, the lack of funding (and time) can even affect the overall magazine. For example, Renay explained that their photo shoots for the magazine are limited to the cover story, and even that takes time and resources (such as money and the need for equipment).

Challenges with Cooperation: International Linkages

Along with the difficulty in securing funds, another challenge facing some of the activists and LGBTI rights-based organizations in Turkey has to do with cooperation with other nongovernmental organizations. Earlier in the book, I spoke about some of the ways that organizations in Turkey are working together to advocate LGBTI rights. Yet despite the various forms of success that network linkages have brought for LGBTI rights in Turkey, it also seems that there have been times where working with others internally, as well as outside of Turkey, has led to challenges, particularly with regard to strategy, influence over policy, and disagreements on prioritization of issues on which to work.

Regarding the question of whether there were any challenges in international cooperation with other activists, Çakmak spoke about the care that domestic activists have taken to ensure that international organizations do not dominate the LGBTI agenda within Turkey, saying that the only attitude which we never allowed is that some of the international organizations try to be bossy ... This is a huge no-no in the non-hierarchical environment. This was one of the things that we fought in the past ... [for example] ... [in] 2004 we would ... [have] lots of [contact] with [NGOs] ... from various countries and especially these big ... wide gay men organizations, we generally question[ed] them a lot ... But now ... with many organizations we come to the point that they ... recognize us and ... they just say that ["]we just want to be supportive so tell us what you need,["] etcetera. So, I mean ... now I would say that we are on extremely good terms but ... in 2004 and 2006 we would be having lots of fights.

To Çakmak, these arguments were due to how the international actors were framing what they perceived to be the situation in Turkey. Çakmak explained what was happening, saying:

[F]or example ... I would be meeting lots of journalists or people from other organizations, again in 2004 or [2005], [2006], and they would be asking m,e "[I]s it hard to be a gay women in a Islamic world,". .. and then I would be thinking, here I am an atheist, I grew up in an extremely secular family ... I mean the only religion lesson I took was when I was in high school ... no one even cares about it ... So, I mean, if you ask me religion has no place in my life[,] so when you ask me like that[,] "Islamic world[,]" I will be like ... what Islamic world are you talking about...? Or, for example, when you look at ... all the press releases, you ... [see] the LGBT movement in Turkey, we are highly secular, actually. We just talk about equal rights, social rights, economic rights, we would be always be referring to the rule of law ... We would ... [state] that we ... keep the same distance from all kinds of religion.

So, while many of the activists do not focus on religion as part of their message when advocating for LGBTI rights, she also saw that some from the outside solely wanted to frame the issue merely as one of religion, when, in reality, it is obviously much more than that. We saw this attention to culture over politics in the lead-up to the US intervention in Afghanistan, when arguments for involvement were not based on political conditions but rather on culture and "saving Muslim women" (Lughod, 2002) when the government showed little in the way of actually working to provide women's rights before 2001. In fact, there has been a large debate amongst scholars as to the interests, motivations, and agendas of Western organizations in general, and specifically on the question of LGBT rights (see Massad, 2002 and Schmitt, 2013 for more on this matter).

This concern that the LGBTI rights movement is one largely set by European actors and language was something also expressed by Kalan of Pembe Hayat. As I discussed earlier, the organization has many linkages with international NGOs and international organizations in Europe. Kalan spoke about the importance of having Turkish NGOs shape the discourse. Yet, Kalan felt that "this queer language and queer activism at the global level has been dominated by Anglo-Saxon language[,] which is very European dominated[,] which most of the times doesn't reflect on the language and on the criticisms of the countries, which [don't] ... speak a European language ... So we try to criticize their work." Also, because the "European Union doesn't have [a] direct effect ... on the developments...[in Turkey]," Pembe Hayat's work has also been urging organizations such as Transgender Europe "to include [a] UN level of advocacy and [a] Counsel of Europe level of advocacy because these are more relevant to Turkish cases."

One other challenge when working with international NGOs on LGBTI rights has been choosing the level of priority for advocating a particular LGBTI issue. This can be seen when looking at the question of depathologization of transgender individuals. Pathologization is the idea that something is categorized as a disease in the medical community. Many European LGBTI organizations, such as Global Action for Transgender and Global Action for Trans Equality (GATE) have been advocating for a transgender depathologization campaign. Kalan said that this topic of "depathologization of transgender identities itself is ... a very problematic discussion here in Turkey," the reason being that

[b]ecause the only access to the healthcare services and to the equal legal services in Turkey for transgendered people [is] usually or most of the times ... during the transition processes. There's a law[,] which is defined in terms of sexuality and in terms of transgendered, legally and medically in Turkey since 1987, and although it is very problematic, it is the only access opportunity. And ... the access opportunity itself is created on the [basis] ... of ICD – International Classification of Diseases, which is classifying transgendered identities under the section of psychological and behavioral disorders.

Yet, as Kalan noted in one of our interviews,

The global network which is working on the issue is discussing ... the issue as [a] separate section, separate title under the ICD to exclude transgendered identities, to actually get transgendered identities from behavioral and psychological disorders to a different, a new chapter, which is called sexual health ... [While] this is something that we[']re encouraging, and on some level of supporting ... departmentalization itself per [se] could create obstacles, a lot of problems for countries like Turkey.

Again, the reason that Kalan believes that this could cause some problems is that in Turkey, "the state provides some sort of social security and funding for gender transition processes as well as ... social services on the basis of pathologization." So, while it is good to recategorize transgendered individuals as not having psychological and behavioral disorders (since of course it is none of those things), if this happens in Turkey, then any financial support a person might have gotten to undergo a gender transition might be in jeopardy. Thus, Kalan noted that because of this, there have been "some discussion[s] going on between [those in Turkey] and the international community." Again, while there is an understanding and agreement with European transgender advocacy organizations that it is not a disease to be transgendered, there is a concern that this will close one of the few opportunities for transgendered individuals to have access to doctors. Thus, Kalan wants to have Pembe Hayat be able to state their position to the international community of activists, and not only explain their stance, but also to explain "why we cannot get direct[ly] involved with the campaign itself."

Additional Concerns

Another concern that activists brought up as it pertains to cooperation is the ability to successfully keep all LGBTI activists together, working on common issues together in Turkey. This was a particular issue when discussing lesbian, gay, bisexual, intersex, and transgender rights. Historically in Turkey, many of the early LGBTI rights organizations were working on gay, lesbian, bisexual, and transgender rights; there was no division on these issues (there exist cases in other parts of the world where LGBTI rights were not always inclusive of everyone) (Taylor, Lewis, Jacobmeier, and DiSarro, 2012). As Çakmak points out, Lambda International in the 2000s was very diverse, with different gendered and also transgendered individuals within the organization. Speaking on this, Çakmak says that

[t]hat's one of the things which I really like about Turkey, it was never LGB and T, it was always LGBT together. So in that respect, I really ... see the differences in Turkey. In some ways ... the LGBT movement here in Turkey is more progressive than the one in the Netherlands or even one in the States in some ways ... And as I said ... there were lots of women, gay and transgender, women and at that time in 2004 we were getting ready to ... conduct a survey with ... the gay people ... then two years later, we conducted another survey ... for the transgender women."[2]

The work on all LGBTI issues has continued with human rights organizations in Turkey. However, there was a concern by Cihan Hüroğlu about what the future might look like between LGBI organizations and primarily transgender organizations. For Hüroğlu, the reason has to do with feelings as it pertains to transgender rights in all organizations. There are some within the transgender community that feel that LGBTI organizations are not giving as much specific attention to transgender rights, and that, in turn, this might cause a split among activists. He stressed the importance of keeping the LGBTI together to fight for these issues as one.

One of the other continued threats facing the LGBTI community is the resistance posed by the AKP-led government and the police. While an ongoing concern, this became quite clearer during the police brutality during the 2015 Pride March in Istanbul. Again, it was here that authorities used force to disperse individuals from marching. It would be interesting to examine whether the different NGO strategies would be altered following the events that transpired during the Pride March. I wanted to know if such public and violent events alter the strategies employed by these rights-based organizations, and if they themselves felt concerned about the future of LGBTI rights, given the way the police was willing to use force against marchers.

The response was not unanimous; different activists had various viewpoints on the effects of the police violence during the 2015 march. Regarding whether the police actions during the 2015 Pride March would have an effect on how the LGBTI rights movement's strategies and tactics would proceed in the next year, Çakmak responded that

[p]robably we will take more precaution in the pride parade next year ... I also have several strategies in my mind in order to make it more secure and we definitely need to learn more about the security of the activists. There are

various organizations working on this issue in Europe or in the States but it is ... unfortunately, we're just too daredevil to think about our own security or we have other mechanisms.

For Çakmak, the concern was not just the police but also political parties that she felt the LGBTI community does not have strong ties with, which could further hurt the cause. For example, Çakmak said,

I am so worried but I will be relieved if the coalition will be made between AKP and CHP. I will be even more worried [if] it is between MHP [Nationalist Movement Party] and AKP because those are the two parties which we, the LGBT movement, has no contact [with] whatsoever. And those are the two parties ... even though we have some individual contacts from, one or two MPs, they would be saying that, they say to us that they cannot say this openly because it's not ... party politics, etcetera. So, a coalition which does not get into contact with LGBT movement, that scares me ... You can wait for the next election to wait for the government to change in order to push more legislative measurements. But it is ... fearful that they will decide to pursue a more aggressive strategy towards the LGBTs like in Russia or like in many African countries.

Çakmak said that the call for the LGBTI-only prison is one sign of the deteriorating conditions, and he is worried that this could then lead to targeting sex workers. Çakmak spoke of the state, saying there is a "lack of trust [of] our government ... that there is no guarantee that they will not pursue a more aggressive strategy".

When I asked Yakar whether the police actions against Pride marchers in 2015 affected the way that he and the mayor were approaching LGBTI issues, Yakar replied: "Not really actually. [At] the local level we are supported. In the party politics, we are supported as well. So all the things we are doing [are] ... kind of protected by CHP. So if they say [to] us don't do it openly, do it discretely, we will keep on going this way." And he went on to say that despite attempts by some within the government to argue that the march should be stopped because of Ramadan, "[y]ou cannot stop anything because [of] Ramadan in Turkey. So a huge case is going to happen on it, I'm sure about that. And we are going to win it somehow." Yakar even discussed the possibility of using the court system to hold authorities responsible for their actions during the 2015 Pride March. On this issue, he said that they are considering other approaches as well.

Yakar even thought that, in a way, what the police did was helpful and could actually help mobilize more people to become LGBTI activists. He explained that the government would always use human rights rhetoric when dealing with other countries and international organizations. However, following the use of violence, the government could no longer hide behind words: "[T]he world learned how brutal they are." So while Yakar was understandably not happy with what the government did, he explained that the LGBTI community was

the very last democratic group who has the chance to do whatever on the streets as a political thing. So they stopped us as well. So it was important because we're not the only one who is banned[;] with us, tons of people from democratic groups ... were coming to th[e] streets ... So it was important they banned all of them again. So ... I think from the other perspectives, it seems like it's not the only war of LGBTIs right now, [but] it's the war of everybody.

The false image of Turkish democracy was now exposed. This has led various civil society groups to work together in Turkey, since the government is going after not only LGBTI individuals but also those advocating democracy, equal gender rights, ethnic minority rights, etc.

Janset Kalan also discussed whether the increased level of government and police violence changes the strategy employed by Pembe Hayat, saying that

we are still continuing with our existing strategies, trying to formulate them in a better way, [a] more progressive way. And we are trying to focus on more how to engage with the state authorities and the bureaucrats. This is something new for [the] LGBTI movement in Turkey. We are trying to build solidarity with a couple of MPs in the parliament and make them bring out ... our voices in the parliament on the parliament agenda ... and other new strategies ... This is something which we as activists and as [a] movement feel is going backwards actually.

Kalan pointed out that many of the conversations center not on a variety of LGBTI issues but mostly about security issues during the marches, that this

has become almost like the only agenda that they're discussing when it comes to any parades, [and the] LGBTI community in Turkey. And this is something demotivating actually, but I think that most of the activists as well as the communities itself are fearless, and they build the strategies of including more international participation, more MP participation, more institutional participation in the parades, so they can decrease the risk of violence from the police officers in case of ... rejection from the governor of the city.

When asked about any other big challenge (or challenges) that the organization faces in their work, Kalan replied that state violence in areas such as southeast Turkey against the Kurdish minority actually has a great negative effect on transgender rights in the country, stating that

the biggest challenge right now is the ... increasing state violence against [the] Kurdish population in country, as well as with the ... Syrian crisis, because these two things are directly reflecting on the everyday life in [the] trans community in Turkey. I can say that since [the] 7th of June general elections [2016] ... until the first of November general elections ... [there have] probably been more than ... eighty, eighty to one hundred attacks on trans people in the streets. And ... just in [the] last two weeks, there ha[ve] been two trans women murdered. And I think that the social psychology of this increasing state violence as well as trends... [in] society ... are increasing the hatred and violence attacks from the society as well from the law enforcement agencies towards trans community ... They see trans people ... [and] especially trans women, as ... open targets, easy to reach. And if ... the perpetrators just attack or... commit any type of crimes, or they murder a trans person, they know that they will not be punished properly.

Kalan added:

There is ... impunity in the legal system, in the justice system, especially for the law enforcement agencies, for the police officers. There is impunity in general when it comes to trans issues[;] if the victim is a trans person it becomes even doubled so it becomes a very difficult process of a court case for LGBTI organizations[,] for trans organizations to follow and make some sort of pressure on the judges to give a proper decision, proper court verdict, which will be matching with the crime itself. But it doesn't happen most of the times, so I think that [at] the psychosocial level the Turkish society itself is full of hate, full of violence right now, and it's reflecting on us, if it's reflecting on women, it is reflecting on children. There's an increase of hate crimes. There's increase of rapes, and there's increase of murders right now. I think this is the biggest challenge [to] us right now. Because, when you deal with the violence it becomes less probable for you to deal, for you, as an organization, to focus on advocacy [at] both national or international level [s]. So [this] attracts some disappointment and some reactions from the community because they say the violence should be your only priority right now, you should only work on that and if you're ... not working enough to change this current situation, if you're powerless, then you're nothing, you're doing nothing.

So, while some might tend to think of matters such as the Kurdish conflict as completely separate issues from LGBTI rights, this is not the case. The more the government abuses citizens in the country, whether the Kurds, journalists, political dissidents, or others, the more a culture of impunity that exists, which makes it even harder to hold the state accountable for their unwillingness to support transgender rights. The state has shown its willingness to go after ethnic minorities, journalists, and to ignore abuses against the transgender community. If people see this, they will know that committing a crime against someone who is transgendered is unlikely to get them into serious trouble; it is rare that stiff penalties are handed out, which leads to further fear within the transgender community.

As Kalan added,

[T]he state itself is encouraging all [this] violence ... in the society. They're actually benefitting from it, so when there is chaos, when there is pressure in the society, on the society[,] and there is fear in the society, it is easy to manage. It's easy to administer. [The state is] ... also encouraging all the negative attitudes and negative policies, [and] sometimes they are making it publicly. Sometimes they are making it indirectly, not publicly, and then they are benefitting from it. And ... impunities of police officers inside Turkey itself is also, of course, another point which we need to consider because this attack on the pride parade in Istanbul this year by police officers where they used extreme violence and injured, wounded, several people, several protest-ers there, and all the LGTBI organizations went to court and applied for courts to take up this case, but [the] court refused it very recently ... [this] shows the level ... of understanding from the state, from the justice system from the government, also.

Again, it is quite evident that the state's attitude of indifference and negativity has created and fostered a culture of violence against the transgender community.

Given the hostilities between activists and police – especially since the 2013 Gezi Park protests, the 2015 police crackdown of Pride marchers, the breakup of the transgender and Pride marches in 2016, and the police actions during the 2017 march – it is interesting to see if there is any possibility of police and rights-based organizations working together to better understand one another. Following the discussion about increased state and police violence in Turkey, when asked whether they have considered dialoguing with police officers, Kalan replied:

[T]hat's a good question. We are not working with police. This is something very difficult I think, something they refuse. But what we do from time to time, most of the time informally[, is] we come together and discuss ... the issues and ask them questions and give some recommendations so they can at least behave like ... human[s]. But this year [2016] ... recently a couple of LGBTI organizations started negotiating with some departments of the police department such as a human right departments ... under the section of the international relations department. I don't know why they did that in the international relations department, but they think at this point something alien to the policy work they put it there and we had a meeting with OSCE [Organization for Security and Co-operation in Europe] ... it was about ... the possibility of OSCE giving ... hate crimes and hate speech training to ... the police academy in Turkey. And they wanted to meet with us previously and to ... discuss some of the issues and in order to discuss how to build a ... proper curriculum.

Kalan went on to add that there were negotiations also taking place "within [groups like] the police academy and [with the] minister of interior" on the matter. As I have written in the conclusion of the book, there is a lot of potential for improved relations, especially if police are open-minded and willing to speak with human rights organizations and open to hearing all of the challenges that the LGBTI community faces. But of course this is difficult, especially when the police culture in Turkey has been discriminatory towards members of the LGBTI (and especially transgender) community.

The Threat of Terrorism and LGBTI Rights

The threat of terrorism has been one that has continued to worry the LGBTI community in Turkey (and elsewhere in the world, for that matter). A number of my interviews occurred just days after the terror attacks that occurred on July 20, 2015, in Suruç, a Turkish town near the border with Syria, where thirty-three people were killed and many more injured. Sadly, Turkey has witnessed many more acts of terror since July 2015. This led many of the activists to say that the situation in Turkey was dire.

For example, in a follow-up interview with Cihan Hüroğlu in the spring of 2016, he spoke about the situation in the summer of 2015, comparing it to months later, saying that then "we had more hopes ... because the war had not really started that badly. And now it is all about the war. All about terror, bombs, and you cannot discuss it." He went on to say that

additionally, now, positions of the politicians have been sharpened. Very recently politicians have declared again that "we are not going to allow in the new constitution any phrase on LGBTI discrimination because we are conservative. And we are not going to do that." They were not that clear on that before, they were not that clear when they were trying to do the constitution with the concession that the four parties in the government [must be involved in the process], [but] now the commission of the constitution has been abolished. Parties who were supposed to work on it, they quit, because they thought it's not [a] neutral process.

What has made matters worse for the LGBTI community is that Hüroğlu believes that leaders are attempting to push their own constitutional changes where no mention of sexual orientation and orientation rights would exist.

The recent conflicts in Turkey have had a direct negative effect on the advocacy of LGBTI human rights organizations; they have not been immune to what has occurred in the country. For example, the Islamic State has openly threatened LGBTI organizations in Turkey. As Kalan of Pembe Hayat noted, a leaked government document stated that ISIS has threated to attack a series of actors that included human rights organizations (and named Kaos GL as one of the groups). But while the reference was directed towards Kaos GL, Kalan explained that after speaking with the secretary of the national defense, Kalan saw the reference as towards the greater LGBTI community. And because of concerns of being attacked, Pembe Hayat employees and volunteers were unable to work from the office for two weeks. For them, even after going back to the office, Kalan said that

Pembe Hayat started/had to start opening their office because there has ... been simply an escalating violence against trans women in the streets, especially by the police forces and the forces with some cooperation from racketeering gangs. A couple of trans women were beaten up, a couple of them were kidnapped, and a couple of them were seriously injured. So, we have to open our office to combat [this] and to bring all these cases to the legal system. But on the other hand, when we are going to the office we still are a little bit scared because we don't know for sure what will happen if ISIS, or if an ISIS militant[,] comes and I don't know, attacks us; there's not actually much that we can do. We feel only secure a little bit because our office is [equipped] with [a] camera system and also outside our office, on the building we have camera systems, so we think that that kind of recording thing might be some sort of a security back-up plan. But, on the other hand, everything [does not seem to be] okay."

Because of this threat, groups like Pembe Hayat discussed cancelling the Pride Marches for 2016. In April 2016, Kalan spoke to this question:

"the 17th of May is approaching for Ankara, because in Ankara, the 17th of May is when we march. It is [the] international day against transphobia and we are discussing (with other LGBTI organizations in Ankara) whether to go on with the parade or not ... We are going to have the week with events and panels, but with the parade, its not certain if police can provide some sort of security for people attending. So ... last year it was nearly like [a] couple thousand people marching, and you can imagine that if some kind of bomb attack happens to that kind of a crowd, there will be like hundreds of dead people. So we are not still sure. And also, some discussions are going on in Istanbul about [the] trans pride parade and LGBTI parade in June. They still don't know how to hold it, like whether to hold it in [the] Taksim area or whether to move it to another area, [or] whether to cancel it ... Nobody has decided yet, actually.

Following up on this, when asked if one strategy was better than the other, Kalan responded,

No. I am not clear about it actually. I am for doing the parade, because it is symbolically important to show ... that we do not give up and we are not scared of all these threats. But on the other hand, it is very difficult to find some sort of negotiation table with public authorities, with law enforcement agencies about how to provide security for all those people, especially for [the] LGBTI parade, which reaches to hundreds of thousands of people. And if [the] police doesn't provide concrete security for these people ... it could be a massacre.

Hüroğlu also spoke about whether the terror has changed SPoDs' approach toward LGBTI rights advocacy, stressing the importance of being cautious. Hüroğlu also discussed the issue of the leaked document, saying:

[T]here was a document that was leaked on social media that said ... that KAOS GL, the organization in Ankara might be one of the targets. So, among all the other neighborhoods where we have to be careful, there was also a named organization which was actually quite rare because they were describing all the neighborhoods where you shouldn't go, and a possible attack on KAOS GL was also expected, something like that. An LGBT organization to be listed on such [a] list of course ... I don't know if that's a fake document or not ... but ... that is a threat as well. [T]he threat is ... [not from] the government, but from other forces, conservative forces. I don't know how many people from the LGBT movement have really seen that document.

He went on to say that "[w]e did not talk about it very much. But ... that gives you a feeling that ... ISIS ... has a possible target, the LGBTI community." He also said that some activists have brought up the idea of moving the Pride March to other venues, given the feeling that Taksim is no longer secure. However, others have disagreed with this suggestion, wanting instead to keep the Pride March where it has always been; it is not guaranteed that moving to another area will make the marchers any more safe. He then went to talk about how the police could also use this threat to disperse individuals from protesting at the Pride Parade, saying, "[Y]ou can say, in the last Pride Parade, there might be a possible threat from ISIS to the LGBTI Pride Parade, so that the police forces have to disperse the group to avoid any bombings." The conditions have affected their activities and how they have thought about organizing events like the Pride Parade.

Because of the worsening conditions facing the LGBTI community, as well as the deterioration of human rights in general within Turkey, there has been an examination of what approaches to take moving forward. For example, there has been less working with political authorities at the national level and more of a move towards cooperation with local authorities, as well as additional grassroots work. Hüroğlu said of this

that the general political agenda is so depressive, we are focusing more on our daily basis work. We are continuing our trainings, we are continuing our ... more micro-level work. I mean we are not ... engaging [much] with politicians because ... our goals may not fit very well ... It is not the right time to campaign for LGBTI rights. It's not all bombings, but in Southeast Turkey ... just terrible things are happening. So ... we have noticed less connections with the parliamentarians, for example ... But on the other hand, we are working more actively with local governments, that I can say, that works.

Again, because of the climate in Turkey, Hüroğlu believed that there are few opportunities to work with national leaders on LGBTI rights issues. This has led them to continue other avenues of their work.

In late spring 2016, Murat Köylü also spoke about how the threats by the Islamic State may have affected Kaos GL's activities. Köylü said that the organization was unable to go to their office for weeks[3], and while they appealed to the government and military, they received no response from authorities. However, Köylü explained that "it's not a matter of being on the document or not. We already knew that [the] LGBTI movement, LGBTI organizations [were targets]." Köylü then went on say is that, for him, while ISIS is a concern, the AKP government is also a threat to the LGBTI community. Of course while the government and the Islamic State "are different in their nature and in their own context," they have a similar strategy of "attack[ing] the marginalized groups." Köylü gave an example of Islamists with banners in Ankara calling for the killing of gay people and how there was "no response from Turkish police, [the] Turkish government, AKP government, no one." Again, while Köylü made it clear that the two groups are not the same, neither believe in supporting LGBTI rights; both seem to be very much opposed to such rights. With regard to terror organizations, he believed the situation with the Islamic State will be one that will continue to cause problems for the LGBTI community for quite some time; he saw their statements as "a very ... realistic threat and it will go on for many years." Thus, when asked if this would affect activities related to Pride Marches, he said "of course ... There isn't any protection." So, in our late April conversation, Köylü explained that while they used to have the yearly celebration on May 17th for roughly the past ten years, they decided, "for the first time," against holding the event in 2016. When asked if this was a difficult decision for the organization to make, Köylü replied, "It is so difficult but so easy at the same because we don't want to die. And in Ankara people are dying because of these bombs ... It's a very difficult question, of course, but yeah." But for him, "we [Kaos GL] are open targets." Köylü views the situation as much worse for the LGBTI community than in years past. It is not hard to understand this point of view by activists, who have seen the numbers of marchers grow, and the visibility increase, only to find conditions worse today than they were a decade ago.

In this chapter, I discussed some of the challenges facing activists and LGBTI rights-based NGOs in Turkey. As we see, this includes funding shortages, which can affect grant writing, programming, among other issues. In addition, there are also concerns to ensure that the rights-based platform is a Turkey-dominated one and not one controlled and dictated by organizations outside of the country. There are also worries about whether LGBI rights activities will include transgender rights. Lastly, there exist security concerns in Turkey. With increased conflict between the government and Kurdish forces, as well as the continuing war in Syria, the threats of violence against the LGBTI community are making them alter previously adopted strategies. ISIS mentioned Kaos GL as a possible target, and the Istanbul Pride March was cancelled because of threats to security. Additional concerns about increased state power are only making advocacy that much more difficult in Turkey. While it is important to note all of the great advancements that these LGBTI rights-based groups have made in Turkey, it is also necessary to understand continued challenges these activists and organizations face.

Conclusion

[W]e are doing our best in extremely difficult situations.

Sedef Çakmak

In this book, I have discussed the history of human rights abuses against LGBTI individuals, showing just how oppressive the state and police have been (whether in statements or in actions). In addition, I have laid out the laws and how they are interpreted, and what this has done to further limit LGBTI equality in Turkey. The situation has been and, arguably, continues to get worse for the LGBTI community in the country. As Sedef Çakmak explained, "[T]he LGBT movement is facing lots of challenges," and thus it is a great challenge to do advocacy work in such conditions. Çakmak added,

[W]e are doing our best in extremely difficult situations with extremely difficult psychology, actually... When your girlfriend is beaten and as an activist when you feel so desperate and so helpless because she refuses to go to a police station because if she goes to the police station she will be insulted by the police and that will not help ... And when you feel helpless in that situation it is very hard to carry on with your activism too. So, in that respect, I don't see any failures and I see a huge success.

So many within the LGBTI community do not feel like they are viewed as equal members of society. For example, following the murder of Hande Kader, Emirhan Deniz Çelebi, who serves as the director of SPoD, was quoted as saying, "We are not equal." Deniz Çelebi added, "We are being murdered and they do not hear our voices, because the rules in Turkey don't protect us" (Trian, 2016). There is a concern that minorities are being further mistreated, and even more so following the failed military coup (Trian, 2016).

Currently, the actions of the Turkish state, police, and individuals who are attempting to quell any LGBTI rights movement (and are going to great lengths to ensure that people from the community are not only not seen as equal but are carrying out actions that are causing long-term pain) have created conditions in which the situation for the LGBTI community and LGBTI rights no doubt remains a concern, especially with the increased authoritarianism in recent years, and even more so since the failed military coup in July 2016. Some, such as Andrew Gardner have felt that the situation is not getting better, saying (in Jamieson and Akyavas, 2015) that: "I'm very pessimistic about the prospects from this government of bringing [equality] laws into force." "There was a time, up until a few years ago, when generally there was legislation improving protection for human rights. During the last couple of years generally we have seen new laws presented that actually weaken human-rights protection so the trend is definitely negative" (Jamieson and Akyavas, 2015). The situation in Turkey with regard to LGBTI rights abuses has been so bad that "[t]he [United Nations] expressed deep concern over attacks and discriminatory acts on Turkey's lesbian, gay, bisexual and transgender (LGBT) community, while also calling for active measures to be taken in an effort to combat homophobic and transphobic violence and discrimination" (*Hurriyet Daily News*, 2015b). I believe it is important that that international community continue to express their concern with the conditions facing the LGBTI community inside Turkey.

Again, there definitely exists a feeling that the situation has gotten worse in recent years. As Çakmak noted in our interview over the summer of 2015, there were not many concerns about the government pursuing a more aggressive strategy against the LGBTI community until 2013 onwards:

[B]efore the Gezi incidents [we] weren't thinking that what will happen if the government pursues a more aggressive strategy. We weren't thinking that because that wasn't the case back then ... they were just ignoring our move ... We would be saying "Oh, what, why [are] they ... ignoring us[?]" because now we know 10,000 people walking in the parade and they're still ignoring us. That's ... [what] we were saying to [ourselves] but now we are thinking what will happen if they pursue a more aggressive strategy and even if the government openly pursues an aggressive strategy, like in Russia. Of course there are ways to fight against this because Turkey is not Russia. But I am more afraid of the fact that the government will encourage the civil groups to pursue a more aggressive strategy. This is one of the things of which I am afraid because, for example, right after the pride parade for two weeks we have dealt with issues where lots of LGBTs were beaten or raped on the streets.

When I was finishing the interviews in 2016, the mood among human rights activists in Turkey was one of worry. Since I began the interviews in the summer of 2015, Turkey has not only moved toward further authoritarianism, but the war with the PKK and affiliated groups in the country has intensified; the human rights abuses the government has committed against the Kurdish population have also increased greatly, as have terror attacks within the country. In addition, the Islamic State has not only carried out attacks within Turkey and neighboring Syria but they have also specifically called out LGBTI rights organizations. Yet, despite all of this, LGBTI activists and pro-LGBTI human rights organizations have been able to improve upon the conditions facing LGBTI members in Turkey since the earlier years of advocacy. Through media, elections, established networks, workshops, publication of research, and overall visibility campaigns, they have been able to show those in Turkish civil society that LGBTI individuals are also members of the same society and that their human rights matter.

Continued LGBTI Activism

Despite the conditions in Turkey, none of what has transpired is stopping SPoD, Pembe Hayat, Kaos GL, or other human rights organizations from continuing to press forward. They understand that this work is vital if the LGBTI community is going to be seen and treated as equal in Turkey. So, despite the challenges and the high risks, these activists have and are continuing to place their lives on the line in the hopes of ensuring equality for all people in Turkey. In addition, the LGBTI activist community still looks for new strategies and approaches to improve conditions for the LGBTI community. LGBTI rights-based activists are working to learn about new ways and approaches to make a difference. Historically, their strategy was very grassroots centered; marches and information campaigns were a central part of the outreach and rights advocacy. However, in recent years, as discussed, the strategies have expanded to include additional grassroots work like more education and workshop programs, along with other approaches, such as lobbying and working with political figures, constitutional reform, running in elections, and working within municipalities and as political advisors. These initiatives, as well other approaches, such as additional education campaigns and anti-bullying programs in Turkey (Göksel, 2013), will continue to be important. The expansion into the electoral space, while equally important, is not without challenges. With much of the activist experience in Turkey historically centered on noninstitutional advocacy (working outside of the electoral political system or outside of government institutions), the adoption of new strategies will also require the addition of new learning and skills. Plus, with the rise of authoritarianism in Turkey, especially following the failed coup of July 2016, there are even more risks for speaking out against the government.

Since the coup, Erdoğan and his forces have went after those he suspects of being tied to Fethullah Gulen, an Islamic cleric that Erdoğan has viewed as a threat (Muedini, 2015). There have been over 70,000 arrests (as of early October 2016) (Fisk, 2016), along with suspensions and employee firings (whether in the police force, in education, in medical health professions, or in the private sector). Furthermore, the government has also continued its negative campaign against the freedom of the press, detaining journalists and closing down outlets that are deemed to be against the state. There has been a concern that Turkey has slid further and further into authoritarianism since the failed coup attempt. There is of course a worry regarding what this will mean for the rights of the LGBTI and human rights in general. Right now, it is difficult to know. But the signs are not positive, since Erdoğan has gained even more presidential power. These sorts of developments tend not to bode well for minorities in a country, especially with Erdoğan's positions on LGBTI and Kurdish rights.

Municipality Work

It seems that, given the unwillingness of cooperation by the national AKP government,[1] as well as Erdoğan's strong political hold on power, activists are turning much of their attention to the local. Thus, I expect the grassroots activism and municipality work will continue to be a centerpiece of LGBTI rights-based activism moving forward. When Murat Köylü of Kaos GL was asked what can be done at the municipality level to help advance LGBTI rights, particularly given the difficulties of working on these issues at the national level with a government who continues to oppress LGBTI rights, Köylü said that not only are activists "socially and psychologically supporting [LGBTI individuals]," but that it doesn't mean that because we don't expect anything from this government [that] we are not doing anything. ... Our work on local administrations, especially for CHP and HDP has increased ... because there are good things going on at the same time in Turkey too, especially in universities, in local municipalities, in [the] private sector. As the authoritarianism increases, of course ... our strategy is giving more importance ... or weight to working with municipalities now and [the] private sector, especially organizational capacity development ... Because [these] legislative and political actors are in total avoidance at the moment, we will increase our work in [the] judiciary too [as the] ... European Council of Human Rights and the Constitutional Court of Turkey is ... [still] more objective in that regard. So yes, we are shifting a bit of our strategies.

Köylü also said that one can work towards "political representation in the municipalities, they can become council members, they can become mayors, they can work as ... municipality officials, [on] visibility issue [s], empowerment issue[s]." He went on to say that there is also an opportunity where "these municipalities can network with other countries, with other international ... other municipalities from other countries."

Less than a year earlier, in my 2015 interview, Boysan Yakar also spoke about the overall importance of municipality work, saying,

[W]hen you're an MP, the only thing you do is this, representing a group of people. And I'm [an] MP. It's not easy ... to have a candidate and an MP in Turkish assembly, but [until] ... that moment, we have to learn bureaucracy ... it has to be achieved ... I think at the moment, we are going really fine. We did a lot in 23 years. This is important.

Again, this is just part of the advocacy expansion process. The LGBTI rights-based activists understand the importance of using multiple methods – and gaining a series of skills – to better advocate for LGBTI issues in Turkey.

Çakmak and Yakar are two examples of how individuals from within the LGBTI community are working within municipalities to improve the rights of the LGBTI community. Along with this, NGOs have also found ways to create and foster linkages with local administrators. This has been something on which organizations such as Pembe Hayat have concentrated a great amount of time. As mentioned, one of the key components to the advocacy of the organization has been working on providing social services for transgendered individuals. However, a related advocacy position has been to create networks with local administrators. They do so for a number of reasons, and it is important work. As Kalan mentions, "[L]ocal administrations working on social services … as well as professionals from in the field … come together and … discuss … these mechanisms … in regard to providing services or providing inclusive services towards trans identities." So, by talking things like gaps and/or inefficiencies, they can improve upon the overall services for the transgender community.

As noted, for transgender individuals, one of the biggest challenges they face is the ability to access these resources. So, by speaking with officials, there is a hope that groups like Pembe Hayat can communicate continued challenges and can work with officials to remedy any problems that might exist. For them, changing opinions matters. Kalan noted the importance of this, saying, "[S]tate institutions are resisting because of the bureaucracy. We hope that it will change, because if the mentality changes then the services will be more open, more inclusive. Even though the bureaucracy and the legislation is something to be changed very slowly." Yet, the fight continues on this front. When asked how Pembe Hayat can change minds and attitudes of local administrators, Kalan replied,

[O]ur strategy is to … focus on specific professionals in that institution in the local administration as well and build solidarity with them, and call them, and inform them, email them constantly, and not to give up … [another] part of the strategy to make every communication and every meeting with the administration and these institutions public and whatever they say is being recorded, so if they promise something in a meeting, they cannot refuse it.

Kalan went on to add:

[W]e are also doing official applications … to the ministries and the relevant … administrations in the bureaucracy … we are forcing them to provide us with the information and very recently … we are trying to get engaged with them and to make them take up some of the cases, where we cannot have any further progress with the administrative system. So we are at least … making them notice all the cases, we are making them record all the cases, and if we are not recording it, we are bombarding them with emails and with information, providing information and with … postal services. Sometimes we are sending them information notes.

Kalan believed that many of the documents were ignored but also that someone would have to take notice of them.

Again, the problem is that the transgender community activists do not have sufficient resources to work against prosecution, life prison sentences, among other things. Resources are so small that it is difficult to even know just how much violence against the transgender community takes place in Turkey (Carter, 2015). For this reason the state must be proactive and prioritize the rights for this group. They must publically recognize the equality of transgender individuals and also to provide the necessary resources to ensure the safety of this community and also resources for socioeconomic rights that include, but are not limited to housing rights, job access, help with education, food and anti-poverty support, etc. Furthermore, they must send a strong message that they have no tolerance for hatred of or violence against the transgender community. They must condemn the notion of "dishonor" and also ensure that perpetrators stand trial, and if found guilty, pass sentences commensurate with the crime committed.

Visibility

The importance of continued visibility as a strategy is something on which all of the interviewees agreed. Based on the research, it seems that in some way or another, everyone is working on improving the visibility of the LGBTI community. This activism has been successful in Turkey. As Murat Köylü said, "[V]isibility is very important. And in Turkey the visibility problem is much less when you compare it with five years ago, much more than five years ago now." Köylü also spoke about the importance of having success stories, and how the LGBTI community, along with other groups, has been included in society. Köylü went on to add that "[t]wenty years [ago] . . . you couldn't even get an example from England or United States or even ten years ago maybe. So we can make this more visible."

The Role of International Actors

Along with the work of local activists, there is still a place for international actors to have a role in LGBTI rights work in Turkey. For example, countries like the United States can do a lot more, particularly on the front of accepting LGBTI refugees (Grungras, 2016; although such a positive change looks highly unlikely given the Trump presidency). Given the persecution that refugees face in countries like Syria and elsewhere, opening its doors to those in dire need will send a clear and positive message that the US government truly stands by its belief in full freedom and protection of LGBTI individuals (along with non-LGBTI individuals, of course). As mentioned earlier, LGBTI refugees are facing quite a dire situation in Turkey. It is imperative that refugee camps are properly staffed with individuals who can work to improve the conditions for all refugees and marginalized groups. If LGBTI refugees are afraid to identify themselves as LGBTI while at the camps for fear of what might happen to them it is necessary that they are fully supported, whether it is through resources or just a community of other LGBTI individuals with whom they can share their experiences. As Grungras (2016) writes:

A rainbow flag and a concerned look are a good start. But for an LGBT refugee escaping certain death after being hounded by decades of external and internal homophobia, these gestures are not nearly enough. To collect the courage to come out – even in order to save their own lives – most refugees need to derive strength and solace from other LGBT people. Yet in most places, this essential touchstone is nowhere to be seen.

International actors can be involved in other ways. They can contact NGOs in Turkey and ask them what they can do to help. Again, as mentioned earlier, this should not be a Western-driven discourse but an open dialogue on what steps can be taken to improve the situation for the marginalized in Turkey. This might take the form of fundraising, project collaboration, workshops, or the use of the boomerang pattern to lobby one's own national governments about what is taking place in Turkey. Other actions still might include international visibility campaigns or research on LGBTI rights in Turkey and elsewhere. Again, activists in Turkey are very open to working with others abroad, and they have done and continue to do this sort of collaborative work. However, the key must be to not frame it through an "outsider"-based model that does not understand what is most needed in Turkey for sexual minorities.

Private Sector

Murat Köylü of Kaos GL also advocated building networks and linkages with private sector actors. Köylü believed that given the power of private entities in the international system today, these private sector actors could aid in LGBTI rights activism in Turkey by "empowering LGBTI employees [through] visibility, by offering them positions, th [ese] kind of [things]." He also added that these companies can offer social benefits. Furthermore, "visibility of role models from countries like United States and Europe is very important to, again, communicate with the constituencies of Turkey and other countries, standard stuff." So, he sees a place for these private sector companies to not only work with local activists to promote LGBTI rights but also to help with overall visibility and serve as a good marker for actors within Turkey.

Working through the Prism of Religion

Approaching LGBTI rights advocacy from an Islamic perspective is not only an innovative strategy but, as I also believe, a quite effective strategy when approaching individuals who use religion to make arguments about sexuality. It becomes easy for some to dismiss secular arguments, particularly if those arguments (for rights, democracy, etc.) are bound up in other, abusive actions (such as what was done in the name of "civilizing" the nonwhite and non-Christian in the minds of Europeans during imperialism and colonialism). However, if one can make arguments within the traditions of those in the country (be they cultural or religious), then others may be more likely to listen. It is this "insider" approach that does not try to place an exterior culture onto the existing one or does not aim to replace domestic culture with "foreign" culture (s); rather, it cites references within the religion and/or culture itself to show that even within "your" religion, which you make the argument from, there exists evidence to support overarching ideas of love. This provides greater weight for some who only look to religion, and in this case Islam, for answers to these (and many other) questions.

In terms of strategy, NGOs and activists should continue to also take this line of approach. But this in no way suggests an abandonment of secular arguments, references to international human rights law, or even a reduction in the level of secular-based activism. However, there does exist some challenges with a strategy that chooses not to engage with the issue of religion. As Carroll (2010) notes:

In societies where religion significantly underpins much social and political discourse and public policy, there may be much overt hostility and denial of

LGBT claims. Personal safety is paramount as right wing nationalist forces can be quite well organized and tend to run counter-demonstrations when they hear of LGBT public manifestations. Political opponents also profit from denouncing LGBT targets to varying degrees.

Opposition forces will tend to garner support from the widest constituency available and harness that energy against your advocacy action when they have the chance to. Although public representatives are charged with the protection and promotion of human rights in their societies, they will often denigrate human rights concepts and the language and logic of human rights to their own constituents, portraying human rights as irreligious, un-nationalistic and undesirable ... it may often be wise not to focus too much on theoretical human rights standards when working with the public, but to root your arguments in illustrative experience and real cases of what human rights violations look like.

Again, if we recall from the first chapter, when asked if they employ specific strategies for those with what are seen as conservative viewpoints on Islam and homosexuality, the activists, while not in disagreement with the idea, don't prefer it since they are not as knowledgeable about issues of Islam. Therefore, it is necessary to have people from within the Islamic tradition, speaking in the "language of Islam," to advocate for LGBTI rights. Activists from these NGOs do not have to alter their entire strategy or ignore what has worked in the past. But what might be missing is the importance of Islamic-based human rights NGOs with progressive values that can speak about the need for embracing LGBTI (and all other) human rights.

Again, none of this will be easy in Turkey. Hüroğlu argued that the issue of same-sex rights in Turkey is difficult given the issue of religion in the country. He argues,

Everything, all of the caricatures, all of ... whatever [is] found in Turkey, has to do with the conflict of Eastern and Western values. Because we are really in the middle of that ... people live with that conflict, and they do conflictual things, and all these Western arguments, if you see [this] from [a]Western point of view, see people in their lives, and you want to criticize them[,] showing them how inconsistent they are doesn't bring anything because everything is built on that kind of inconsistencies because you always try to find a middle way between those traditional values, and its almost impossible. So most of those things you do is actually conflictual in itself, and that [is] the common acceptance in Turkey, and its very hard to change. And Islam and LGBT rights is such an issue.

Even though it is difficult, Hüroğlu, as well as others, understood the importance of potentially using religious arguments for individuals as a strategy for promoting LGBTI rights in Turkey, particularly when he pointed out that while many of the activists within the LGBTI movement may not necessarily be Muslim or may not be religious, many in wider Turkish society are. And thus, to him, it is important to use Islam, to frame the discussion in religious terms, in order to help shift opinion among those in society who may identify more with their Islamic faith. So, Hüroğlu explained that

we are trying to do ... some work on that ... Lambda [Istanbul] had a workshop on Islam with LGBTI people, and it was very interesting they say. They started [this] again ... There are one or two people who are very interested in Islamic thought and they are trying to interpret Islam for LGBTI-friendly perspective[s].

However, Hüroğlu also noted that they as an organization are somewhat limited in this approach, since "we don't have arguments, we don't prefer to approach it." Hüroğlu felt that approaching the topic from a position of religion "only polarizes the society, because everyone knows there is a big conflict" on this issue. Plus, Hüroğlu said that approaching it from this position might make matters more difficult for those in the LGBTI community who are religious. Thus, the sentiment was that "until there are LGBTI-friendly interpretations of Islam, until that becomes more strong," that the preference was to not discuss it from a religious perspective.

Again, although he did believe that the overall idea of using Islamic-based arguments for same-sex rights in Turkey is a good thing, he stressed that it has to be done a certain way, and to him, a strategic choice would be to work on the issue but to do so rather quietly. He spoke about approaching LGBTI rights from religious arguments, as well as his position on doing so more under the radar, saying:

I think it's a good thing, but they are also doing it in a right way, by not too much publishing of that ... You work on that, but if those people who come to you and say they need that kind of workshops, but you do not create a media discussion on homosexuality and Islam ... It's not the right approach to do that. And there is a big conflict. And this conflict, at this time, with this interpretation of Islam, the normal interpretation of Islam would say[,] "[N]o, Islam doesn't in anyway accept homosexuality, and if possible, punish them, and if possible, kill them." You cannot have enough reference to fight on that so, you should be silent on that. You cannot overcome that obstacle by advocacy anyway.

Because of this belief, Hüroğlu again stated that one can still speak with those in the religious community about LGBTI issues, but that they these discussions should be done quietly, "without making it public," although he argued that "in the short run, we should be rather silent and we should leave that work for those that are religious themselves, [to converse about] new ideas on Islam and homosexuality." Thus, there is a view that approaching the topic from a religious perspective should be done by those from within the "in-group," and that while SPoD itself would not "take any initiative to create a discussion," they would be there to help them along the way if they would like. Related to this, when asked whether SPoD had such a plan in place to take the approach that he was speaking about with regard to using religion, he said that they currently did not. He said that he thought "[they] had some proposals on that matter, and we refused that because ... [they were] not reliable people ... They want to create ... kind of a scandal discussion, and ... make their own names, [have] their own organizations names being heard. And that doesn't really help anybody."

In fact, he also recognizes the risk associated with a nonreligious-based organization trying to apply this tactic of making religious-based arguments by having Muslim speakers on the issue. This is a common discussion in the literature, and it revolves around this idea of "insider-outsider." While SPoD is clearly an "insider" when it comes to Turkish society (as they are a Turkish-based NGO), given their secular-based arguments for LGBTI rights in the past, they may actually be viewed as "outsiders" with regard to the issue of Islamic law and how it relates to issues of homosexuality. Throughout the history of the human rights movement, there have existed examples of "outsiders" trying to make a particular rights-based argument. Now, that alone is not necessarily an issue, but where it becomes problematic is when that "outsider" believes that they understand what is best for said society and then try to implement a policy, when in reality that person does not have a solid understanding of the society and all of the issues around that human rights topic. Again, this is not to say that someone outside of a specific culture or country cannot work on human rights in a country; it is however critical that they are well-versed in all of the issues surrounding the topic that they are addressing. It is clear from speaking with Hüroğlu that he understands the value of approaching LGBTI activism from an Islamic perspective in Turkey but also realizes, as he says, that there are challenges to having a secular NGO work on these issues. This is quite clear to him when he says that although they may adopt such a strategy in the future,

I don't know, we are close to that date or not, but I won't take the initiative for that. I mean, maybe one day . . . it is very risky . . . you can try that and you can bring in a very interesting voice of a Muslim person who is respected, and speaks out in a good way about homosexuality, and you have the right media to support that idea and present that, in a good way. And then you can have that, but it's not easy right now. [It is] very risky. If you don't do it in a good way, [then] it backfires. So, I'd rather be very careful with that and let the initiative [come] from the people who are Muslim.

Again, it is important to note that the direction of this approach should not be one-sided. While I believe LGBTI rights-based organizations should consider the possibility of approaching LGBTI rights through religious arguments, it is equally important for those within Islamic faith-based community to speak out in defense of LGBTI rights. As long as public opinion in the Muslim world is so strongly against LGBTI rights, it will be difficult to make progress on this front. Overall, there is reluctance in many of Muslim communities around the world to accept homosexuals and homosexuality. However, the unwillingness to support homosexuals is even stronger in areas where the citizens measure high on religiosity – how central religion is to one's life. While the religiosity measurement can and does vary in academic and policy studies, some dictate that religiosity is "measured by whether they consider religion to be very important, whether they believe it is necessary to believe in God in order to be moral, and whether they pray at least once a day" (Pew Research Center, 2013). Thus, it seems those who place religion as a key element of their life have much more of a negative view of homosexuality. As I argue, it should be for this reason that activists should also be making religious arguments to those in society – namely, how homosexuality is not a sin and how religions such as Islam don't condemn homosexuality in the Quran, while also emphasizing other elements of the faiths (such as ideas of love and family) that are clearly related to homosexual relationships, for example.

Therefore, it is necessary to have Muslims speak out, call for full LGBTI rights, and condemn any hate crimes against LGBTI individuals. Some, such as Bariş Sulu, who ran for MP in the June 2015 elections, spoke about the need for imams and other Islamic religious leaders to alter the current discussions about homosexuality in the Islamic communities to better fit with Western religious worldviews and said this could help readjust the way people in the LGBTI community are viewed; this approach could alter negative stereotypes (Tokyay, 2015). There exists a responsibility on Muslims to call for the equal rights of all human beings. They must be adamant that LGBTI rights clearly fall within Islam, and that notions of peace, acceptance, and justice advocated in Islam are for everyone.

Again, given the developments in Turkey since 2015, the situation is one in which democracy looks to be in decline. The failed military coup in 2016 – and the backlash that followed (and continues to affect the country), concerns about terrorism, and the government's fighting with Kurdish forces, have led to conditions of instability in Turkey. Because of the recent developments in Turkey, the government has offered even less support for LGBTI rights. The conditions are among the worst that they have been for the LGBTI community in a long time. Not only that, but Turkey is, as Öz says, "[A] patriarchal society with a government that is financing conservatism," and she admits that "I worry the next generation will become only more conservative and less tolerant (Bohn, 2015). The government is clearly not on the side of LGBTI rights, and it continues to make conditions that much more difficult. Yet, despite the worsening trend in recent years, activists are still pushing for the rights of all in Turkey. Therefore, it is imperative that these groups not only are recognized for their work but are also given the much-needed support for continuing their work. In addition, there must continue to be attention given to any human rights violations in the country. We must make it clear that there will be no toleration for any rights abuse of any individual whatsoever. It is only when everyone is given their full set of human rights, which of course includes sexual identity rights, that a community can truly live in peace and prosperity.

There is hope. Despite the current situation in Turkey, people continue to fight for their human rights, demanding social and economic equality. For example, in the summer of 2017, citizens of Turkey began a 250-mile walk from the capital, Ankara, to Istanbul. They carried out this "March for Justice" to protest the increased authoritarian conditions in Turkey under Erdoğan (Tuysuz and Dewan, 2017). The march included members of opposition parties (such as the CHP and the HDP) and, according to the estimates, had upwards of a million people involved. The LGBTI community and women's rights organizations were also a part of this march. Many of them chose to join the demonstrations in the city of Gebze. It was here that the Italian artist and human rights activist Pippa Bacca was found killed in 2008 (*BirGün*, 2017a). Bacca's work centered on bringing different people and cultures together around messages of peace (Povoledo, 2008). These protests illustrated that people are not giving up the struggle for freedom and justice. So, despite what has taken place in Turkey, the LGBTI community continues to fight. They continue to speak out against sexual inequalities, patriarchal structures, and other inequities in Turkey.[2] While the path is far from easy, the LGBTI community has shown no sign of letting up. They maintain their struggle with their work in local community activism, workshop organization, in the halls of government, through the media with increasing visibility, and through fighting for education, employment, and health rights for the LGBTI in Turkey.

Notes

Introduction

1 In Turkey, activists reference sexual minority rights as LGBTI rights, including the "I", which stands for Intersex (persons with reproductive organs that are not either clearly "male" or "female.") The human rights organization Lambda Istanbul (2013) speaks of the importance of fighting for Intersex rights in Turkey, saying, "Intersex people are among us and they number more than we know, so much so that they can uproot accepted gender models but they are being ignored precisely because they pose a danger to solidified and outdated social norms. One in every 2000 births is an intersex baby … Everyday, intersex people are being forced to fit into dualistic gender models by means of medical procedures such as surgeries and chemical interventions without any psychological support, information or consent. They are ignored, left alone and, usually, they cannot grow into independent adults." In the book, I shall use the acronym LGBTI unless quoting someone who used another acronym, such as "LGBT."

2 There has been work on homosexual identity issues in Turkey (Bereket and Adam, 2006; Bakacak and Oktem, 2014) and on LGBTI and transgender issues in other countries such as Iran (see Najmabadi, 2005, 2013; Afary, 2009).

3 Lambda Istanbul LGBTI Solidarity Association is one of the most important volunteer organizations with regards to LGBTI rights. The association is different than other nongovernmental human rights organizations in Turkey (and elsewhere, for that matter) primarily because of its organizational structure. While most organizations operate in a vertical, hierarchical fashion, Lambda Istanbul does not; it has a horizontal structure that avoids leadership chains of command, and instead is centered on a series of issue-based commissions. These are created, organized, and ran by volunteers of the organization (Lambda Istanbul, 2015). With regard to its origins, "Lambdaistanbul is an organization that was formed by a group of gays and lesbians, right after the governor of Istanbul banned the Christopher Street Day Sexual Liberation Activities that were

attempted to be held in July 1993. After this, the group that used to gather under the name 'Gokkusagi' (Rainbow) took the name Lambdaistanbul" (Lambda Istanbul, 2015). However, it was not until 2006 that Lambda Istanbul became registered. In 2007, as I shall discuss later in the book, the local prosecutor's office in Istanbul tried, unsuccessfully, to close their association. While a part of its early work was of course in terms of LGBTI advocacy, it was also an organization that brought together members of the LGBTI community. For example, as mentioned on their website, "in [their] early years, [Lambda Istanbul] ... organized regular Sunday meetings for queer people who need to find each other to share their experiences, and to realize that they are not alone. For this reason, we have also prepared a radio show that lasted for a year and a half (1996–97) on a prestigious local station of Istanbul, Acik Radyo (www .acikradyo.com.tr)" (Lambda Istanbul, 2015).

Chapter 1

1 Muslim groups in Britain criticized the study, arguing that it was not representative of the true feelings of Muslims in Britain, and questioned the "academic rigor" of the study. There were specific issues with how the examiners decided on the sample; a spokesperson for the Muslim Council of Britain (MCB) said that "[c]hoosing specifically to poll in areas that are poor and more religiously conservative skews the results and makes it indicative of these areas and not of British Muslims nationally." The organization stood by their study and approach towards conducting the survey (Hume and Greene, 2016).

2 It should also be noted that many Christian denominations in the USA and the world also have varying levels of support for homosexuality. See Pew Research Center (2015) and Murphy (2015) for a discussion on Christian groups and homosexuality in America.

3 There have been some studies that have interviewed LGBTI individuals in Turkey about the social problems they have experienced. For example, Biçmen and Bekiroğulları (2014) interviewed thirty people within the LGBT community on how they felt within Turkish society and how moving to a new city compared to their hometowns.

4 The work resulting from the public opinion data was entitled "The Global Divide on Homosexuality," in which they summarized some of their key findings on country-trends with regard to opinions on homosexuality.

5 People in Turkey have noticed this discrimination and unwillingness to accept members of the Turkish LGBTI community. For example, Barış Sulu, who ran for a MP position under the HDP, spoke about Turkish public opinion with regard to the LGBTI community, saying, "I have been

in Diyarbakır several times. There's a different atmosphere there. The perception of LGBTIs doesn't change wherever you go. Maybe the current process will soften that perception. It will help people understand more. We're being killed despite our right to live. That's what we're talking about. We say, we can't receive an education, we're kicked out of schools, we experience bullying. We experience a whole other set of issues at hospitals. We can't find work. People are forced to do different kinds of work. They are pushed to the margins of society. We're trying to talk about these issues and I believe that our voice is heard here and there" (Akan, 2015).

6 Hostile attitudes towards homosexuality have led many in Turkey (and elsewhere) to often either hide their actions, or to be very careful, especially when there are also additional pressures of "family honor" (see Bereket and Adam, 2008).

7 Of course, the allowance of slavery is reprehensible, a direct violation of human rights, and, as Kugle (2010a) accurately notes, "the vast majority of Muslims no longer recognize these practices as morally allowable in Islam" (203).

8 Fishman (2013) writes that one reason that the Ottoman Empire was able to establish protections for sexual minorities was due to the lack of colonization by a direct outside power. Many colonialist countries were highly influential in advocating laws that criminalized homosexuality.

Chapter 2

1 While it might be the case that the conservative elements of society are pushing their agenda with support, from members of society, it must be noted that there is also a strong movement for the human rights of the oppressed, which include the LGBT community (Nigar Goksel, 2014).

2 There is a small conservative group within the LGBTI community that has continued to support Erdoğan and the AKP government. This group has formed a twitter page called the "Pro-AKP LGBTI Individuals" (Lee, 2014). Here, they post comments of support for Erdoğan and the AKP, statements such as "[t]he homosexuals stand with Tayyip Erdogan. We are at the rallies, we are everywhere – get used to it" (Kutahyali, 2014). They have also taken the rainbow flag to AKP rallies (Kutahyali, 2014).

With regards to explaining their support for Erdoğan and the AKP, Kerem, the founder of the group, spoke of the relationship between Erdoğan and the AKP and their group, saying, "There are people in our group who are highly influential within the AKP. In the days we created the group, we received a congratulation message from an AKP mayor. And we are in contact not only with the AKP." Regarding the negative comments the AKP has made about the LGBTI community, he added, "As a homosexual who votes for the AKP, I have been offended and saddened by statements AKP lawmakers make. Hence, our goal is to change the perceptions of rightist and conservative quarters who think likewise" (Kutahyali, 2014, in Lee, 2014).

Despite their attempts at trying to change the minds of those who have such feelings towards the LGBTI, this group has been highly criticized by others within the LGBTI movement. In my first interview with Cihan Hüroğlu, he brought up the group, saying that those who within the LGBTI community who support Erdoğan are "terrible; they are supporting the police attacks on people."

He went on to explain that many of them are not active in the LGBTI marches, as they opposed them being held during Ramadan. There is even discussions among some of the "more religious ... rather conservative gay/lesbian people that the LGBTI movement are not really representing them."

Members of this group, such as Melih Neseli Gunes, have argued that the AKP has actually allowed many more rights for the LGBTI community and that they could be much more restrictive; the fact that they have allowed rights for LGBTI is positive (Lee, 2014). However, while they have allowed more rights than governments fully repressive against all LGBTI rights, as I have argued, there are many human rights violations against the LGBTI community, many of which the AKP-led government have been directly or indirectly carried out.

3 Kaos GL also held their 12th Anti-Homophobia Meeting in May 2017, in which activists Ceyhun Güler and Murat Köylü of Kaos spoke about LGBTI conditions in the workplace in Turkey (Uzun, 2017).

4 Grindr is a dating app for those who are gay, lesbian, bisexual, or transgender. The state argued that stopping the app from being used in Turkey was a "protective measure"; they make similar arguments for pornographic websites that they block (Feldman, 2014).

5 Murat Köylü mentioned this information to me in a 2017 email after I asked about the current status of this prison.

6 Turkey's position towards asylum seekers and refugees can be seen in their response to the Syrian conflict. Turkey, while helping millions of Syrians fleeing the country, will not use the term "refugees"; instead, the government calls the Syrians "guests."

7 Pemebe Hayat (2015b) also reported on the response that activists received when they were in contact with the police about the killing, noting that "Kivilcim Arat from Istanbul LGBTI Solidarity Association said that they have kept calling police offices all night after they heard about the attack in order to get concrete information. However, they were

not informed by the police officers. Arat [was quoted as saying], "Police officers talked to me in a very disrespectful manner and mockingly. We were trying to get information for legal follow-up procedures, but they did not provide us any information. They said 'he is already dead, his throat is cut open, why do you care.'"

8 Amnesty International (2011) also reported that "every transgender woman that Amnesty International spoke to in early 2011 described being subjected to extreme violence – including sexual violence – by police officers in police stations in previous years" (12). Furthermore, we must keep in mind the power dynamics in these situations; many are quite afraid to report any police abuse for fear of retribution (Amnesty International, 2011).

Chapter 3

1 For a discussion on the debate surrounding Article 10, see Engin (2015).

2 For discussion on their application as organizations, the complaints by the Directory of Associations, the year of the complaints to the prosecutor's office, and additional details, see Öz (2010).

3 See Akdeniz's 2010 OSCE report for a detailed discussion of the articles and regulations within the legislation.

4 See Drescher (2015) for a discussion on the evolution of the American Psychiatric Association's decision to take out "homosexuality" as a diagnosis within the *DSM*.

5 It is also important to note that for many who speak Lubunca also do so as a way to express their LGBTI identity. By showing that they speak Lubunca, it indicates to others that they are members of the LGBTI community. For example, an individual by the name of Turgay Bayındır made this point, saying, "It's a subculture. When you use it, you are actually emphasizing that you belong to this subculture and you are also stressing your difference from the mainstream culture" (Mortada, 2015).

6 The People's Democratic Party (Halkların Demokratik Partisi; HDP) has quickly become one of the most noted and influential political parties outside of the AKP in Turkey, emerging as a very real challenge to the politics of Erdoğan and his party. They have been outspoken about the rising authoritarianism of Erdoğan and the AKP, and they have also called for an end to Erdoğan's presidential discretionary fund, and additional increases in presidential powers (Werz, Hoffman, and Bhaskar, 2015). And while they are currently not a full electoral threat to the government (in the sense of overall votes), they are gaining support throughout the country (their support is currently primarily in Kurdish areas, as well as pockets in Istanbul) and have made crucial gains in terms of the

2015 parliamentary elections (MacDonald, 2015), winning 13 percent of the vote (Berman, 2015). And because of their strong criticism of Erdoğan, various authoritarian institutional elements of Turkish government, and their calls for equality amongst all citizens, it has led Lale Kemal (2015), in *Today's Zaman*, to call the HDP the "only party with [a] real democratic agenda," saying that "[i]t would not be wrong if we describe the election manifesto of the HDP as the most democratic of the three parties comprising the HDP, the AKP and the Republican People's Party (CHP)" (Kemal, 2015). The 2015 results have been viewed as a major milestone for the party, as they will have the ability to at least challenge AKP dominance in Parliament, something that the AKP themselves have not been used to for a number of years.

But what also makes the HDP a rising political party in Turkey is its continued statements and actions with regards to the importance of women's rights. Namely, the HDP has been highly outspoken against what they see as gross human rights violations against women in various aspects of Turkish society. And because of the continued calls for women's rights, Mehtap Erol, who is the co-founder as well as the spokesperson for the HDP outlet in Berlin, is quoted as saying that "[t]here needs to be a fundamental rethink in Turkey concerning the regard and treatment of women." Erol and the HDP are appalled at the cases of rape in Turkey and with a lax law that does not adequately punish those who commit such heinous crimes (Nurtsch, 2015). But it is not just the cases of rape that are the problem in Turkey but a more endemic overall way of thinking that sees women as unequal to men, which in turn creates a variety of other inequalities in the country. Speaking more on this issue, Erol states that "[i]t is a question of awareness and mindset. The prevailing mood is a macho attitude that allowed the former Prime Minister Erdoğan to tell me how many children I should have" (Nurtsch, 2015). Erol (and the HDP) advocate the importance of independent decision making for women and fighting the discrimination that takes place against women (Nurtsch, 2015).

The party has been able to attract attention and increase the number of supporters by its criticism of both the AKP-led government and the increased role of religion in the government. Furthermore, they have also been outspoken about the AKP party's main rivals, the Republican People's Party (CHP), for its nationalistic platform, which has often come at the expense of any significant concessions to Kurdish political goals (MacDonald, 2015). They have been able to attract support from various minority groups who have all been discriminated against in Turkey; this includes the Kurdish population (which is at roughly fifteen million people, or 20 percent of Turkey's entire population; Lowen, 2015), Alevi and Ismaili Muslims, Greeks, Jews, Armenians (MacDonald, 2015), and the LGBT community.

Along with its popularity amongst often marginalized minority groups in the country, the HDP "has also prided itself on socially liberal policies – it maintains a 50 percent quota of female parliamentary candidates and has promoted feminist policies, promising the creation of a national ministry for women. It has also promised to create a ministry for the youth and to lower the voting age to 16" (MacDonald, 2015). In addition, the HDP has also been one of the most supportive of LGBT rights within its party, as it has a specific quota for LGBT members, which is at 10 percent. It is also an active participant in LGBT marches in Istanbul and advocates for rights protections for the LGBT community in Turkey (MacDonald, 2015). Thus, the party aims to be quite inclusive, and for this reason, seems to be picking up support.

HDP has been willing to take any backlash that those who are critical of LGBTI rights may offer in order to stick to principles of LGBTI and gender equality. This could be seen with regards to their willingness to nominate Sulu as an HDP MP candidate. In fact, leaders of the party called Sulu from their headquarters, explaining their decision to nominate him, saying: "Demirtaş is already talking about the rights of LGBTI individuals. He asserted, 'If this is a risk, then we're taking that risk.' The HDP has an LGBTI committee, just like a women's committee and a youth committee. It's in a state of dialogue. We have an election manifesto, a section of which reads 'We're the rainbow.' This is a pamphlet that has been distributed to all provinces for all the party members to read and learn from" (Akan, 2015). In their published manifesto, the section that is related to LGBTI issues reads: ""Our party ensures that LGBTI people will live an equal and proud life by eliminating discrimination and oppression based on sexual orientation and gender identity against a system rising upon the prevalent heterosexism which denies and ignores the diversity of sexual orientation and gender identity." In the manifesto, the party goes on to speak about issues of equality, saying:

A new constitution which recognizes the peoples of Turkey and all differences living in this region is also crucial for establishing the equality of LGBTIs. The HDP, which considers the issue of LGBTI recognition as a problem, will take steps to guarantee equal citizenship in the constitution as well as developing the fight to transform the homophobic and transphobic social culture.

Local and central governing structures bodies, where LGBTIs have their say and can directly be represented in administrative and political decision-making mechanisms both in individual and organized ways, will be founded. (Kaos GL, 2015c; LGBTI News Turkey, 2015a).

The support for LGBTI rights continues in the manifesto, as it states that "[s]ocial policies will be implemented to eliminate social inequalities by extensively regulating all legislation, particularly regarding education, health, employment and housing, based on the principle of acknowledging that LGBTIs are equal citizens and that they should be protected from attacks. Accessible and effective mechanisms will be established regarding discrimination and violation against LGBTIs" (Kaos GL, 2015c; LGBTI News Turkey, 2015a).

HDP political leaders such as Selaattin Demirtaş have consistently supported LGBTI rights in statements. For example, in the 2013 parliamentary discussion on LGBTI rights, Demirtaş (under the Peace and Democracy Party) said, "LGBTI individuals who are targeted, killed, repressed, or ostracized because of their sexual orientations and sexual identities are ignored by the system. LGBTIs' mere existence is seen as a crime. Homophobia and transphobia are fed. 'New Life' calls for equal citizenship rights for all sexual identities to live free and honorable lives in society without fear of discrimination" (quoted in Engin, 2015: 848).

In an interview with HDP co-chair Figen Yuksekdag, Pinar Tremblay of *Al-Monitor* asked Yuksekdag about when the HDP first thought that they could represent all individuals in Turkey, Yuksekdag explains that

The HDP was established as the party of all oppressed and all peoples. All factions find a voice in the HDP. We must accept that the LGBT community is real. We give all groups, including LGBT community members, access on the basis of merit at all levels. So they feel welcome here. It is difficult to bring together sections of society so different from each other, but as the HDP we always believed in a unified movement of the oppressed in these lands. That is why the HDP was established, so our success and effect on society is a result of this unifying power (Tremblay, 2015).

And as researcher Zulfukar Cetin explains, the LGBTI human rights movement is similar in various ways with the HPD, saying that the "[LGBTI] is a movement with many identities – and in this respect, it has much in common with the HDP. This is because the party aims to bring together groups that have been marginalised by society and to demonstrate that these form the majority" (quoted in Nurtsch, 2015).

In fact, the organization publicizes their support for LGBTI rights in many ways. They do this through public events, campaign speeches and information posted on their website. The party has been active in using online platforms for their call of LGBTI rights. For example, one such statement was placed on their website on June 26, 2015, following the June 2015 parliamentary elections, and during the LGBTI Pride Week in Turkey. The post was entitled "We Can Overcome Prejudices, Hatred, and Violence Only with a Culture of Equal and Free Life." In their post, the HDP (2015) party wrote:

LGBTI people of Turkey have been resisting for years against social disregard, being prisoned to a life of oppression, and hate murders.

Pride March[es] are organized in the final week of June, where the LGBTI demands of freedom, justice and peace are voiced stronger every year.

Once again, [the] Pride March on June 28 is the final event of the 23rd Pride Week, which will strengthen LGBTI's search for equality and freedom.

The struggle for "New Life," together with the values of "Great Humanity," which were strengthened by the June 7 elections[,] aim to achieve progress to end human rights violations, discrimination and oppression, based on sexual orientation and gender identity.

We believe in the importance of the fight for a free society in which none would be subject to persecution for their identity and sexual orientation, everyone would be equal under law and would have access to their social rights.

26.06.2015
HDP Central Executive Committee

Thus, they continue to place LGBTI rights as a foundational point of their message as a political party in Turkey.

In terms of its political history, The HDP, while a newer political party in Turkey, actually has its roots in the Democratic Society Party (DTP). The DTP was banned in the year 2009. The Turkish government accused it of being counter to Article 68 and Article 69 of the Turkish constitution, which calls for unity of the state. The government believed that the DTP, with its history of being tied to the Kurdish Worker's Party (PKK), and its history of Kurdish nationalism, was a threat (MacDonald, 2015). And while the group operates separately from the PKK, there is some overlap in activities, such as both being a part of the "the transnational democratic body the Koma Civakên Kurdistan (KCK)" (MacDonald, 2015). Furthermore, PKK leader Abdullah Ocalan has made comments about the HDP, saying that this party would maintain the "historical legacy of revolutionary struggle" and that "[t]he HDP marks an important stage in our common struggle for democracy ... The experience of our struggle will evolve into democracy" (MacDonald, 2015). Some have suggested that the HDP is evidence that the PKK is serious about its movement away from violent measures with regard to their political activities in Turkey and elsewhere in the region. Regardless, it seems that the HDP, while increasing their popularity in recent years, still faces challenges, at least in terms of association. There are some in the country that continue to worry about any possible ties to the PKK, but the HDP continues to advocate for human rights for everyone in Turkey (MacDonald, 2015), something that seems to have resonated with voters in 2015.

However, the HDP has not cornered votes with regard to the Kurdish minority in the country. The AKP– since coming to power – has been more willing to negotiate with the PKK and introduce new measures of support for the Kurdish minority; language classes, schools, and Kurdish media have all helped to increase the AKP's support in Kurdish majority areas of Turkey. They have also tried to use economic growth to help Kurdish groups (MacDonald, 2015), which has helped with regard to electoral support. In addition, it has not helped the HPD's cause that Erdoğan and his allies have used an extensive negative campaigning strategy in attempts to undermine the HDP's (as well as the CHP's) credibility in the eyes of the electorate. For example, Erdoğan and the AKP party have tried to frame the HDP, along with the CHP, as parties with little faith in Islam, attempting to win voters who have a high saliency for issues related to religiosity. In the case of the HDP, "[s]eeking to win over pious Kurds, Erdogan has devoted much time to questioning the HDP's Muslim credentials, describing them as followers of the Zoroastrian religion and accusing them of an insulting reference to the Kaaba, the most sacred site in Islam which worshippers face when praying" (Butler and Pamuk, 2015). And at a rally in Istanbul in early May, when speaking about the HDP, he said that "[t]hese people have nothing to do with Islam," and that "I believe my pious Kurdish brothers will give them the necessary answer on June 7 [the day of the 2015 parliamentary elections]" (Butler and Pamuk, 2015). Erdoğan has continued to use religion and religious sentiment as a way to minimize the level of support that the HDP could receive in Turkey, often painting the HDP and their leadership as non-religious. In addition, he has continued to try to tie the HDP to terrorism (and indirectly, to the PKK), with statements such as the party is "supported by terrorism" or that the HDP is "ran by a terrorist organization" (Uras, 2015).

Along with the smear campaign that Erdoğan used both to challenge the HDP's political ties and its religiosity and religious identity, exact financial statements for all parties are not known, and some believe that the HDP also has far less electoral funds than the AKP or the CHP, with these parties being able to receive money from the state for campaigning – something that the HDP cannot do. And because of this challenge, Erdem Yörük of the HDP explains that their fundraising strategy has to adapt to the situation, noting, "That's why we have to raise money from the people." Erdem continued, "And since we are the party of the Kurds and the workers ... these are the lower classes in the country. So we are doing what Obama did. Small amounts of money from everyone, like five lira, ten lira, twenty lira. We never get support from big corporations, from companies, but from the people" (Reilly, 2015). However, their concerns are not merely financial. In fact, they have been the target of dozens upon dozens of attacks during the most recent election cycle (Reilly, 2015).

Chapter 4

1 In fields like political science, there has also been a resistance to place LGBTI studies and questions within the field, since scholars have often questioned the values and relevancy of these studies to broader political science topics (see Novkov and Barclay, 2010; Mucciaroni, 2011 for a discussion of this issue).
2 While there are not many larger works on LGBTI rights in Turkey, for a recent work on issues of prostitution, sexuality, gender, class, and masculinity, see Özbay (2017).
3 For a study on this issue of contact as it relates to Turkey, see Sakallı and Uğurlu (2001; 2002).

Chapter 5

1 In our interview, Çakmak explained that when she first began working with Lambda International in 2004, there were about twenty members in the organization.
2 As I have discussed before in the section on the Turkish government's response to LGBTI rights – and more specifically, their history of rights abuses, they have tried to shut down many of these human rights organizations. And yet, despite these attempts, these LGBTI NGOs have been able to continue to not only exist but thrive, offering much-needed advocacy on these rights issues.
3 Sadly, given the importance of her position at IMC TV for the LGBTI community, in September of 2014, Demishevich was fired following being discriminated against at work (Busey, 2014). Speaking to Pembe Hayat, Demishevich discussed some of the things that happened to her leading up to her firing, saying:

I was employed at a low salary, without insurance. Recently I was getting warnings about my clothes and the color of my hair. Finally even my use of red lipstick started to be a problem. These things are totally different from motives arising from transphobia. It is on account of my identity as a woman that I was subjected to discrimination and marginalization.

Women working at the organization are living witnesses to the fact that I was subjected to mobbing. When they learned that I had been sacked, they gave me great support; they encouraged me to fight (Busey, 2014).

Demishevich went on to say of the situation,

They decided that we should part ways because they thought that I had violated professional ethics. According to what the general manager said, there was no problem with gender identity. My attitude and conduct reportedly caused a disturbance. It was not my gender identity, but my attire, the color of my hair, and my use of red lipstick that was considered intolerable. They tried to make me sign a paper stating that I waived my employee rights. My lawyer warned me and I did not sign it. At the moment I am an unemployed journalist" (Busey, 2014).

She said that her employer kept bringing up how she was dressed, as well as her hair color. She says that the issue in her case here was not about transphobia but discrimination against women.

   IMC TV disputes that there was discrimination, saying that among other things, Demishevich "had an argument with some of their representatives and allegedly told them inappropriate things – which was the last drop in the bucket" (Busey, 2014). A number of people were outraged at how Demishevich was treated by her employer. Some members and volunteers from the LGBTI human rights activist group Pink Life showed their support for Demishevich by wearing red lipstick (Busey, 2014), which is again why many believe Demishevich was fired. After being fired, Demishevich herself took a picture in which she was wearing red lipstick and said that she was "smiling in a way against the morals with her red lipstick and blonde bleached hair" (Tahaoğlu, 2014).

   What is also unfortunate about Demishevich's situation is that she also reported facing other forms of discrimination while at work. For example, she did not have health insurance from her employer, her pay was low, and she was frequently last to be chosen for new stories (Kellaway, 2014). Nonetheless, despite these setbacks and continued discrimination against her, Demishevich continues to speak out for her (and other transgendered individuals') rights in Turkey. For example, she has been critical of imams who did not allow transgendered individuals to be buried in Muslim cemeteries, saying: "Even after death, you continue your life, or whatever it is, on the fringes of society. So you live your life rejected by society, and even after death, you are excluded" (Heffernan, 2014). Demishevich has stated that she will continue to fight for LGBTI rights, even possibly considering entering into electoral politics (Heffernan, 2014).

4 Ertetik (2010) has done research on the issue of coming out in Turkey in a non-digital-media setting.

5 For more detail on Legato and its history regarding LGBTI Internet activism in Turkey, see Görkemli (2015).

6 Along with the Turkish language publication, Renay and a partner who works on *GZone Magazine* run a site called GaysofTurkey.com. He explained that this site is "full English and it's all about the issues of LGBT Turkey but not in a political way. For example, when you think about Turkey gay life but you think of Turkish bands or song it's in there. Or gay bars, they're all in there and it's something like that." But he hopes that they will also move to provide *GZone Magazine* in English in the very near future.

7 Although Renay's publications are focused on celebrities and cultural issues, politics are not completely absent from his online publications (particularly his online portal). He explained that they "cannot always focus only focus on the fashion [or] style[,]" and that politics have to be discussed, at least somewhat.

8 For a discussion of Bulent Ersoy as it relates issues of transgender identity, see Altinay (2008).

9 As Pearce (2014a) noted, "In 2013, gay rights gained visibility in the music world in Istanbul, during a concert by the Turkish singer Sezen Aksu, who unfurled a rainbow flag and asked the audience, 'Where are you, my dear?', the line that had been the chosen theme for the June 2013 Istanbul Pride parade, to audience cheers of recognition" (Akpınar, 2013).

10 According to Renay, one other criticism for this approach – namely, using celebrities for visibility – has not come from the public per se but from other LGBTI rights activists and NGOs. Renay and I were speaking about NGOs in the country, and he said that many of the NGOs may not see his approach toward using celebrities as effective. He said that "[t]hey think that is lame or they think that it's a little bit useless, but we don't think that. Our news, it relates to issues, we try to have all the famous celebrities." Or, he also said that some may think that his publication borders on that of tabloids. Renay explained "that he listens to the criticism from the LGBT community in the world [as they do inspire Renay and his team], and [they are] willing to change their actions, but only if [his team] agrees. He said that they "are okay because we are really confident that what we are doing."

11 Again, the organization's activities have not primarily been on film documentaries. Rather, LİSTAG has worked with family members of those who are LGBTI. This advocacy has taken various forms. Some organizations have established a support group in order to provide an outlet for those with questions and have put together booklets for families of LGBTI persons (LİSTAG, 2011). Moreover, NGOs have also

organized monthly therapy sessions with volunteer psychologists who offer to speak with family members to discuss whatever issues the persons may have (LİSTAG, 2011).

Chapter 6

1 The BDP later became a part of the HDP in Turkey.

Chapter 8

1 At the time of the interview, Kalan explained that it was almost three weeks without the Solidarity Center in Ankara actually helping.
2 While this has been argued is the case in terms of activism, Saruhan (2013) points out that "[t]ranssexual and transvestite subjects in Turkey belonged to a social group disconnected from lesbians and gay men. They formed their own group, as a subculture, different from that of homosexual subjects. They usually were not included in the activities and activism of homosexual subjects, even discriminated by those groups, which led them to create their own activism, in order to survive in the society," but Saruhan also notes that "[a]lthough the trans subculture still exists, it is now more accepted in homosexual activism" and that the LGBI and transgender have worked together, forming organizations for LGBTI rights-based advocacy.
3 At the time of my interview (April 29, 2016), it had been three weeks since Kaos GL were able to work from their offices.

Chapter 9

1 There was hope pinned on electoral successes in order for constitutional changes for LGBTI rights. Yılmaz (2013) argued "that the success of [the] LGBT rights movement in promoting LGBT equality in Turkey, definitely shares the same fate with the electoral success of the political parties on the left side of the spectrum" (140).
2 The women's rights organizations put out the following statement:

As women, we give importance to join this Justice March with our own demands for justice because since the time of the murder of Pippa – just as it had been the case before it – thousands of women have been buried under the ground while the crimes of men against them have ... at times gone unpunished and, at other times, been abated in the name of "general moral norms." LGBT individuals have been subjected to hate crimes – even been killed – and thousands of children have been abused. The state of hating and lynching those who are "different" [has come] to be defined as a "sensible" act; and, it has even been applauded at certain times ... We, the women, want to march for real justice; not a patriarchal justice. The injustices especially felt lately under the state of emergency laws have increased violence of men even more. On top of dismissals of hundreds of people, detention of women MPs, politicians, and local governors[,] shutting down of women's shelters, women's associations, and women's news sources have put women and children into a even more fragile situation in the face of men's violence. Women are being pushed away from politics. We are going to fight until women get equal rights and opportunities as men in all field of life! If there is no equality, there will be no justice! (*BirGün*, 2017b)

References

Abu-Lughod, L. (2002). Do Muslim Women Really Need Saving? Anthropological Reflections on Cultural Relativism and Its Others. *American Anthropologist*, Vol. 104, No. 3, pages 783–790.

Afary, J. (2009). *Sexual Politics in Modern Iran*. Cambridge: Cambridge University Press.

Afrol News (2010). Desmond Tutu: "Homophobia Equal Apartheid." *Afrol News*. July 7, 2010. Available online: www.afrol.com/articles/13584.

Agence France Presse (2014). Turkey's Separate Gay Prisons Plan Angers Local LGBT Groups. April 15, 2014. Available online: www.huffingtonpost.com/2014/04/15/turkey-gay-prison-plan-_n_5153478.html.

Ajansı, E. H. (2013). LGBTs Forgotten in the Democracy Package! Etha.com.tr. Available online in Turkey: www.etha.com.tr/Haber/2013/09/30/politika/demokrasi-paketinde-lgbtler-unutuldu/. Translated in LGBTI News Turkey: https://lgbtinewsturkey.com/2013/09/30/lgbt-not-in-democracy-package-of-akp/.

Aksoy, H. A. (2015). Invigorating Democracy in Turkey: The Agency of Organized Islamist Women. *Politics & Gender*, Vol. 11, No. 1, pages 146–170.

Akan, A. K. (2015). "HDP'yi seçtim çünkü LGBTİ'liler baştan beri varlar" ["I Chose the HDP, Because LGBTIs Have Been in the HDP since the Beginning"], *Anadolu Agency*, May 25, 2015. Available online: www.aa.com.tr/tr/rss/516349–hdp-yi-sectim-cunku-lgbtililer-bastan-beri-varlar.

Akdeniz, Y. (2010). Report of the OSCE Representative on Freedom of the Media on Turkey and Internet Censorship. January 11, 2010. Available online: www.osce.org/fom/41091?download=true.

Akpinar, Ö. (2012). The New Constitution in Turkey: Not for Gays! Kaos GL. September 15, 2012. Available online: http://kaosgl.org/page.php?id=12282.

(2013). Turkish Singer Gave Support to LGBTs during Concert. Kaos GL. Available online: www.kaosgl.org/page.php?id=14555.

(2015a). LGBTI Activist Candidate for Nomination from HDP: Peace Must Also Be Made with the LGBTI in the Resolution Process. Kaos GL. March 2, 2015, Available online: http://kaosgl.org/sayfa.php?id=18855.

(2015b). Trans Pre-Candidate for Turkish General Elections: I Am in This Race to Get Our Rights Once and for All. Kaos GL. February 28, 2015.

Akyol, M. (2015). What does Islam Say about Being Gay? *New York Times.* July 28, 2015. Available online: www.nytimes.com/2015/07/29/opin ion/mustafa-akyol-what-does-islam-say-about-being-gay.html.

Al Jazeera (2016). Timeline: A History of Turkish Coups. July 15, 2016. Available online: www.aljazeera.com/news/europe/2012/04/20124472 814687973.html.

(2017). Detentions as Police Break up Istanbul Pride Parade. June 26, 2017. Available online: www.aljazeera.com/news/2017/06/detentions-police-break-istanbul-pride-parade-170625182611340.html.

Alkaç, F. (2014). Gay Couple Faces Threats after Symbolic Wedding. *Hurriyet Daily News.* October 13, 2014. Available online: www .hurriyetdailynews.com/gay-couple-faces-threats-after-symbolic-wedding .aspx?pageID=238&nID=72879&NewsCatID=339.

Altinay, R. E. (2008). Reconstructing the Transgendered Self as a Muslim, Nationalist, Upper-Class Woman: The Case of Bulent Ersoy. *Women's Studies Quarterly,* Vol. 36, No. 3/4, pages 210–229.

Amnesty International (2009). Turkish LGBT Organization Wins Appeal against Closure. January 21, 2009. Available online: www.amnesty .org/en/latest/news/2009/01/turkish-lgbt-organization-wins-appeal-against-closure-20090121/.

(2011). Not an Illness nor a Crime: Lesbian, Gay, Bisexual and Trans-gender People in Turkey Demand Equality. June 21, 2011, pages 1–50. Available online: www.amnesty.org/en/documents/EUR44/001/2011/ en/.

(2013). Gezi Park Protests: Brutal Denial of the Right to Peaceful Assem-bly in Turkey. October 2013, pages 1–70. Available online: www .amnestyusa.org/files/eur440222013en.pdf.

(2015). Republic of Turkey. Amnesty International Report 2014/2015. Available online: www.amnesty.org/en/countries/europe-and-central-asia/turkey/report-turkey/.

(2016a). Bangladesh: Authorities Fail to Curb Brutal Killing Spree as LGBTI Editor Hacked to Death. April 25, 2016. Available online: www.amnesty.org/en/latest/news/2016/04/bangladesh-authorities-fail-to-curb-brutal-killing-spree-as-lgbti-editor-hacked-to-death/.

(2016b). Case Study: Ahmet Yıldız. Murdered for Being Gay. May 2016. Available online: www.amnesty.org.uk/files/power_of_the_pen_may_ 2016_-_ahmet_yildiz_0.pdf.

Anadolu Agency (2016). Erdogan Criticizes West's Insensitivity towards Syrians. May 13, 2016. Available online: http://aa.com.tr/en/turkey/erdogan-criticizes-wests-insensitivity-towards-syrians-/572010.

Arat, Z. F. K. and Nuñez, C. (2017). Advancing LGBT Rights in Turkey: Tolerance or Protection? *Human Rights Review.* Vol. 18, No. 1, pages 1–19.

Ashdown, N. (2015). "This Is What Being a Kurd Is About." *Al Jazeera.* January 10, 2015. Available online: www.aljazeera.com/news/mid dleeast/2015/01/what-being-kurd-about-2015165576342191.html.

Ataman, H. (2011). Less than Citizens: The Lesbian, Gay, Bisexual, and Transgender Question in Turkey. *In Societal Peace and Ideal Citizenship for Turkey, Rasim Ösgür Dönmez,* ed. Pinar Enneli, pages 125–158. Lanham, MD: Lexington Books.

Ayyıldız, F. (2015). SPoD's Volkan Yılmaz: Political Parties Must Ban LGBTI Discrimination in Their Organizations. (Partilerde LGBTI'lerin Dışlanması Yasaklanmalıdır), *Evrensel,* February 4, 2015. Available online: www.evrensel.net/haber/103777/partilerde-lgbtilerin-dislanmasi-yasaklanmalidir.

Baba, H. B. (2011). The Construction of Heteropatriarchal Family and Dissident Sexualities in Turkey. *Fe Dergi,* Vol. 3, No. 1, pages 56–64.

Bagirov, E., Fernandez, B., Fabeni, S., and Tripp, D. (2009). The Violations of the Rights of Lesbian, Gay, Bisexual, Transgender Persons in Azerbaijan: A Shadow Report. Submitted during the Third Periodic Report to the UN Human Rights Committee, July 2009. Available online: www.globalrights.org/sites/default/files/docs/LGBT_Shadow_Report_Azerbaijan.pdf.

Bakacak, A. G. and Otem, P. (2014). Homosexuality in Turkey: Strategies for Managing Heterosexism. *Journal of Homosexuality,* Vol. 61, No. 6, pages 817–846.

Banco, E. (2015). Turkey's Transgender People Fight for Recognition, Run For National Election for First Time. *International Business Times.* May 28, 2015.

Banner (2011). World News: Allan Boesak Quits Church Posts over Homosexuality Policy, Belhar. January 18, 2011. Available online: www .thebanner.org/news/2011/01/world-news-allan-boesak-quits-church-posts-over-homosexuality-policy-belhar.

Barrionuevo, A. (2010). Argentina Approves Gay Marriage, in a First for Region. *New York Times.* July 15, 2010. Available online: www .nytimes.com/2010/07/16/world/americas/16argentina.html.

Baş, E. (2015). From Self-Effacement to Confrontation: The Emergence of Queer Theatre in Istanbul. *Asian Culture and History,* Vol. 8, No. 2, pages 126–134.

BBC (2013). Archbishop Tutu "Would Not Worship a Homophobic God." July 26, 2013. Available online: www.bbc.com/news/world-africa-23464694.

(2016a). LGBT Groups Barred from Attending UN AIDS Conference. May 18, 2016. Available online: www.bbc.com/news/world-us-canada-36325578.

(2016b). Turkey LGBT: Scuffles at Banned Istanbul Transgender Event. June 19, 2016. Available online: www.bbc.com/news/world-europe-36571303.

Beck, J. (2013). Turkey's Violent Homophobia. *Daily Beast.* July 1, 2013.

Behind the Mask (BTM). n.d. "Benin."

Bereket, T. and Adam, B. D. (2006). The Emergence of Gay Identities in Contemporary Turkey. *Sexualities.* Vol. 9, No. 2, pages 131–151.

(2008). Navigating Islam and Same-Sex Liaisons among Men in Turkey. *Journal of Homosexuality*, Vol. 55, No. 2, pages 204–222.

Berman, I. (2015). Turkey's Political Earthquake. CNN. June 8, 2015.

Bianet (2015). LGBTİ Aktivistleri Boysan Yakar ve Zeliş Deniz'i Kaybettik. September 6, 2015. Available online: http://bianet.org/bianet/lgbti/167397-lgbti-aktivistleri-boysan-yakar-ve-zelis-deniz-i-kaybettik. Translated in LGBTI News Turkey, 2015: https://lgbtinewsturkey.com/2015/09/13/we-have-lost-lgbti-activists-boysan-yakar-and-zelis-deniz/.

BirGün (2017a). Women in Turkey to Join Justice March in Gebze Where Activist Pippa Bacca Was Murdered. July 5, 2017. Available online: www.birgun.net/haber-detay/women-in-turkey-to-join-justice-march-in-gebze-where-activist-pippa-bacca-was-murdered-168356.html.

(2017b). Women's Associations in Turkey Call for Support to Justice March. July 6, 2017. Available online: www.birgun.net/haber-detay/women-s-associations-in-turkey-call-for-support-to-justice-march-168463.html.

Biçmen, Z. and Bekiroğulları, Z. (2014). Social Problems of LGBT People in Turkey. *Procedia: Social and Behavioral Sciences.* Vol. 113, pages 224–233.

Bohn, L. (2015). Lacking a Supportive Community, Many LGBT People in Turkey Live Double Lives. Public Radio International. July 4, 2015. Available online: www.pri.org/stories/2015-06-04/lacking-supportive-community-many-lgbt-people-turkey-live-double-lives.

Boon, S. D. and Lomore, C. D. (2001). Admirer-Celebrity Relationships among Young Adults: Explaining Perceptions of Celebrity Influence on Identity. *Human Communication Research.* Vol. 27, pages 432–465.

Botelho, G. (2014). Egyptian Men Seen in Alleged Same-Sex Wedding Video Get Three Years in Jail. CNN. November 1, 2014.

Bouchaud, M. (2015). A Human Rights Group Says It's Not Safe to Be Gay in Cameroon. *VICE News*. February 25, 2015. Available online: https://news.vice.com/article/a-human-rights-group-says-its-not-safe-to-be-gay-in-cameroon.

Bozkurt, G. (2012). Protection For Gay Rights Vetoed. *Hürriyet Daily News*. September 14, 2012. Available online: www.hurriyetdaily news.com/protection-for-gay-rights-vetoed.aspx?pageID=238&nID=30096&NewsCatID=339.

Brooks-Pollock, T. (2015). First-Ever Openly Gay Parliamentary Candidate Stands for Election in Turkey. *Independent*. May 27, 2015. Available online: www.independent.co.uk/news/uk/firstever-openly-gay-parliamen tary-candidate-stands-for-election-inturkey-10274746.html.

Brydum, S. (2015). Turkish Army Adopts "Don't Ask, Don't Tell" Policy for Gay Recruits. Advocate.com, November 23, 2015. Available online: www.advocate.com/world/2015/11/23/turkish-army-adopts-dont-ask-dont-tell-policy-gay-recruits.

Burton, N. (2015). When Homosexuality Stopped Being a Mental Disorder. *Psychology Today*. September 18, 2015. Available online: www .psychologytoday.com/blog/hide-and-seek/201509/when-homosexuality-stopped-being-mental-disorder.

Busey, K. (2014). Michelle Demishevich, First and Only Turkish Transgender TV Reporter Fired for Red Lip Stick. Planet Transgender. September 17, 2014. Available online: http://planettransgender.com/michelle-demishevich-first-and-only-turkish-trans-reporter-fired-for-red-lip-stick/

Butler, D. and Pamuk, H. (2015). Islam Center Stage as Turkish Election Campaign Enters Final Week. Reuters. May 30, 2015.

Butt, R. (2009). Muslims in Britain Have zero Tolerance of Homosexuality, Says Poll. *Guardian*. May 7, 2009. Available online: www .theguardian.com/uk/2009/may/07/muslims-britain-france-germany-homosexuality.

Canada: Immigration and Refugee Board, Canada (2003). Benin: Laws Regarding Homosexuality and the Treatment of Homosexuals by the Public and the Authorities. December 17, 2003. Available online: www.refworld.org/docid/403dd1e28.html.

Carroll, A. (2010). Make It Work: Six Steps to Effective LGBT Human Rights Advocacy. ILGA Europe. October 2010. Available online: www.eidhr.eu/files/dmfile/advocacy_manual_www1.pdf.

Carter, W. (2015). Suffering and Loss in Istanbul's Transgender Slum. *Middle East Eye*. July 28, 2015. Available online: www.middleeast eye.net/in-depth/features/silence-suffering-and-dispossession-istanbul-s-transgender-slum-1343803757#sthash.2tbCG7qi.dpuf.

Çetin, Z. (2015). The Dynamics of the Queer Movement in Turkey. Heinrich-Böll Stiftung. European Union. September 30, 2015. Available online: https://eu.boell.org/en/2015/09/30/dynamics-queer-movement-turkey.

(2016). The Dynamics of the Queer Movement in Turkey before and during the Conservative AKP Government. Working Paper Research Group EU/Europe Stiftung Wissenschaft und Politik German Institute for International and Security Affairs. January 2016. Available online: www.swp-berlin.org/fileadmin/contents/products/arbeitspapiere/WP_RG_Europe_2016_01.pdf.

Cohn, J. (2015). Why Indiana's Religious Freedom Law Is Such a Big Deal. *Huffington Post*. April 1, 2015. Available online: www.huffington post.com/2015/04/01/indiana-religious-freedom_n_6984156.html.

Cole, J. (2015). The Truth behind the Turkish Police Attack on Istanbul's Gay Pride Parade. TruthDig, June 29, 2015. Available online: www.truthdig.com/report/item/interpreting_the_turkish_police.

Concannon, L. (2009). Developing Inclusive Health and Social Care Policies for Older LGBT Citizens. *British Journal of Social Work*. Vol. 39, No. 9, pages 403–417.

COWI: The Danish Institute for Human Rights (2010). Study on Homophobia, Transphobia, and Discrimination on Grounds of Sexual Orientation and Gender Identity. Sociological Report: Turkey. Pages 1–18. Available online: www.lgbti-era.org/sites/default/files/pdfdocs/0028%202010%20ENG%20Sociological%20LGBT%20Report%20Turkey.COWI_.pdf.

Currier, A. M. A. (2007). The Visibility of Sexual Minority Movement Organizations in Namibia and South Africa. Ph.D. Dissertation. University of Pittsburgh. Available online: http://d-scholarship.pitt.edu/8254/1/CurrierAMetd2007.pdf.

(2012a). Invisibility and Its Advantages: Why LGBT Rights Activists in Africa Sometimes Strategize to Remain Hidden. UMP University of Minnesota Blog. August 29, 2012. Available online: www.uminnpressblog.com/2012/08/invisibility-and-its-advantages-why.html.

(2012b). *Out in Africa: LGBT Organizing in Namibia and South Africa*. Minneapolis, Minnesota. University of Minnesota Press.

Curry, A. (2014). Archbishop Desmond Tutu: Oppression of Gays Is "New Apartheid." NBC. June 27, 2014. Available online: www.nbcnews.com/watch/ann-curry-reports/archbishop-desmond-tutu-oppression-of-gays-is-new-apartheid-290683459580.

Daily Beast (2015). Even in Repressive Contexts, Online Activism Makes LGBT Lives Visible. *Daily Beast*. April 20, 2015. Available online: www.thedailybeast.com/articles/2015/03/11/even-in-repressive-contexts-online-activism-makes-lgbt-lives-visible.html.

Daily Sabah (2016). Trans Women's Brutal Death Sparks Outrage. August 18, 2016. Available online: www.dailysabah.com/nation/2016/08/19/trans-womans-brutal-death-sparks-outrage.

Day, A. (2013). Turkey: Court Bans Access to Gay Dating App Grindr as a "Protection Measure." *PinkNews.* September 12, 2013. Available online: www.pinknews.co.uk/2013/09/12/turkey-court-bans-access-to-gay-dating-app-grindr-as-a-protection-measure/.

Deese, M. A. and Dawson, B. L. (2013) Changing Attitudes toward LGBT Students: An Analysis of an Awareness Training Paradigm Aimed at Increasing Pro-LGBT Attitudes. *Papers & Publications: Interdisciplinary Journal of Undergraduate Research.* Vol. 2, Issue 7. Available online: http://digitalcommons.northgeorgia.edu/papersandpubs/vol2/iss1/7.

Diva, M. (2015). Din ve Eşcinsellik. July 1, 2015. Pembe Hayat. Available online: www.pembehayat.org/yasam.php?id=799.

Doğan News Agency (2015). LBGTI Protest against Hate Crimes in Turkey's Aegean Province. May 4, 2015. *Hurriyet Daily News.* Available online: www.hurriyetdailynews.com/lgbti-protest-against-hate-crimes-in-turkeys-aegean-province-.aspx?pageID=238&nID=81937&NewsCatID=339.

Drescher, J. (2015). Out of DSM: Depathologizing Homosexuality. *Behavioral Sciences.* Vol. 5, No. 4, pages 565–575. Available online: www.ncbi.nlm.nih.gov/pmc/articles/PMC4695779/.

Duffy, N. (2014). UN: Human Rights Council Passes Landmark LGBT Rights Resolution. *PinkNews.* September 26, 2014. Available online: www.pinknews.co.uk/2014/09/26/un-human-rights-council-passes-landmark-lgbt-rights-resolution/.

(2016). Top Saudi cleric: Homosexuals Should Not Be Punished. PinkNews. May 3, 2016. Available online: www.pinknews.co.uk/2016/05/03/top-saudi-cleric-homosexuals-should-not-be-punished/.

Durgun, A. (2015). "Bu saatten sonra kimse bizi belediyeden atamaz" ("No One Can Kick Us out of the Municipality at This Point"). Milliyet.com.tr, January 17, 2015. Available online: www.milliyet.com.tr/-bu-saatten-sonra-kimse-bizi/pazar/haberdetay/18.01.2015/2000113/default.htm. Translated in LGBTI News Turkey: https://lgbtinewsturkey.com/2015/01/20/lgbt-in-municipality.

Engin, C. (2015). LGBT in Turkey: Policies and Experiences. *Social Sciences.* Vol. 4, pages 838–858.

(2016). Transgender Sex Work in Turkey. Working Paper. Available online: www.researchgate.net/publication/296641938_Sex_Work_in_Turkey_Experiences_of_Transwomen.

Enguix, B. 2009. "Identities, Sexualities and Commemorations: Pride Parades, Public Space and Sexual Dissidence." *Anthropological Notebooks*. Vol. 15, pages 15–33.

Equal Rights Association for Western Balkans and Turkey (2017). Turkey. Available online: www.lgbti-era.org/content/turkey.

Ertetik, I. (2010). Coming Out as a Political Act in LGBT Movement in Turkey. Gradate Thesis, Department of Sociology, Middle East Technical University. June 2010. Available online: http://etd.lib.metu.edu.tr/upload/12611923/index.

Esmer, Y. (2009). *Radicalism and Extremism*. Istanbul: Bahcesehir University.

European Commission (2013). Turkey: 2013 Progress Report. Extract from the Communication from the Commission to the European Parliament and the Council "Enlargement Strategy and Main Challenges 2013–2014." Pages 1–80. Available online: http://ec.europa.eu/enlargement/pdf/key_documents/2013/package/brochures/turkey_2013.pdf.

European Court of Human Rights (2015). Refusal to Authorise Transsexual to Have Access to Gender Reassignment Surgery Breached Right to Respect for Private Life. ECHR 075 (2015) Press Release. October 3, 2015.

Feder, J. L. (2015). This Is What It Is Like to Be an LGBT Syrian Fleeing for Your Life. Buzzfeed. October 22, 2015. Available online: www.buzzfeed.com/lesterfeder/this-is-what-its-like-to-be-an-lgbt-syrian-fleeing-for-your#.mkxMgWKPAn.

Felice, W. (2016). *The Ethics of Interdependence: Global Human Rights and Duties*. Lanham, MD: Roman and Littlefield.

Feldman, E. (2014). What One Magazine Means for Gay Life in Turkey. August 6, 2014. Available online: http://mashable.com/2014/08/06/turkey-gay-magazine/.

Fishman, L. A. (2013). Turkey and LGBT Rights: A Historical and Global Perspective. *Turkish Policy Quarterly*. Vol. 11, No. 4, pages 149–159.

(2015). How Erdogan Spurs LGBT Hatred for Political Gain. *Haaretz*. July 17, 2015. Available online: www.haaretz.com/opinion/.premium-1.666544.

Fisk, R. (2016). The 70,000 Post Coup-Arrests Are Now at the Heart of the Turkish Government's Propaganda War. *Independent*. October 8, 2016. Available online: www.independent.co.uk/voices/turkey-coup-purge-recep-tayyip-erdogan-arrests-latest-a7351781.html.

Gentile, C. (2016). Meet Three LGBT Syrian Refugees Who Fled ISIS Brutality. Vocativ. January 30, 2016. Available online: www.vocativ.com/277828/isis-lgbt-refugees.

Göksel, D. N. (2013). Gay Rights: Where is Turkey Going? On Turkey. The German Marshall Fund of the United States. March 28, 2013.

Golebiowska, E. A. and Thomsen, C. J. (1999). Group Stereotypes of Individuals: The Case of Gay and Lesbian Political Candidates. In *Gays and Lesbians in the Democratic Process: Public Policy, Public Opinion and Political Representation*, ed. Ellen D. B. Riggle and Barry L. Tadlock, pages 192–219. New York: Columbia University Press.

Gomillion, S. C. and Giuliano, T. A. (2011). The Influence of Media Role Models on Gay, Lesbian, and Bisexual Identity. *Journal of Homosexuality*. Vol. 58, No. 3, pages 330–354.

Gordon, N. (2011). A Case Study Approach to LGBT Interest Group Strategies: The 2009 D. C. Marriage Campaign. *Critique: A Worldwide Student Journal of Politics*. Fall 2011. Available online: https://about.illinoisstate.edu/critique/Documents/Fall%202011/GORDON.pdf.

Görkemli, S. (2012). "Coming Out of the Internet": Lesbian and Gay Activism and the Internet as a "Digital Closet" in Turkey. *Journal of Middle East Women's Studies*. Volume 8, No. 3, pages 66–88.

(2015). *Grassroots Literacies: Lesbian and Gay Activism and the Internet in Turkey*. Albany, NY: State University of New York Press.

Grungras, N. (2016). Stop Neglecting the True State of LGBT Refugees. Advocate.com. January 12, 2016. Available online: www.advocate.com/commentary/2016/1/12/stop-neglecting-true-state-lgbt-refugees.

Güler, H. (2012). Portrayal of Transgenders in Turkish films, or Lack Thereof. *Hurriyet Daily News*. July 2, 2012. Available online: www.hurriyetdailynews.com/portrayal-of-transgenders-in-turkish-films-or-lack-thereof-24492.

Güneş, A. (2014). Interview with Sevda Yılmaz. İlk Eylemden Bug üne LGBTİ Hareketi. T24. Available online: http://t24.com.tr/haber/ilk-eylemden-bugune-lgbti-hareketi,262152.

Gurcan, M. (2015). Gays Seeking Military Exemption in Turkey No Longer Need to Provide Visual Proof of Their Homosexuality. Al Monitor. November 17, 2015. Available online: www.al-monitor.com/pulse/origin als/2015/11/turkey-military-gay-rights-homosexual-picture.html.

Gutierrez, G. and Schuppe, J. (2015). Rowan County Clerk Kim Davis Isn't Kentucky's Only Gay Marriage Holdout. NBC News. September 9, 2015. Available online: www.nbcnews.com/news/us-news/why-arent-other-defiant-kentucky-clerks-joining-kim-davis-jail-n423496.

Harper, R. (2012). National Coming Out Day and Achieving Progress through Visibility. *Huffington Post*, October 11, 2012. Available online: www.huffingtonpost.com/robyn-harper/national-coming-out-day-a_b_1956574.html.

Harrison, B. F. and Michelson, M. R. (2015a). God and Marriage: The Impact of Religious Identity Priming on Attitudes toward Same-Sex Marriage. *Social Science Quarterly* Vol. 96, No. 5, pages 1411–1423.

(2015b). How to Change Minds about Same-Sex Marriage. *Washington Post* Monkey Cage. May 26, 2015. Available online: www.washingtonpost.com/blogs/monkey-cage/wp/2015/05/26/how-to-change-peoples-minds-about-same-sex-marriage/.

Hashimi, F. (2016). Turkey LGBTI Resources. International Refugee Rights Initiative: Rights in Exile Programme. Available online: www.refugee legalaidinformation.org/turkey-lgbti-resources.

HDP (People's Democratic Party) (2015). We Can Overcome Prejudices, Hatred and Violence Only with a Culture of Equal and Free Life. HDP Website. June 26, 2015. Available online: https://hdpenglish.wordpress .com/2015/06/29/we-can-overcome-prejudices-hatred-and-violence-only-with-a-culture-of-equal-and-free-life/.

Heavy.com (2015). Watch: Turkish Police Water Cannon Istanbul Celebrators. June 28, 2015. Available online: http://heavy.com/news/2015/06/turkey-police.

Heffernan, D. (2012). The APA Removes "Gender Identity Disorder" from Updated Mental Health Guide. GLAAD. December 3, 2012. Available online: www.glaad.org/blog/apa-removes-gender-identity-dis order-updated-mental-health-guide.

(2014). Michelle Demishevich, Transgender Turkish TV Reporter, Talks to AFP about Activism. GLAAD. July 23, 2014. Available online: www.glaad.org/blog/michelle-demishevich-transgender-turkish-tv-reporter-talks-afp-about-activism.

Henschke, R. and Ginanjar, G. (2016). The Sudden Intensity of Indonesia's Anti-Gay Onslaught. BBC., February 29, 2016. Available online: www.bbc.com/news/world-asia-35657114.

Human Rights Campaign (2014). 10 LGBT Candidates Running for Office in Turkey. HRC Blog. March 11, 2014.

Human Rights First (2014). Report: The State of Human Rights For LGBT People in Africa. July 2014. Available online: www.humanrights first.org/sites/default/files/HRF-HRC-Africa-Report.pdf.

Human Rights Watch (2009). They Want Us Exterminated: Murder, Torture, Sexual Orientation and Gender in Iraq. August 2009. Available online: Available online: www.hrw.org/sites/default/files/reports/iraq0809web.pdf.

Hume, T. and Greene, R. A. (2016). 52% of British Muslims in Poll Think Homosexuality Should Be Illegal. CNN. April 12, 2016. Available online: www.cnn.com/2016/04/11/europe/britain-muslims-survey/.

Hurriyet Daily News (2009). Gay Web Site Block Reveals No Limit to Censorship in Turkey. October 5, 2009. Available online: www .hurriyetdailynews.com/default.aspx?pageid=438&n=still-no-limit-about-censorship-2009-10-05.

——— (2010). Homosexuality Is a Disease, Says Turkish Minister. March 7, 2010.

——— (2012). Calling Gay People "Perverts" an Insult, Top Court Says. January 9, 2012. Available online: www.hurriyetdailynews.com/calling-gay-people-perverts-an-insult-top-court-says-.aspx?pageID=238&nID=11040& NewsCatID=339.

——— (2014). Four "LGBT friendly" Mayors Elected in Istanbul and Mersin. April 1, 2014. Available online: www.hurriyetdailynews.com/four-lgbt-friendly-mayors-elected-in-istanbul-and-mersin-64410.

——— (2015a). Turkish LGBTI Associations Condemn Homophobic News Items against Openly Gay HDP Candidate. May 27, 2015. Available Online: www.hurriyetdailynews.com/turkish-lgbti-associations-condemn-homo phobic-news-items-against-openly-gay-hdp-candidate–83048.

——— (2015b). UN Concerned over LGBT Rights in Turkey, Calls Gov't to Take Action. July 15, 2015. www.hurriyetdailynews.com/un-concerned-over-lgbt-rights-in-turkey-calls-govt-to-take-action-.aspx?pageID=238&nid= 85465.

Hurtas, S. (2015). Turkey's "Pink Prisons." Al-Monitor. January 21, 2015.

Idiz, S. (2014a). Turkey's first "Gay Marriage." Al Monitor. October 14, 2014. Available online: www.al-monitor.com/pulse/originals/2014/ 10/turkey-lgbt-first-gay-marriage-nightmare.html.

——— (2014b). Turkey's LGBT Fight Uphill but Not Hopeless Battle. Turkey Democracy Index. July 15, 2014. Available online: http://turkey democracyindex.wordpress.com/2014/07/.

İnce, E. (2014). LGBTİ: Kaldırımın Altından Gökkuşağı Çıkıyor (LGBTI: The Rainbow is Peaking Out from the Pavement). Bianet, 8 December 2014. Available online: http://bianet.org/bianet/lgbti/160544-lgbti-kal dirimin-altindan-gokkusagi-cikiyor. Translated in LBTI News Turkey: https://lgbtinewsturkey.com/tag/bianet/page/2/.

International Federation for Human Rights (FIDH) and World Organisation against Torture (2015). Homophobia and Violence against Defenders of the Rights of LGBTI Persons. February 2015. Available online: www.fidh.org/IMG/pdf/report_cameroun_lgbti_eng_final.pdf.

International Gay and Lesbian Human Rights Commission (IGLHRC) (2015). LGBTI People Gain Ground on Rights Advocacy in Turkish Parliamentary Elections. June 10, 2015.

International Justice Resource Center (IJRC) (2015). ECTHR: Refusal to Authorize Gender Reassignment Surgery Violates Convention. March

23, 2015. Available online: www.ijrcenter.org/2015/03/23/ecthr-refusal-to-authorize-gender-reassignment-surgery-violates-convention/.

(2016). Turkey's Seizure of LGBT Magazine Issue Violated European Convention. November 29, 2016. Available online: www.ijrcenter.org/2016/11/29/turkeys-seizure-of-lgbt-magazine-issue-violated-european-convention/.

International Lesbian and Gay Association (ILGA). (2002). Benin: World Legal Survey. July 21, 2002.

(2009). A Brief History of the LGBT Movement in Turkey. October 1, 2009. Available online: http://ilga.org/a-brief-history-of-the-lgbt-move ment-in-turkey/.

(2013). ILGA-Europe Annual Review 2013: Turkey. Pages 218–222. Available online: www.refworld.org/pdfid/5195f1290.pdf.

Jafari, F. (2013). Silencing Sexuality: LGBT Refugees and the Public-Private Divide in Iran and Turkey. Ph.D. Dissertation. University of Arizona. Available online: http://arizona.openrepository.com/arizona/bitstream/10150/311697/1/azu_etd_13115_sip1_m.pdf.

Jama, A. (2015). 5 Times Turkey Stood Up for LGBT People. Islamandho-mosexuality.com. May 21, 2015. Available online: http://islamandhomo sexuality.com/5-times-turkey-stood-up-lgbt-people/.

Jamieson, A. and Akyavas, A. (2015). Turkey Elections: Gay, Transsexual Candidates Spotlight LGBT Rights. NBC News. May 24, 2015. Available online: www.nbcnews.com/news/world/turkey-elections-gay-trans sexual-candidates-spotlight-lgbt-rights-n363076.

Jaspers, J. (2004). A Strategic Approach to Collective Action: Looking for Agency in Social-Movement Choices. *Mobilization: An International Journal*. Vol. 9, No. 1, pages 1–16.

(2006). *Getting Your Way: Strategic Dilemmas in the Real World*. Chicago: University of Chicago Press.

Jean-Jacques, S. (2014). Gay and Lesbian Mobilization in Algeria: The Emergence of a Movement. Muftah.org. December 15, 2014. Available online: http://muftah.org/gay-and-lesbian-mobilization-in-algeria/#.VLro T74yBUQ.

Johnston, L. (2005). *Queering Tourism: Paradoxical Performances of Gay Pride Parades*. London: Routledge.

Jones, S. (2013). 76 Countries Where Anti-Gay Laws Are as Bad or Worse than Russia's. Buzzfeed. August 9, 2013. Available online: www .buzzfeed.com/saeedjones/76-countries-where-anti-gay-laws-are-as-bad-as-or-worse-than#.wlWqPzRV9O.

(2016). Transgender Woman's Mutilated Body Found Burnt in Street Follows Streak of Gay Hate Crimes in Turkey. *Irish Mirror*. August

15, 2016. Available online: www.irishmirror.ie/news/world-news/trans gender-womans-mutilated-body-found-8638180.

Kafanov, L. (2015). Is Turkey Ready to Elect Its First Openly Gay Lawmaker? *Christian Science Monitor*. May 5, 2015.

Kaos GL (2005). Lesbian, Gay, Bisexual, and Transgender (LGBT) Rights in Turkey: An Overview of Issues. September 2005.

(2015a). 40 MP Candidates Signed the LGBTI Rights Pledge. Kaos GL. May 27, 2015. Available Online: http://kaosgl.org/page.php?id=19507

(2015b). Gays and Lesbians Are Changing the World by Making News. Kaos GL. May 28, 2015. Available Online: http://kaosgl.org/page.php?id=19514

(2015c). Pro-Kurdish HDP Pledges LGBTI Equality. April 21, 2015. Available online: http://kaosgl.org/page.php?id=19240.

(2016a) AKP'li vekil: "Eşcinsellik en büyük tehditlerden biri." February 17, 2016: Available online: www.kaosgl.org/sayfa.php?id=21120.

(2016b). Istanbul LGBT+ Pride Committee: We Will Not Be Able to Hold the 14th Pride March. June 24, 2016. Available online: www .kaosgl.org/page.php?id=21960.

Kaos GL, LGBTI News Turkey, and International Gay and Lesbian Human Rights Commission (IGLHRC) (2014). Republic of Turkey: Human Rights Violations of LGBT Individuals in Turkey. Submission to the United Nations Universal Periodic Review. November 2014. Available online: https://ilga.org/wp-content/uploads/2016/02/Shadow-report-16.pdf.

Kaplan, S. (2015). Priests Are Bucking Catholic Church Leadership to Support Same-Sex Marriage in Ireland. *Washington Post*. May 20, 2015. Available online: www.washingtonpost.com/news/morning-mix/wp/2015/05/20/priests-are-bucking-catholic-church-leadership-to-support-same-sex-marriage-in-ireland/.

Keck, M. and Sikkink, K. (1998). *Activists beyond Borders: Advocacy Networks in International Politics*. Ithaca, New York: Cornell University Press.

Kellaway, M. (2014). Turkey's First Trans Reporter Fired after Alleged Dispute Over Lipstick. Advocate.com. September 20, 2014. Available online: www.advocate.com/politics/transgender/2014/09/20/turkeys-first-trans-reporter-fired-after-alleged-dispute-over.

Kemal, L. (2015). Only Party with Real Democratic Agenda. *Today's Zaman*. April 23, 2015. Available Online: www.thefreelibrary.com/Only+party+with+real+democratic+agenda.-a0410912513.

Kollman, K. (2007). Same-Sex Unions: The Globalization of an Idea. *International Studies Quarterly*. Vol. 51, No. 2, pages 329–357.

Kollman, K. and Waites, M. (2009). The Global Politics of Lesbian, Gay, Bisexual and Transgender Human Rights: An Introduction. *Contemporary Politics*. Vol. 15, No. 1, pages 1–17.

Koopmans, R. (2004). Movements and Media: Selection Processes and Evolutionary Dynamics in the Public Sphere. *Theory and Society*. Vol. 33, pages 367–391.

Köksal, N. (2015). Being Transgender in Turkey: Some Say They Live in "Empire of Fear." CBC News, August 15, 2015. Available online: www.cbc.ca/news/world/being-transgender-in-turkey-some-say-they-live-in-empire-of-fear-1.3175570.

Köylü, M. (2014). Turkish Ministry of Justice: We Do Not Have Any Work on LGBT Citizens' Human Rights. Kaos GL, December 30, 2014. Available online: http://kaosgl.org/page.php?id=18377.

Korkmaz, Ö. (2016). A Turkish Call to Massacre LGBT Community. *Hurriyet Daily News*. June 18, 2016. Available online: www.hurriyetdailynews.com/a-turkish-call-to-massacre-lgbt-community-.aspx?PageID=238&NID=100537&NewsCatID=497.

Krajeski, J. (2014). Loud and Proud: After Turkey's Massive Park Protests Last Summer, LGBT Candidates Are Now Taking Their Fight to The Political Arena. Slate. March 28, 2014. Available online: www.slate.com/articles/news_and_politics/roads/2014/03/lgbt_rights_in_turkey_after_gezi_park_lgbt_candidates_are_now_running_for.single.html.

Kugle, S. S. H. (2010a). *Homosexuality in Islam: Critical Reflections on Gay, Lesbian, and Transgender Muslims*. Oxford: Oneworld Publications.

(2010b). Sexual Diversity in Islam: Is There Room in Islam for Lesbian, Gay, Bisexual and Transgender Muslims? Muslims for Progressive Values. Available online: www.mpvusa.org/sexuality-diversity/.

(2014). *Living Out Islam: Voices of Gay, Lesbian, and Transgender Muslims*. New York: New York University Press.

Kutahyali, R. O. (2014). Pro-Erdogan LGBT Individuals Get Organized in Turkey. Al-Monitor. August 11, 2014. Available online: www.al-monitor.com/pulse/originals/2014/08/kutahyali-lgbt-erdogan-akp-freedoms-human-rights.html#.

Kutty, F. (2014). Why Gay Marriage May Not Be Contrary to Islam. Huffington Post, March 27, 2014. Available online: www.huffingtonpost.ca/faisal-kutty-/gay-marriage.

Lahey, K. A. (2010). Same-Sex Marriage, Transnational Activism, and International Law: Strategic Objectives: Beyond Freedom to Marry. *Proceedings of the Annual Meeting (American Society of International Law)*, Vol. 104, pages 380–383.

Lambda Istanbul (2013). Kız görünümlü erkek, erkek görünümlü kız değil: İNTERSEKS! (Not a Girl That Looks Like a Boy, or a Boy That Looks Like a Girl: Intersex!). October 1, 2013. Available online: https:// lgbtinewsturkey.com/category/intersex/.

——— (2015). Lambda Istanbul LGBTI Solidarity Association. Available online: www.lambdaistanbul.org/s/lambdaistanbul-lgbti-solidarity-associ ation/.

Law Library of Congress (2014). Laws on Homosexuality in African Nations. February 2014. Available online: www.loc.gov/law/help/criminal-laws-on-homosexuality/laws-on-homosexuality-in-african-nations.pdf.

Lee, S. (2014). Turkey's Gay Community Rallies in Support of Newly Elected President Recep Tayyip Erdogan. *LGBT Weekly*. August 14, 2014. Available online: http://lgbtweekly.com/2014/08/14/turkeys-gay-community-rallies-in-support-of-newly-elected-president-recep-tayyip-erdogan/.

LGBTI News Turkey (2015a). In School, at Work, in the Parliament: LGBTIs Are Everywhere! LGBTI News Turkey. Feburary 25, 2015. Available online: https://lgbtinewsturkey.com/2015/02/25/in-school-at-work-in-the-parliament-lgbtis-are-everywhere/.

——— (2015b). LGBTI Activist Sedef Çakmak Is Now a Municipal Assembly Member. March 2, 2015. Available online: https://lgbtinewsturkey. com/2015/03/02/lgbti-activist-sedef-cakmak-is-now-a-municipal-assem bly-member/.

——— (2015c). Politics School for LGBTI Begins. February 25, 2015. Available online: http://lgbtinewsturkey.com/2015/02/25/politics-school-for-lgbti-begins/.

——— (2015c). Pro-Kurdish and Minority Rights HDP Pledges to Eliminate Discrimination against LGBTIs. April 21, 2015. Available online: http://lgbtinewsturkey.com/2015/04/21/pro-kurdish-and-minority-rights-hdp-pledges-to-eliminate-discrimination-against-lgbtis/.

——— (2015d). We Ask MP Candidates: Will You Defend LGBTI Rights in the Parliament? Available online: http://lgbtinewsturkey.com/2015/04/23/ spod-lgbti-mp-pledge-for-elections-turkey/.

——— (2016). AKP MP: "Homosexuality is one of the biggest threats." Kaos GL. January 17, 2016. Available online: http://lgbtinewsturkey.com.

LGBT Rights Platform (2009). Human Rights Violations against LGBT Individuals in Turkey in 2008.

Likmeta, B. (2013). Albania is Europe's Most Homophobic Country, Survey Says. *Balkan Insight*. 25 March 2013. Available online: www .balkaninsight.com/en/article/albania-is-the-most-homophobic-country-in-europe-survey-says.

Lipka, M. (2015). Muslims and Islam: Key Findings in the U.S. and around the World. Pew Research Center. December 7, 2015. Available online: www.pewresearch.org/fact-tank/2015/12/07/muslims-and-islam-key-findings-in-the-u-s-and-around-the-world/.

Liptak, A. (2015). Supreme Court Ruling Makes Same-Sex Marriage a Right Nationwide. *New York Times*. June 26, 2015. Available online: www.nytimes.com/2015/06/27/us/supreme-court-same-sex-marriage.

LİSTAG (Lezbiyen, Gey, Biseksüel, Trans, İnterseks Bireylerin Aileleri ve Yakınları Grubu) (2011). About Us. Available online: https://listag .wordpress.com/english/about-us/.

(Lezbiyen, Gey, Biseksüel, Trans, İnterseks Bireylerin Aileleri ve Yakınları Grubu) (2017). LİSTAG. Available online: https://listag.org/english/.

Littauer, D. (2013a). Albania Passed Landmark Gay Hate Crime Laws. *Gay Star News*. May 5, 2015. Available online www.gaystarnews.com/art icle/albania-passes-landmark-gay-hate-crime-laws050513.

(2013b). Burkina Faso Bishop Warns Gay Marriage Will Destroy the World. February 12, 2013. Available online: www.gaystarnews .com/article/burkina-faso-bishop-warns-gay-marriage-will-destroy-world 120213.

Los Angeles Times (2016). Turkey Uses Tear Gas to Break up Gay Pride Gathering. June 26, 2016. Available online: www.latimes.com/world/la-fg-turkey-gay-pride-20160626-snap-story.html.

Lowen, M. (2015). Turkey Election: Kurds, Women, Gays Put Faith in Upstart Party. BBC. June 1, 2015.

MacDonald, A. (2015). Kurdish Political Party Launches Colourful Election Campaign in Turkey. Middle East Eye. May 19, 2015.

Markoe, L. (2016). Muslim Attitudes about LGBT Are Complex, Far from Universally Anti-Gay. *USA Today*. June 17, 2016. Available online: www.usatoday.com/story/news/world/2016/06/17/muslim-lgbt-gay-views/ 86046404/.

Massad, J. A. (2002). Re-Orienting Desire: The Gay International and the Arab World. *Public Culture*. Vol. 14, No. 2, pages 361–385.

Mchugh, L. (2014). Meet Michelle Demishevich – Turkey's First Transgender News Anchor. Her.ie. Available online: www.her.ie/life/meet-michelle-demishevich-turkeys-first-transgender-news-anchor/159288.

Mertus, J. (2007). The Rejection of Human Rights Framings: The Case of LGBT Advocacy in the US. *Human Rights Quarterly*. Vol. 29, No. 4, pages 1036–1064.

Milliyet (2008). Eşcinseller de eşitlik istiyor, verecek miyiz? January 28, 2008. Available online: www.milliyet.com.tr/2008/01/28/siyaset/ asiy.html.

Mincheva, I. (2012). Beyond Equality and Non-Discrimination: Escaping Narrow Human Rights Framings in the Context of Sexual Orientation and Gender Identity. Master's Thesis. Masaryk University, Brno, Czech Republic.

Morrison, A. (2015). ISIS LGBT Persecution: At UN Security Council Meeting, Gay Islamic State Victims in Syria and Iraq Discussed. *International Business Times*. August 24, 2015. Available online: www.ibtimes .com/isis-lgbt-persecution-un-security-council-meeting-gay-islamic-state-victims-syria-2065987.

Mosbergen, D. (2015). Brunei's LGBT Community Faces Terrifying Future. *Huffington Post*. October 15, 2015. Available online: www.huffington post.com/entry/lgbt-brunei_us_561501f9e4b0fad1591a1167.

Mortada, D. (2015). Turkish Sex Worker Dialect Lubunca Liberates, Stigmatizes LGBT Community. *Al Jazeera English*. January 17, 2015. Available online: http://america.aljazeera.com/articles/2015/1/17/turkish-languagesexworkers.html.

Mucciaroni, G. (2011). The Study of LGBT Politics and Its Contributions to Political Science. *PS: Political Science and Politics*. Vol. 44, No. 1, pages 17–21.

Muedini, F. (2015). Environmental Politics and the 2013–2014 Protests in Turkey. *Islam and Muslim Societies: A Social Science Journal*. Vol. 8, No. 1, pages 1–17.

Murphy, C. (2015). Most U.S. Christian Groups Grow More Accepting of Homosexuality. Pew Research Center. December 18, 2015. Available online: www.pewresearch.org/fact-tank/2015/12/18/most-u-s-christian-groups-grow-more-accepting-of-homosexuality/.

Mutua, M. (2011). Sexual Orientation and Human Rights: Putting Homophobia On Trial. In *African Sexualities: A Reader*, ed. Sylvia Tamale, pages 452–462. Nairobi, Kenya: Pambazuka Press.

Najmabadi, A. (2005). *Women with Mustaches and Men without Beards: Gender and Sexual Anxieties of Iranian Modernity*. Berkeley, University of California Press.

——— (2013). *Professing Selves: Transexuality and Same-Sex Desire in Contemporary Iran*. Durham, North Carolina: Duke University Press.

NBC News (2016). Turkish Police Fire Rubber Bullets at Pride Parade. June 19, 2016. Available online: www.nbcnews.com/slideshow/turkish-police.

NEOnline (2015). Turkey's Upcoming Elections Highlight Gay Rights. May 25, 2015.

New Europe (2014). Turkish Prime Minister Recep Tayyip Erdogan Has Backtracked on a Threat to Shut Down Facebook and YouTube in Turkey. *New Europe*.

Nigar Goksel, D. (2014). Turkey's Elections and Gender Politics. *Al Jazeera English*. April 3, 2014.

Nigerian Government (2013). Same Sex Marriage (Prohibition) Act, 2013. December 17, 2013. Available online: www.refworld.org/docid/52f4d9cc4.html.

Novkov, J. and Barclay, S. (2010). Lesbians, Gays, Bisexuals, and the Transgendered in Political Science: Report on a Discipline-Wide Survey. *PS: Political Science and Politics*, Vol. 42, No. 1, pages 95–106.

Nurtsch, C. (2015). The Role of the HDP in the Turkish General Election: Beacon of Hope for Women and LGBTs. Qantara.de. June 3, 2015. Available online: http://en.qantara.de/content/the-role-of-the-hdp-in-the-turkish-general-election-beacon-ofhope-for-women-and-lgbts.

Organization for Refuge, Asylum and Migration (ORAM) (2011). Unsafe Haven: The Security Challenges Facing Lesbian, Gay, Bisexual and Transgender Asylum Seekers and Refugees in Turkey. Updated ed. June 2011. Available online: www.oraminternational.org/images/stories/PDFs/oram-unsafe-haven-2011-web.pdf.

OutRight Action International (2016). Timeline of Publicized Executions for Alleged Sodomy by the Islamic State Militias. Available online: www.outrightinternational.org/content/timeline-publicized-executions-alleged-sodomy-islamic-state-militias.

Öz, Y. (2010). Study on Homophobia, Transphobia and Discrimination on Grounds of Sexual Orientation and Gender Identity. Legal Report: Turkey. Danish Institute for Human Rights (COWI). Pages 1–53. Available online: www.coe.int/t/Commissioner/Source/LGBT/TurkeyLegal_E.pdf.

Öz, Y. and International Gay and Lesbian Human Rights Commission (IGLHRC) (2011). LGBT Rights In Turkey. Submission to the Country Report Task Force for the Adoption of Lists of Issues. Initial Report CCPR/C/TUR/1. Available online: https://iglhrc.org/sites/default/files/554-1.pdf.

Özalp, H. (2003). May Homosexuals Be Members of AKP? *Sabah*. April 15, 2003.

Özbay, C. (2015). Same-Sex Sexualities in Turkey. In *International Encyclopedia of the Social & Behavioral Sciences*, 2nd ed., ed. James D. Wright, pages 870–874.

(2017). *Queering Sexualities in Turkey: Gay Men, Male Prostitutes and the City*. London: I. B. Tauris.

Ozer, V. (2013). Turkey's LGBT Community Draws Hope from Harvey Milk. Al-Monitor. December 15, 2013. Available online: www.al-monitor.com/pulse/originals/2013/12/turkey-lgbt-discrimination-legal-protection-public-awareness.html#.

Paton, C. (2016). Gay German MP "Violently Arrested" in Riot-Police Attack on Banned Istanbul Gay Pride March. *International Business Times*. June 27, 2016. Available online: www.ibtimes.co.uk/gay-german-mp-violently-arrested-riot-police-attack-banned-istanbul-gay-pride-march-1567659.

Pearce, S. C. (2014a). "Gej" (Gay) In Southeast Europe: LGBTI Rights in a European-Global Corner. Policy Brief for the Global Europe Program. Woodrow Wilson Center. February 2014, pages 1–10.

(2014b). Pride in Istanbul. *Societies without Borders*. Vol. 9, No. 1, pages 111–128.

Pembe Hayat (2015a). Turkey: Trans Woman Murdered by Stabbing in Her Heart. Email notification. December 2, 2015.

(2015b). Turkey: Trans Woman Stabbed and Strangled to Death! Email notification. November 24, 2015. Available online: https://lgbtinews turkey.com/2015/11/.

Pew Research Center (2013a). The Global Divide on Homosexuality. Pew Research Center: Attitudes and Trends. June 4, 2013. Available online: www.pewglobal.org/2013/06/04/the-global-divide-on-homo sexuality/.

(2013b). Pew Research Center's Global Attitudes Project 2013 Spring Survey Topline Results. June 4, 2013. Available online: www .pewglobal.org/files/2014/05/Pew-Global-Attitudes-Homosexuality-Top line-REVISED-MAY-27-2014.pdf.

(2015). U.S. Public Becoming Less Religious. November 3, 2015. Available online: www.pewforum.org/2015/11/03/u-s-public-becoming-less-religious/.

Pink Life LGBTT Solidarity Association and Kaos GL (2015). Human Rights Violations in LGBT Individuals in Turkey. Republic of Turkey. Submission to the United Nations Universal Periodic Review. Available online: http://ilga.org/wp-content/uploads/2016/02/Shadow-report-16.pdf.

Pittman, M. (2013). Turkey Really Doesn't Want Gay People to Have Sex. *Vice*. October 4, 2013. Available online: www.vice.com/read/grindr-vs-turkey.

Povoledo, E. (2008). Performance Artist Killed on Peace Trip Is Mourned. *New York Times*, April 19, 2008. Available online: www.nytimes .com/2008/04/19/theater/19peac.html?mcubz=1.

Pride Istanbul (2013). 21st LGBT Pride Week. Available online: http:// prideistanbul.tumblr.com.

(2016). Let's Sign the Petition for a Safe LGBTI+ Pride March in Istanbul. Available online: http://en.prideistanbul.org/lets-sign-petition-safe-lgbti-pride-march-istanbul-2/.

Public Opinion (2015). Turkish Police Use Water Cannons to Clear Gay Pride Parade. Available online: www.thepublicopinion.com/news/associ ated_press/world/turkish...de-rally/article_9014df94-c561-57c6-a648-f0afba0694c3.html?mode=jqm.

Pullen, C. and Cooper, M. (2010). *LGBT Identity and Online New Media*. New York: Routledge Press.

QRD.org (2009). Lambda Istanbul: Welcome to Lambda Istanbul. Available online: www.qrd.org/qrd/www/world/europe/turkey/.

Quebec Ministry of Immigration and Cultural Communities (2014). Réalités juridiques et sociales DES MINORITÉS SEXUELLES dans les principaux pays d'origine des personnes nouvellement arrivées au Québec. Guide d'information, 3rd ed. May 30, 2014. Available online: www.quebecinterculturel.gouv.qc.ca/publications/fr/divers/GUI_Info HomosexualiteTranssexualite_FIN.pdf.

Rahman, M. (2010). Queer as Intersectionality: Theorizing Gay Muslim Identities. *Sociology*. Vol. 44, No. 5, pages 944–961.

Ramchurn, R. (2013). Gay Hook-Up App Grindr Fights Back against Turkish Ban with Threat of Legal Action. *Independent*. September 20, 2013. Available online: www.independent.co.uk/life-style/gadgets-and-tech/gay-hook-up-app-grindr-fights-back-against-turkish-ban-with-threat-of-legal-action-8829360.html.

Reilly, P. (2015). The Election of the Middle East. Gate. May 25, 2015.

Research Turkey (2015), Interview with Sedef Çakmak from the CHP: November 1st Elections from the Perspective of an LGBTI Activist. Vol. 4, No. 12, pages 58–79. Available online: http://researchturkey .org/?p=10324.

Reynolds, A. (2013). Out in Office: LGBT Legislators and LGBT Rights around the World. Pages 1–35. Available online: http://globalstudies .unc.edu/files/2013/11/Annual-Report_May20FinalVersion.pdf.

Rimmerman, C. A. (2014). *The Lesbian and Gay Movements: Assimilation or Liberation?* Boulder, CO: Westview Press.

Romero, S. (2013). Brazilian Court Council Removes a Barrier to Same-Sex Marriage. *New York Times*. May 14, 2013. Available online: www.nytimes.com/2013/05/15/world/americas/brazilian-court-council-removes-a-barrier-to-same-sex-marriage.

Sakallı, N. and Uğurlu, O. (2001). Effects of Social Contact with Homosexuals on Heterosexual Turkish University Students' Attitudes towards Homosexuality. *Journal of Homosexuality*.Vol. 42, No. 1, pages 53–62.

—— (2002). The Effects of Social Contact with a Lesbian Person on the Attitude Change toward Homosexuality in Turkey. *Journal of Homosexuality*. Vol. 44, No. 1, pages 111–119.

San Diego Gay and Lesbian News (SDGLN). (2015). Turkey: TV Music Channel Fined for Sexual Videos, One Showing Lesbian Kiss. January 15, 2015. Available online: http://sdgln.com/news/2015/01/15/turkey-tv-music-channels-fined-sexual-videos-one-showing-lesbian-kiss.

Schechter, D. (2011). Dateline Istanbul: Defending the Internet and Exposing Symbolic Politics. *Huffington Post*. November 26, 2011. Available online: www.huffingtonpost.com/danny-schechter/dateline-istanbul-defendi_b_973908.html.

Schmitt, A. (2013). Gay Rights versus Human Rights: A Response to Joseph Massad. *Public Culture*, Vol. 15, No. 3, pages 587–591.

Seattle Gay News (2014). Pro-Gay Mayors Elected in Turkey. April 4, 2014.

Sezer, S. (2016). Istanbul Riot Police Disperse "Trans Pride" March. June 19, 2016. Yahoo! News. Available online: www.yahoo.com/news/istanbul-riot-police-disperse-trans-pride-march-172549687.html.

Saruhan, H. (2013). Transexuality in Turkey – The Representation of Transexual Identities in Contemporary Turkish Films. Master's Project, September 2013. Available online: www.academia.edu/6368123/Trans exuality_in_Turkey_-_The_Representation_of_Transexual_Identities_ in_Contemporary_Turkish_Films.

Selek, P. (2001). *Maskeler, Süvariler, Gacılar* (Masks, Calvalry, Women). Istanbul: Aykırı Yayıncılık.

Sheill, K. (2009). Losing Out in the Intersections: Lesbians, Human Rights, Law, And Activism. *Contemporary Politics*, Vol. 15, No. 1, pages 55–71.

Şimşek, H. (2016). Cinsiyet geçişinde kritik görüşme (Critical Deliberation on Gender Reassignment). *BirGün*, January 31, 2016, Available online: www.birgun.net/haber-detay/cinsiyet-gecisinde-kritik-gorusme-102380.html.

Social Policies, Gender Identity and Sexual Orientation Studies Association (SPoD) (2013). 2012 Report of Human Rights Violations Based on Sexual Orientation and Gender Identity. Project to Strengthen Mechanisms of Access to Justice for LGBT people in Turkey. Available online: https://lgbtinewsturkey.files.wordpress.com/2013/09/2012-sogi-rights-violations-in-turkey1.pdf.

——— (2014). SPOD's LGBTI-Friendly Municipality Protocol. Available online: https://lgbtinewsturkey.com/2014/03/09/spod-lgbti-friendly-municipality-protocol/.

Social Policies, Gender Identity and Sexual Orientation Studies Association (SpoD), Kaos GL Association, and International Gay and Lesbian Human Rights Commission (2012). Human Rights Violations of Lesbian, Gay, Bisexual and Transgender (LGBT) People in Turkey: A Shadow Report. Submission to the 106th Session of the Human

Rights Committee (United Nations CEDAW Committee). October 15–November 2, 2012. Available online: www.outrightinternational .org/sites/default/files/turkey_report.pdf.

Sterling, J. (2017). Chechen Leader: No Gays Here – But if There Are, Take Them Away. CNN. Monday, July 17, 2017. Available online: www.cnn.com/2017/07/17/europe/russia-chechnya-gays/index.html.

Stewart, C. (2014). Gabon Releases Men after Arrested Gay Wedding. Erasing 76 Crimes. January 17, 2014. Available online: http://76crimes .com/2014/01/17/gabon-releases-men-arrested-after-gay-wedding/.

Swiebel, J. (2009). Lesbian, Gay, Bisexual and Transgender Human Rights: The Search for an International Strategy. *Comparative Politics*. Vol. 15, No. 1, pages 19–35.

Tahaoğlu, Ç. (2014). IMC TV Lays Off Trans Reporter Demishevich. September 17, 2014. Available online: http://bianet.org/english/media/ 158558-imc-tv-lays-off-trans-reporter-demishevich.

Tar, Y. (2015). From Lynching and Attacks to the Parliament: LGBTI Candidates for Nomination. Kaos GL. March 6, 2015. Available online: https://lgbtinewsturkey.com/2015/03/05/from-lynching-and-attacks-to-the-parliament-lgbti-candidates-for-nomination/.

(2016). Human Rights Observation Report of 19 June 2016 Trans Pride March. Kaos GL. Available online: www.kaosgldernegi.org/resim/ yayin/dl/human_rights_observation_report_of_19_june_2016_trans_ pride_march.pdf.

(2016b). Syrian Gay Refugee Killed in Istanbul. Kaos GL. August 4, 2016. Available online: http://kaosgl.org/page.php?id=22071.

Taylor, J. K., Lewis, D. C., Jacobmeier, M. L., and DiSarro, B. (2012). Content and Complexity in Policy Reinvention and Diffusion: Gay and Transgender-Inclusive Laws against Discrimination. *State Politics & Policy Quarterly*, Vol. 12, No. 1, pages 75–98.

Terkel, A. (2015). Mike Pence Signs Revised Indiana "Religious Freedom" Law. *Huffington Post*, April 2, 2015. Available online: www .huffingtonpost.com/2015/04/02/mike-pence-religious-freedom_n_699 6144.html.

Transgender Europe (TGEU) (2015). ECtHR to Announce Verdict on Turkish Gender Reassignment Law. February 25, 2015. Available online: http:// tgeu.org/ecthr-to-announce-verdict-on-turkish-gender-reassignment-law/.

Today's Zaman (2015). Demirtaş: AK Party Preparing Crackdown on All Dissidents if It Wins Strong Majority. *Today's Zaman*. June 01, 2015.

Tokyay, M. (2015). Turkey's LGBT Crusaders Marching Onward Despite Huge Obstacles. *International Business Times*. June 25, 2015. Available online: www.ibtimes.co.uk/turkeys-lgbt-crusaders-marching-onward-despite-huge-obstacles-1507924.

Tremblay, P. (2015). Kurdish Women's Movement Reshapes Turkish Politics. Al-Monitor. March 25, 2015.

Trew, B. (2013). Egypt's Growing Gay Rights Movement. Daily Beast. May 21, 2014. Available online: www.thedailybeast.com/articles/2013/05/21/egypt-s-growing-gay-rights-movement.html.

(2014). Al-Sisi's Egypt Is Worse For Gays Than the Muslim Brotherhood. Daily Beast. 06. 28. 2014. Available online: www.thedailybeast.com/articles/2014/06/27/egypt-targets-gays.html

Trian, N. (2016). Turkey Transgender Activist's Death Highlights Rise in Hate Crimes. France 24. August 19, 2016. Available online: www .france24.com/en/20160819-turkey-lgbt-trasgender-activist-death-high lights-rise-hate-crimes-hande-kader.

Turkish Criminal Code (2004). Criminal Code, Law Nr. 5237. Passed On September 26, 2004. Available online: http://legislationline.org/documents/action/popup/id/6872/preview.

Turkish Weekly (2014). LGBTI Candidates Vie for Local Office. March 8, 2014.

Tuysuz, G. and Dewan, A. (2017). Turkey: Anti-Erdogan Marchers "Scream" for Justice in Istanbul. CNN. July 9, 2017. Available online: www .cnn.com/2017/07/09/europe/turkey-istanbul-protests-march/index.html.

Uhlmann, A. J. (2005). Introduction: Reflections on the Study of Sexuality in the Middle East and North Africa. *Social Analysis: The International Journal of Social and Cultural Practice*, Vol. 49, No. 2, pages 3–5.

UN General Assembly, 56th Session (2001). Report of the UN Special Rapporteur on the Question of Torture and other Cruel, Inhuman or Degrading Treatment, Sir Nigel Rodley, Special Rapporteur. UN Doc. A/56/156, July 3, 2001.

United States State Department (2014). Benin 2013 Human Rights Report. February 27, 2014. Available online: www.state.gov/documents/organ ization/220294.pdf.

Uras, U. (2015). Pro-Kurdish party Seeks Wider Reach in Turkish Vote. *Al-Jazeera English*. June 1, 2015. Available online: www.aljazeera .com/news/middleeast/2015/06/pro-kurdish-party-seeks-wider-reach-turkey-polls-150601191117208.html.

(2016). Hardliner Groups Vow to Prevent Istanbul Gay Pride. *Al Jazeera*. June 16, 2016. Available online: www.aljazeera.com/news/2016/06/groups-vow-prevent-istanbul-gay-pride-160616151056179.html.

(2017). Istanbul LGBT March Banned over "Security Concerns." *Al Jazeera*. June 24, 2017. Available online: www.aljazeera.com/news/2017/06/istan bul-lgbt-march-banned-security-concerns-170624181917813.html.

Uzun, D. U. (2017). IDAHOT 2017 at Ankara: Queer Politics of Labor! Kaos GL. May 14, 2017. Available online: www.kaosgl.org/page .php?id=23771.

Weise, Z. (2015). Deva Ozenen: What It's Like to Be Transgender Election Candidate in Turkey. *Independent*. May 16, 2015. Available Online: www.independent.co.uk/news/world/middle-east/deva-ozenen-what-its-like-to-be-a-transgender-election-candidate-in-turkey-10255812.html.

Werz, M., Hoffman, M., and Bhaskar, M. (2015). Previewing Turkey's General Election. Center for American Progress. June 2, 2015.

Williams, S. (2016). Istanbul Bans Gay Pride March on Security Grounds. Yahoo! News. June 17, 2016. Available online: www.yahoo.com/news/ istanbul-bans-gay-pride-march-security-grounds-002156626.html.

Williamson, H. A. (2016). Turkish Activists look to Germany for Support on Rights Crackdown. Human Rights Watch. February 3, 2016. Available online: www.hrw.org/news/2016/02/03/turkish-activists-look-germany-support-rights-crackdown.

Wilson, C. (2012). The Opposite of Being Visibly Out: Hiding in Plain Sight. *Huffington Post*, November 9, 2012. Available online: www .huffingtonpost.com/chana-wilson/the-opposite-of-being-visibly-out-hiding-in-plain-sight_b_2089707.html.

Yackley, A. J. (2015). Gay, Christian, Roma Election Candidates Show Turkey's Changing Face. Reuters. June 5, 2015.

Yılmaz, V. (2013). The New Constitution of Turkey: A Blessing or a Curse for LGBT Citizens? *Turkish Policy*. Vol. 11, No. 4, pages 131–140.

Yip, A. K. T. (2008). Researching Lesbian, Gay, and Bisexual Christians and Muslims: Some Thematic Reflections, *Sociological Research Online*, Vol. 13, No. 1, page 5.

Index